ABIGAIL CARTER

THE ALCHEMY OF LOSS

A YOUNG WIDOW'S TRANSFORMATION

Health Communications, Inc.
Deerfield Beach, Florida

www.hcibooks.com

Library of Congress Cataloging-in-Publication Data
is available through the Library of Congress.

© 2008 Abigail Carter
ISBN-13: 978-0-7573-0790-6
ISBN-10: 0-7573-0790-4

Publisher: Health Communications, Inc.
            3201 S.W. 15th Street
            Deerfield Beach, FL 33442-8190

for Arron

[CONTENTS]

PREFACE

The collapse of the World Trade Center and the death of my husband, Arron, on September 11, 2001, began a process of personal growth that I could never have foreseen. I faced the dark demon of grief, endured its crippling physical effects, and was occasionally surprised by moments of clarity and optimism. I likened myself to the Hero undertaking a circular journey from despair through numerous challenges before finally conquering the ultimate challenge, which I now realize was myself.

Driven to write my story despite never having written before, I sat down at my computer shortly after the second anniversary of Arron's death and simply wrote "September 11, 2001." Words spilled onto the pages. I told myself I wanted to record the events for my children, who would someday ask for details, but I also secretly hoped my story would be more—something that could help others to cope with their own losses. I wanted to write the book I had not found, the one that would give me hope that my grief would not be permanent and that a whole new life might emerge from the ashes of loss.

During this time I found a book by Kathleen Brehony called *After the Darkest Hour*, which provided me with some insight into enduring loss. She maintains that loss is a form of "spiritual alchemy" and can offer us an opportunity to change and grow.

Alchemy is an ancient science and form of spiritualism that combines chemistry, metallurgy, physics, and medicine. Its followers aimed to turn lead into gold.

This transmutation process follows three steps. First there is a "blackening" where the lead is stripped of its original alloys and broken down to its barest essential elements to prepare it for transformation. The original form ceases to exist. In spiritual terms, this is the loss of what is familiar and is often characterized by a state of confusion, where we feel disoriented and anxious.

The next stage is the "whitening" process whereby the metal (or the human spirit) is cleansed and purified, transforming its original chemistry. The confusion and chaos become regulated, more predictable, and we begin to see opportunities in our transformation to develop a fuller awareness of ourselves and our spirituality. Kathleen Brehony describes this stage in the journey as a "baptism . . . a spiritual and psychological awakening."

A red powder made from the mythical philosopher's stone mediates the final stage, the "reddening," resulting in a superpure form of gold. An individual rises above his old, earthbound beliefs and values and achieves a higher level of enlightenment. He is transformed into his gold, pure, or awakened state.

What follows is my journey from the loneliness and isolation of my early days after September 11 through my understanding of the rewards that suffering and tragedy offer us all. It is my own transformation of lead into gold.

PART ONE

THE BLACKENING

Be helpless, dumbfounded,
Unable to say yes or no.
Then a stretcher will come from grace
to gather us up.

"Zero Circle" by Rumi

SEPTEMBER 11, 2001

I was carrying Carter, my two-year-old, and standing in the kitchen putting my daughter Olivia's lunch into her back-pack when the phone rang. I hesitated, debating whether to answer it, knowing we had only a few minutes to catch her school bus. "Here, finish this." I handed her the bag so she could zip it up and grabbed the phone. "Hello?"

"Ab, Ab! There's an emergency. I'm in the World Trade Center and there's been a bomb. Ab, are you there?" It was my husband, Arron, and he was speaking slowly, articulating his words. I imagined a small firecracker in a bathroom somewhere. Surely Arron was just being dramatic.

I tried to answer him, but he was unable to hear me and hung up. A second later, the phone rang again. I answered before the first ring fully sounded. I could sense his urgency, but I also wanted the call over with. Olivia was about to miss her bus.

"Ab, Ab, I'm at Windows on the World in the World Trade Center," he said slowly. I knew he had to attend a trade show that day in downtown Manhattan somewhere, but I didn't know where exactly he would be. "There's been a bomb. You need to call the police! Ab?" I was still holding Olivia's lunch box, helping her to stuff it into her backpack as he spoke.

"Yes, yes," I said. "I'm here. Okay. Okaaay. I'll call them right now." We hung up. I was exasperated. It was Olivia's second day of first grade. Our nanny, Martha, had taken the day off and I was rushing through my morning without her help. Why couldn't he call 9-1-1 himself, I wondered. Why was he making such a big deal out of this?

My call reached our local dispatcher at the Montclair, New Jersey, police department. I felt silly explaining that my husband thought there had been a bomb in the World Trade Center.

"I haven't heard anything about a bomb, but we will call NYPD and call you back," the dispatcher said calmly. Our town, a bedroom community for New York, was only twelve miles west of Manhattan.

I stood in the driveway, unsure how far the signal of the cordless phone would travel. "Liv, can you walk from here to the bus stop by yourself?"

"No, Mama! You have to come."

"Okay, okay," I said, annoyed. I rushed her down the street, just as the bus arrived.

She stepped into it and turned to me from the stairs. "Who were you talking to?"

"Daddy called and said there is a bomb in New York! Bye-bye, honey!" She looked confused as I waved, pretending frivolity. Carter was still strapped to my hip and I watched Olivia take her seat.

As I walked back to the house, the police called back. "We have talked to NYPD. A plane has hit the building. I suggest you turn on your TV."

"All right," I said feebly. I pictured something small, like a Cessna, as I rushed into the house and turned the TV on.

Thick smoke both poured down from the top of the impossibly tall building like water and billowed up into the indigo blue sky. The picture switched to a shot of another building, this one a pristine twin of the other. Blinking, I stepped backwards as a sudden burst of orange flame seemed to envelop the TV. Carter clung to my hip and I sensed him looking at me fearfully. I hugged him tighter, not wanting to avert my eyes from the screen.

Suddenly, the screen went blank. I froze for a second, then frantically bent down to fumble with buttons on the TV. "Oh no! No!" I mumbled. Several channels flipped by, all black. Finally I landed on one and the nightmare returned: a building engulfed in sinister black smoke, a second now with an orange flame eating at the wound in its upper floors. "It seems another plane has hit the South Tower," the reporter was saying. A different camera angle proved his point in a replay. The huge plane careened crazily to the right and then slammed into the building. Another groan rose up from the pit of my stomach, and I began to shake.

"Oh, Fabbo . . ." I moaned Arron's nickname, wanting to jump into the TV.

"Please no. No, no, no, no, no," I groaned involuntarily from somewhere deep in my chest. I crouched down onto the floor, sliding my fingers down the screen, as though I might somehow be able to reach Arron. I put Carter onto his feet, but he clung to my waist. I carefully dialed the numbers that I knew by heart.

"This is Voicestream. Due to technical difficulties, we cannot connect your call at this time." The message seemed foreboding. I redialed again and again.

Finally one call got through. "You have reached the voice mail of Arron Dack. . . ." His voice was reassuring. Surely he would pick up his messages.

"Fabbo, please call me. I am so scared for you. I love you. . . ."

I should call others. Alert them to what? It all seemed impossible. I left Arron's mother, Selena, a message at her home in Port Hope, Ontario.

"Call me right away!" I hoped my voice sounded calm. I didn't call anyone else, wanting to leave the line free in case he called me. I wished I had signed up for call waiting. I willed the phone to ring.

On TV, the smoke was still billowing from the tops of the buildings. It would be horrific inside. What could he be thinking?

Was he scared? Did he know yet that planes had hit the building and not bombs? Was he running down the stairs or was he writing me a good-bye letter? "Dear Ab," it would say. "Take care of the kids. I love you all so much. . . ." I choked. Why was I thinking such thoughts? He was dashing down long flights of stairs with hundreds of others joining him at each floor. It would take a while, but he would get down. He would be tired, exhausted by the time he reached home. Did I have beer? Maybe I should take some steaks out to grill tonight, I thought, but I did not get up.

Harley, our golden retriever, barked loudly as two Brazilian nannies, friends of Martha, appeared at the door accompanied by their two young charges. The sun behind them was blinding. They had heard me at Olivia's bus stop and knew things were not right. They had already heard about the planes, the buildings, and came to make sure that I was okay. But they grew silent when they saw my face. Carter and the two other little boys were thrilled at the impromptu playdate and immediately dove into a bucket of noisy cars and fire trucks. Sirens began to blare.

"My uncle, he there, maybe. He sometimes work in building," Maria said, her accent thick.

"Oh no!" I replied. "I'm so sorry."

We sat silent in our thoughts, watching the tragedy unfold on TV.

Then the screen turned white with dust or smoke. "It seems that a bomb has gone off!" the reporter declared. I stopped breathing. The whiteness was billowy, almost beautiful as it slowly draped and caressed the air. "No, it seems that one of the towers is collapsing!" The reporter sounded incredulous.

A loud ring in my hand startled me out of my momentary stasis. I was shaking as I answered. "Hello?" my voice cracked. "Arron?"

"No, it's me, Selena. What's going on?"

"Turn on your TV!" I screamed.

"Okay," she said, annoyingly calm. From her small town in Ontario, she was unaware of what was happening in New York. She could not know the terror that I was witnessing as I spoke to her.

"Is it on yet?" I asked, watching the dust fill the sky.

"Which channel?" she asked, still too calm.

"Any channel! Just turn on the damn TV!" My patience was depleted. "The fucking building is falling down right now! You're missing it! Hurry!"

I don't know what we said to each other once Selena turned on her TV. I did not register her reaction. I just made her get off the line in case Arron called. I walked outside, dazed, still clutching the phone. The nannies hurried away, taking Carter with them.

Minutes later, I was sitting on the steps of our wide front porch, uncomfortable in the too-tight workout gear I had donned that morning for a kickboxing class. Only an hour had passed since Arron's phone call, and yet it felt like it must have been yesterday or last year. The news had spread quickly around the street and some of my neighbors were now milling around my lawn, chatting quietly. None of us were sure where in the building Windows on the World was, though someone thought it was a restaurant at the top, and we did not know if it was in the building that was still standing or the one that had just fallen. There was talk about how handy Arron is . . . was? How he, of all people, could get out of any situation, like MacGyver. There was laughter at the thought of him rescuing himself with duct tape.

I continued to clutch the phone for dear life. Kathleen, the human resources director from Arron's company, Encompys, called to tell me that she had managed to contact Jeff, one of the two people at the trade show with Arron. From Jeff we learned that everyone at the trade show had moved into a corner office and was waiting to be evacuated, on the 106th floor of one of the buildings. Unimaginably high. "Waiting" seemed like a bad word. They needed to get out as fast as they could.

I received another call from the Montclair police dispatch, Officer Wyatt, the same officer I had spoken to when I had initially called 9-1-1.

"I just wanted to see if you had heard from your husband," Officer Wyatt said.

"No, I haven't."

"I'm sorry. Is there anything I can do?"

"Well, I know he's in Windows on the World, but I still don't know which building it's in. Is it in the one that fell down or the one that's still standing? That's what I really need to know."

"I understand. I'm not really sure," he said. "But I'll try to find out. It seems to me that there was a restaurant in both buildings."

"Oh. Well, if you could find out for me, that would be great." I tried to sound upbeat, but I suspect my voice was monotone. In the end, of course, it didn't really matter.

I looked up to see one of my neighbors striding across the street, making a beeline toward me. I knew from the look on his face that it was more bad news even before he told me that the second building had fallen. "I know" was all I could think to say before my world tilted and became a fog.

The sun dropped in the sky. Around four o'clock I saw another one of my neighbors coming home. He crossed the street when he saw me. Brian worked on Wall Street, so I was surprised that he looked so immaculate, unlike the ghostly figures I had seen on TV, covered in dust. His eyes, though, were sad, weary. I hated imagining all the people he must have known who worked in the buildings.

"I heard about Arron. I'm so sorry. But don't lose hope. It's really crazy downtown. I walked out of my building before the South Tower fell and walked to the ferry. I waited hours to get on and then hitched a ride to Montclair. There are long lineups at every phone booth, the subway is closed, the streets are jammed with people walking. I'm sure Arron will get home. It's just going to take a while." He was talking fast, and slightly nervously, trying to convince both of us that Arron was safe.

But Brian gave me some hope. I imagined Arron, filthy,

smelly, unable or too impatient to wait for a phone, his cell phone useless. Like Brian, he would be quiet, shaken, subdued when he arrived. Or perhaps he would be excited, talking incessantly, telling me all the stories, his adventure of getting home, all the people he had helped or who had helped him along the way. It would be over a beer, he would be clean from a shower, and we would be relaxing outside, grilling the steaks that I hadn't taken out of the freezer. He would be worried about some of the people he knew who were missing.

My steak dinner fantasies were interrupted by talk of calling hospitals. Another neighbor was going into the city to look for a friend, using his status as a doctor to visit hospitals. Would I like him to search for Arron, too? But Arron wasn't lost, I thought. He knew his way home and would call. Soon. Or perhaps none of this had happened and he was just away, on another business trip. He wasn't actually in the city. He was fine. Just couldn't get to a phone. Yes, look for Arron if you wish, but he won't be there.

Olivia came home from school to a house full of people. "Mommy, a boy on my bus said that two bad guys drove a plane into some buildings in New York!" she said breathlessly.

"Yes, I know," was my only response. I was relieved that she hadn't made the connection with Arron's call that morning.

As the evening wore on, Carter was returned to me by the nannies, fed and ready for bed. Somehow I managed to give him a bottle, and mercifully he fell asleep without a fight. When I put Olivia to bed, she asked, "Where's Daddy?" All I could say was, "I don't know sweetie, he must be stuck in New York." Thankfully, she seemed content with that answer.

Neighbors had been coming with food that no one ate. Someone made coffee. Now that the kids were asleep, someone else turned the TV back on, which was showing repeats of the day's terrible images. I sat close to the TV so I could watch the crowd scenes for signs of Arron. But there was nothing to see. The newscaster

9

kept repeating the phrases "emergency rooms empty," "rescue efforts underway," "many still missing" over and over while images played of idle doctors pacing outside of hospital doorways. Hundreds, possibly thousands, were said to be dead or missing. Some friends arrived and I ushered them into the kitchen so we wouldn't disturb those watching TV.

"What can we do?" my friends pleaded as they leaned against my counter.

I became calm and rational. I had to attend to the needs of my children, and find a way to help my husband. "The reality is that Arron might not come back. What am I going to tell the kids? I'm going to have to say something tomorrow. I could use a book to tell me how."

An hour later, I was handed three books on grieving in children, fresh from a bookstore. Surely it was too soon to be thinking about grief. Still, I hid in my bedroom and flipped through the first, *When Children Grieve*, by John W. James, Russell Friedman, and Dr. Leslie Landon Matthews. According to the authors, I was in control of how my kids would grieve. My actions would model grieving and they would follow my lead. I had to put the oxygen mask on myself before I could assist my children.

My neighbors were still in my home at 2:00 AM, begging me to go to bed. But I had to wait up for him. I wanted to be awake when he returned. I turned on my computer and sent e-mails to everyone I had an address for. "Please pray for him," I typed. Isn't that what you say in these situations? I had never prayed a day in my life, but now I wished I knew how. "Please God, let him come home." As I wrote my inadequate prayers, it sank in deeper. What if he never came home? What if he really was gone? What if? I squeezed my eyes shut, pushing the thoughts away.

I was still glued to the computer at 4:00 AM. Regular phone service was unreliable, and I had stopped calling Arron's cell phone hours ago. It was too painful to hear his business-like voice telling me to leave a message, or to get a busy signal, as though he might be trying to call me at the same moment. I chastised myself for not thinking of e-mailing him sooner.

> *Fab:*
> *I love you. Please e-mail me if you get this.*
> *Love, lb*

As I always had, I signed "lb," short for Lemonbird, Arron's nickname for me.

I tried not to watch my computer's clock, but I couldn't keep my eyes from darting to it. Each minute that ticked by diminished the possibility of Arron's return. The building was too huge. He was too high up. I did the math. One minute per floor, that's 106 minutes to get down, *if* he left immediately. Too long. The building fell within 90 minutes. He didn't make it. It was impossible. I knew the truth, but I was not yet ready to admit it. I hated my pragmatism.

I found websites with hundreds of "missing person" reports. So many of the postings were the same: "He was on the 105th floor of Tower 1. . . ." I scanned for the words "Windows on the World" but didn't find any.

I posted a picture of us all that my neighbor Diane had just e-mailed me, despite the hour. It had been taken the previous Christmas. In it, we were a whole family. Carter sat in my lap drinking a bottle, and Arron clutched his small foot. Arron's other arm was wrapped securely around a pigtailed Olivia in a red dress, pinching her own cheeks, his hand resting on her knee.

I added a description of Arron. "He was wearing a red tie. . . . He had a large scar on the left side of his forehead. . . . He wore a partial denture. . . ." I wanted to add the more important details: He had an infectious giggle. . . . He had beautiful hands. . . . He used a picture of his kids as his computer's wallpaper. . . . His big toe was the most ticklish part of him. . . .

It was unusual for me to know what Arron was wearing when

he left the house, but today I did. He'd left that morning for the trade show but then come back and changed, unhappy with his outfit. He'd even let me choose his tie. I imagined his hand in mine as we parted, wishing I hadn't let go.

I was haunted by my phone call with him that morning. I replayed it over and over in my head. I wished I had sounded more concerned, told him I loved him. Instead, I had been dismissive, trying to get Olivia on the bus, confused about him wanting me to call 9-1-1 and thinking he was being overly dramatic. I hadn't even asked him if he was okay. I knew his fear of heights. He had once told me about a meeting he had had at the top of the World Trade Center during a windy afternoon when the curtains swayed alarmingly away from the windows.

"The curtains were actually staying still!" he had exclaimed. "It was the building that was moving! I had to get out of there. I don't know how people can work up there all the time."

I regretted now that I hadn't sounded more reassuring over the phone.

The clock continued to betray Arron. The kids would be up soon. With a deflating sigh, the heaviest I have ever sighed, I relented and lay down exhausted, but sleep did not come. I willed Arron into bed next to me. Perhaps if I imagined hard enough, he would just be there. I could roll over and snuggle into his arms and forget this day.

Like on the many nights when he traveled, I imagined what he must be seeing or thinking and wondered if his thoughts were the same as mine. I hugged a pillow as sleep took me away for a little while.

[2]

LIMBO

I woke up at seven when the kids jumped onto my bed. For a moment, there was glee in their faces and I had forgotten our nightmare until Olivia gazed at me with her blue doe-eyes and asked, "Where's Daddy?" I began to cry, reminded, and then she began to cry as well. Carter crawled up beside me and knitted himself into my arms. I knew that I had to tell them the truth.

"Sweetie, you know when you told me about the planes hitting the building?"

"Yes," she said with trepidation.

"Well," I said, "Daddy was in one of those buildings. And those buildings both fell down."

"Is Daddy okay? Is he hurt?" I took a deep breath. I could allow her to have the false hope that I longed for, or I could give her my own truthful opinion. I opted for the truth, as the grief book had suggested.

"No, sweetie, I don't think he is okay."

"Is he dead?" She was crying harder now.

"I don't know for sure, honey, but I think he could be. They were really big buildings and he was at the very top." Tears rolled silently down her cheeks and we held each other for a while.

Carter was unusually quiet. But then he asked, "Daddy boo-boo?"

"Yes, sweetie. Daddy big boo-boo," I replied through my tears.

"Mommy?" Olivia said after a long pause. "Is that why all those people were in our house last night?"

"Yes. They all want to help us."

"Mommy, why did the planes crash into the buildings?"

"Well, there are bad people who don't like the United States and they got into those planes and pushed the pilots away and flew them into the buildings." She was silent for a few minutes and I could see her taking all this in.

Then she asked, "Mommy, are the bad men dead, too?" I was amazed that she had figured it out so quickly.

"Yes, I think they are."

"Good," she said, satisfied.

Suddenly, we heard shuffling on the porch and Harley erupted into a cacophony of barking. We all started at the sudden noise and Carter panicked and cried, his cozy nest disturbed. Could Arron be home? Was it a neighbor? I knew the latter was more probable, but I held my breath hoping to hear Arron's greeting. Olivia bounded down the stairs ahead of us. By the time Carter and I stumbled downstairs, whoever had arrived on the porch was gone.

Olivia appeared in the doorway holding a large brown bag. "Mommy, look! Bagels! And cream cheese!" Her favorite food had appeared as if by magic, instantly changing her mood.

I stepped outside to hide my disappointment and found a big urn of coffee. A bag of bagels would arrive on our porch every morning for the next few weeks, sixteen dozen bagels in all, so many they sat in our freezer for months.

Carter and Olivia settled into an episode of Elmo on *Sesame Street*. I was desperate to watch the news coverage showing the dusty people walking down the street, to see if I could pick out Arron in the crowds. I wanted to begin calling him again on his cell phone, as if the daylight might have repaired my connection to him. I wanted to go to the building site and watch as the firemen dug for survivors, to see Arron emerge from an air pocket dirty but unscathed. I wanted to hunt through hospitals looking for a dazed and disoriented husband, one who had lost his wallet and his bearings, and would beam with recognition the instant he saw me.

I wanted to keep hoping that my nightmare was not real. I wanted to wake up and still be holding Arron's hand.

Instead I made myself a cup of tea and my usual bowl of cereal. I took one mouthful and my stomach lurched. The cereal stuck in my throat. I pushed the bowl aside.

I wondered again how Arron might get home if he *were* alive. "The truck, oh God, the truck," I said to my uneaten, soggy cereal. Arron had driven it yesterday, would have parked in a commuter lot somewhere, and now it had been there overnight. Perhaps it had been towed. I wanted the truck home in the driveway, safe, because if Arron called, he would be relieved to know it was okay. Though I thought perhaps I should leave it at the lot, in case he needed to drive it home.

Martha took the kids out on playdates, avoiding the chaos in the house and ensuring that I wouldn't have to worry about them. After that, my morning became consumed with the truck. I couldn't find my keys, so my neighbor suggested I call the dealership. "They can tow it and make a new key," he said.

By the afternoon, the bright apple-red truck was parked back in our driveway where it belonged. A calmness settled over me when the newly cut keys were dropped into my hand. Somehow the truck seemed like confirmation that Arron was really missing, but it also seemed like proof that he had existed, and I was grateful to have found a real part of him.

Later that day, my father stepped out of his green Le Baron and charged across my wide lawn. The late afternoon sun shone behind him and his face was obscured in the shadow of his straw fedora. I met him halfway and he hugged me aggressively, slightly scarily. Tears were running down my cheeks. My father's eyes were moist. There were no words.

"How was the border?" I asked, to defuse the moment.

"Easy." My father seemed relieved by the diversion. "There wasn't even a line." I was glad they had made it through the border crossing in Kingston. This morning, none of us were sure if they would.

Selena hugged me next. She had carpooled with my father and stepmother, who lived part-time in Port Hope. Airplane journeys were out of the question and she was too distraught, she said, to drive herself. Her hug seemed aggressive, too. Perhaps I was just too fragile for hugs. Selena avoided my tears and certainly her own by swinging the kids around in the air while they squealed with delight, a nearly normal Grandma arrival.

Selena had been widowed twice: Arron's father died in 1978 and then her second husband, Brian, died of cancer in 1991. Both her parents were also dead. Now that Arron was gone, the kids and I were all she had left. Somehow at this moment I felt sadder for her than for myself, maybe because of her other losses or because losing an only child seemed so terrible to me now that I was a mother myself. I felt I ought to comfort her in some way, but I couldn't think of what to say.

Sheilagh, my stepmother, held back, unable to look at me. I walked over and hugged her. There were still no words. I could tell that all she wanted to do was to light a cigarette and hide. I wished I could comfort her, too, tell her it was okay. Instead I stood by her, silent and helpless.

"Would you like a glass of wine?" I offered finally. She looked grateful and we all moved inside.

Later still, my mother arrived, having driven from Montreal. She had spent the summer at my grandfather's cottage in Ste. Lucie and smelled like it when I hugged her, like camphor and home-baked cookies. She seemed older than when I had last seen her, two weeks ago, standing in the dusty gravel road waving us all good-bye. We had driven off, Arron, the kids, and I, oblivious of the short time we had left together.

Everyone was now assembled in my kitchen, subdued, drinking wine. My father and mother were talking like old friends with Selena talking over them. Sheilagh, silent, looked ready to flee. To have this group of people united was abnormal. One of the few times that they had been together in one room since my parents' divorce was at our wedding, eleven years ago, and again at my sister Jill's wedding, two years ago. The wine was unwinding them and they began talking too loudly. All the noises in the house were too loud to me. A *Thomas the Tank Engine* video, seemingly played on a loop, provided a constant background noise. The dog barked and I flinched. More people arrived: Brent and Marie, our friends from Atlanta, with their chocolate lab, Bo. I was surprised and touched that they had driven such a long way. Arron had been in Brent's wedding party, and we had spent their honeymoon with them in Key West, six years earlier, but we hadn't seen them much since. With Marie's help, Brent maneuvered his wheelchair through the narrow doorways of our old house and they joined the impromptu vigil going on in the kitchen.

During the next two days, the phone rang incessantly, and I cringed at every jarring ring. Instead of answering it, I placed a green notebook half full of kids' drawings by the phone, in which messages and important numbers were being written in the various handwriting styles of my guests. "Missing Persons, 1st Precinct, Detective Smith, Lifenet Support Line." "Uncle Ted called. 3 min silence in UK. Work stopped in Adrian's mine." "Stopped by 5:30ish. Sorry to have been absent (been sick). Need extra bedrooms, call me." "Jeff phoned from New Zealand." "Beverley sends her thoughts and prayers (London)."

The days were full of "air pocket" talk. A neighbor told me the story of a man who had jumped from one of the upper floors of the World Trade Center, gotten caught in an updraft, and drifted peacefully down to the ground, breaking only a leg in his fall. I knew it was a myth, but I wanted to believe it. When a 110-story building falls on you, the chances of survival are zero percent. "Pancake" was the word I dared not utter to others. Arron was like the character in a Looney Tunes *Road Runner* cartoon, flattened. But maybe he could pop up whole again in an instant. It was horrible to think of my husband that way, yet I found myself making light of things in supposedly inappropriate ways.

My worries became more real when the Canadian consulate put us in touch with Jim Young, a coroner from Toronto who had come to New York to help Canadian families with collecting DNA and "remains recovery." Selena and I took turns speaking to him on the phone. He was honest and straightforward when we peppered him with questions about what the conditions might have been like that day. "Arron most likely passed out from smoke inhalation. He wouldn't have known that the buildings had fallen," Jim told us. *He died before they fell* is what he omitted from his sentence, but it was what we wanted to hear.

It was Thursday, two days after the towers fell, before I finally remembered that I could leave the house. An entourage followed me to the park and helped me push the stroller and walk the dog. I felt like an invalid. When Harley, in her own form of dog grief, sat down at the corner of the park and refused to continue, a sprightly Marie, used to hauling Brent's wheelchair around, simply bent down and hoisted the sixty-five-pound dog up into her arms and walked her into the park. I think my first smile in three days was the sight of this slim, tiny woman carrying a humiliated ball of yellow fur.

That night, the house was still full of people. I was giving Carter his bath, alone for what seemed the first time since that horrible Tuesday morning. As I sat on the toilet watching Carter play in the bathwater, I realized that Arron had already missed three whole days of his son's life. The thought of this wonderful little boy growing up without knowing Arron brought my first sobs. Arron would miss Carter's first tooth falling out. His first soccer game. He wouldn't see Carter get married, wouldn't have a grandchild. Carter wasn't going to learn to laugh out loud at his father's silly jokes, wasn't going to learn to swing a bat with him, wasn't going to get a goodnight kiss from him tonight. The tears poured down my cheeks as wave after wave of sadness hit me.

After a while I noticed that Carter had stopped splashing and was standing in the bath looking at me. I peeked at him through my wet hands, worried that my display might be upsetting to him.

"Mama sad?" Carter asked.

"Yes, Mama very sad," I said.

Carter came closer to the edge of the tub with his arms outstretched. A hiccup sob escaped from me as I knelt down onto the floor to receive his dripping wet hug. It was strong and purposeful. As he held me I had the sensation that Arron was holding me, as if Arron had entered Carter's little naked body so he could hug me one last time. My tears dripped into the tub. And then he let me go.

After I got Carter to sleep, I sat beside Olivia on her bed, crying again as she looked on wide-eyed. Bedtime with the kids brought the saddest moments of my day. They were the only moments that I had alone with them, and memories seemed to be unleashed in the silence of their rooms. I couldn't help thinking of things they would miss: No more kisses from Daddy. No more of Arron's special Minnie Mouse pancakes. No more Daddy-inspired lacrosse lessons. No more tosses into the pool. I would miss watching the kids ride Arron around the yard like a horse. Olivia would miss her "workouts" in the basement, in her red velvet skating dress she refused to take off, as she negotiated the huge stepper machine. Or Arron using her little body as a barbell, pumping her up and down to the accompaniment of Aerosmith or Phish blaring on the CD player while she squealed with delight.

Let them see you cry. Show them your grief. I thought of *When Children Grieve* again as I cried in front of Olivia, remembering, but unable to share these memories with her. They were stuck in my throat, blocked by my tears.

"When are we going to get a new daddy?" Olivia asked suddenly.

"A new daddy?" I said, stunned.

"Yes. I think if we had a new daddy, we wouldn't be sad any more," she explained.

I stalled, trying to find the right words, trying not to show how shocked I was by her question. I hoped my voice sounded normal as I answered her. "Well, sweetie. That might take a long time. I would have to meet someone else and then get married again. But I need time to feel sad about Daddy first. It's okay for us to feel sad, you know," I said carefully.

"I don't want to feel sad anymore. I want to be a happy person."

"Feeling sad doesn't mean you aren't a happy person."

"I don't want to feel sad any more!" she whined and began to cry.

"I know, sweetie, I know. I don't want to feel sad any more either. I wish it could go away for a while, too." I managed to resist the desire to fix everything for Olivia and make it all better for her, just as the grieving book had taught me.

A tiny accomplishment.

On Friday, September 14, on Kathleen's advice, I went to the Armory to file a missing-person report with the New York Police Department. With me were Selena, Brent, my brother Matt, who had skipped classes at Concordia University and driven from Montreal with our eighty-eight-year-old grandfather, and Bruce, a friend of Arron's from fourth grade, who had driven from Toronto with his wife, Jacquie. Arron had introduced Bruce and Jacquie to each other, and they got married during a visit to see us in London, where we had briefly lived years earlier.

The Armory was an old army barracks in downtown New York City that had been pressed into service during the past three days as the first "Family Assistance Center," a place where the victims' families were asked to come and register their loved ones as missing persons. The entire building was painted a dingy olive camouflage color, but single red and white roses in individual vases on each table relieved the drabness. They seemed both hopeful and mocking among the anguished faces that filled the hall. Family upon family sat in front of nonuniformed police officers, clergy, or Red Cross volunteers. Missing-person posters papered the walls, so many happy, confident, alive people smiling into the room. I could read snippets from where I sat on a hard wooden chair . . . "Dragon Tattoo on left bicep," "Last seen on the 105th floor," "Father of four."

I spent over an hour in the impossibly huge room, being questioned by a police officer. I failed to see how any of this questioning was going to locate Arron. Selena was also sitting with an officer, as though the two of us describing him might find him faster. Selena had a way of making the people helping us, like this police officer, Jim Young, the coroner, and Kathleen from Arron's office, seem like her new best friends, in a way I found unnerving. I knew it was just her way, and she was adept at currying favor, but right now, as I looked over and saw the officer laughing at something Selena had said, I was annoyed.

"Gray flannels?" The officer looked at me quizzically as I tried to describe the pants that Arron had been wearing that morning. I searched my mind for an alternative description. "It's like gray wool," I said dully. I was exhausted and disheartened.

The police officer, disheveled and looking as though he hadn't slept in days, took an inordinate amount of time, writing each word I said in painstakingly precise, tiny handwriting. I watched, fascinated but detached.

"Nationality?"

"British. But he was raised in Canada." My U.S. birth had allowed us to live and work in the States, and now irrationally, I suddenly felt I was to blame for his being in the World Trade Center on the wrong day. Selena had brought Arron to Canada to give him a better life than he might have had in the north of England, where they had lived. I had been the one to take him to the United States, and now he was missing, and possibly dead. I wondered if she blamed me for his misfortune, and for hers.

"What did, um, does your husband do?" This question was a joke among my family because no one really understood what he did. How was I going to explain what Arron did to a man who didn't know what gray flannel was?

"He was the vice president of a global financial software company called Encompys." There. I didn't need to explain the intricacies of middleware and banking networks that I myself barely understood.

"Have you brought anything that might have a sample of his DNA?" the officer asked. I handed him Arron's toothbrush, which I had retrieved from his desk drawer at his office earlier in the day, and the long skinny envelope containing his dental x-rays, supplied by our dentist. "I'm so sorry for your loss. This is the most difficult part of my job," our dentist had said, grimly. These trivial things, toothbrushes and dental x-rays, were the only physical proof that Arron had existed.

The day before, Selena had come upstairs to find me digging in the upstairs garbage cans. "What are you doing?"

"I'm looking for the condom that Arron and I used last weekend. I thought it would be good to bring to the Family Assistance Center when we go tomorrow, so they'll have a sample of his DNA."

Without a word, Selena began digging around in garbage bins with me.

"I can't tell you how happy I am that we made love the weekend before he died. It had been a long time." I didn't know why I was telling Arron's mother this.

"I'm glad for you," Selena had replied, smiling.

We continued to hunt, but nothing turned up. Now I was glad, as I imagined myself handing this officer a used condom.

The report he was filling out was eight pages long. Four days had not been long enough to set up computers, which would no doubt have speeded up the process. Proof of the inefficiency of this system would come several months later, when the police called me to verify that Arron's race was African-American. To think that I had agonized over the gray flannel description! Only then did it dawn on me how strange it was that they never asked for a photograph of Arron. Did they already presume him dead?

Finally the officer looked up tiredly and then scrawled a number onto a yellow Post-it and handed it to me. "You will need this number whenever you talk with the medical examiner's office," he said. "In case they find, um, some evidence of him." I memorized Arron's "P-number" quickly, having to recite it often in the weeks to come to prove our status as 9/11 family members. Arron had been replaced by a number. I wondered what the "P" stood for. Perdition?

I walked stiffly to a table with a sign reading "Victims of Crime." It took a while for me to realize that Arron was the victim the sign was referring to, or perhaps I was. I was so tired and longed to lie down on the floor and sleep for the rest of my life.

A woman was asking me something.

"What is your mortgage payment?" She wanted to know how much I paid each month. Did I have a car payment? Were any other payments due? I dove deep, trying to remember amounts. Arron had recently begun paying the bills. He had been angry with me after finding a late charge on a VISA statement. I was angry back, complaining that I couldn't be expected to do everything: children, working, cooking, bills. So he took over the finances. He neatly arranged folders for each statement, wrote checks, argued with companies over amounts. I was satisfied. Now he understood how much time it took me and how tedious it was. Perhaps he could appreciate me just a little bit more. Instead he was zealous, enjoying his scrupulous control over all the finances.

I worked hard to awake from my reverie. I was still sitting in a hard chair at another table with another red rose, a check now clasped in my hand. I was confused. "What is this for?"

"It's to pay your mortgage, dear," said the kindly volunteer. I was astonished and embarrassed. One doesn't speak about one's finances. I was Canadian, after all. What did these people think of me? I was not poor and yet I was being handed money from the Victims of Crime people. I did not deserve this. I felt both humiliated and grateful.

Suddenly I felt crushed by my responsibility for myself and for my children. It struck me like a blow to the stomach, given that I had lost my job in a restructuring just a month earlier. What would become of us? I stood up and thanked the Victims of Crime volunteers and frantically searched for the door, a way out, an escape. I needed to see daylight. I had gone into the Armory with the hope that Arron would be found, but I came out sensing something sinister. I was as much a victim as he was.

HALLELUJAH

Going to church that first Sunday after 9/11 seemed like the right thing to do. Although I was not raised as a churchgoer, these were extreme circumstances. I groped for spiritual guidance. I needed to know where Arron had gone. It was inconceivable that he could have vanished into blackness, faced a bleak nothingness. He had just been with me, alive, thinking, breathing. We had eaten roast chicken together on Monday night. There had to be more. It seemed to me that the purpose of religion and churches was to give people hope that there was more life, more *something* after death. That week I wanted someone to tell me that Arron wasn't dead, that by some miracle he had been found amid the crushed concrete. If I couldn't have that and he truly was dead, then I wanted assurances that he was safe wherever he was, that a part of him still lived and still loved us as we still loved him. I wanted a community of people to help me, to show me the ropes of dealing with the possibility of his death. If anyone knew how to cope with death, I reasoned, people who went to church would.

The truth was, though, that the idea of going to church scared the crap out of me. It was my mother, really, who pushed the idea. She liked to go to her local Anglican church for the music. It seemed to give her a calmness that I was unfamiliar with, as this was not a habit she had followed during my childhood years. "It might do us all some good, sweetie," she reasoned.

My mother expressed her interest in finding an Anglican church in Montclair, so our ever-helpful neighbor Tom called his Catholic priest and secured the name of a Reverend at a local Episcopal church, the U.S. version of the Anglican church. I imagined a club where they got together and networked, exchanging referrals.

I called the Reverend and was surprised to get the church's message machine. Churches had voice mail?

"Uh, hi. This is Abigail Carter. I got your name from a friend's minister. Um . . . my husband was in the World Trade Center. . . . A group of us would like to attend the 10:00 AM service on Sunday. I just wanted to let you know that we would be there."

It was like making a blind date with God.

The day of the service, I fought with the kids to get them to wear nice clothes and then to leave the house. They did not want to go to church. They wanted to watch *Thomas the Tank Engine*. Again. I didn't want to go either, but an ulterior motive fed my determination: I might need to plan a funeral, and a church seemed like a good beginning. I imagined being greeted by the Reverend, a friendly fellow who would look at me with his kind eyes and take me into his office, where he would offer me tissues as he helped me to figure out how to plan Arron's service. "I'll arrange everything, dear," he would say. "You don't have to worry about a thing."

My legs were rubbery as we climbed the church steps, and I could sense the kids' fear by their sudden silence. The building was imposing, large and stone with massive wooden double doors, which stood open, waiting to swallow us up. Churches were as scary to me as they were to the kids. When I was five, I once declared to my grandmother, after visiting Notre Dame in Montreal, "Grandma, I don't really like all this God stuff very much."

As we walked in the front door, my palms were sweaty and my

heart was beating wildly. My nervousness was also rooted in my fear of the unknown: this was my first public outing as a widow. I was certain that I must look different. Perhaps it was possible to see in my eyes that not only was I a widow but I was a 9/11 widow. I felt I had to act a special way, be demure, or red-eyed, or wear a black band around my arm, or carry a folded flag. I *wished* I could wear something that might explain my strange slow gait, and, what I felt must be, my vacant look.

Eleven of us, my entourage, hovered inside the church door awkwardly, expecting a welcoming committee. Some people at the door smiled at us, but we were clearly on our own. I felt responsible for everyone in our group: my mom; Grandad; Selena; my younger sister, Jill (newly pregnant), and her husband, Dan, who had flown in from Vancouver; my brother, Matt; and Bruce and Jacquie. I felt queasy.

We sat down on the hard pews, and Carter immediately climbed into my lap. Olivia twisted her arm around mine and snuggled close. I hoped the minister would be one of the calming, kindly ones and not one of those fire-and-brimstone types that I knew would make the kids (and me) even more nervous. The organ music began and we all tensed up at the sudden noise. Then the kind-looking minister walked up to the altar and began his sermon.

"It is a time of great Sin . . ." he declared in his loud, strident, wavering voice, like a blue-eyed, white-haired Martin Luther King. I groaned inwardly.

The minister carried on, gesticulating and vociferous, his voice becoming louder and louder with his convictions and his denouncements of the "terrorists." He thanked God that "no one in our congregation has been directly affected." I stared at him, incredulous, hoping to pierce him with my eyes. Did he not know we were here? Had he not picked up his messages? Did we not qualify as his congregation? Were we the interlopers I so feared we were? The kids begged to go home. I shushed them and rooted myself to my seat, forcing myself not to grab them and run.

Finally the minister's voice became softer. I had stopped listening to him but suddenly snapped to attention when he said the words "celebrating this happy event, despite the tragic events going on in the world." A woman joined him and they began walking toward the back of the church singing "Take Me to the River" in a slow rhythmic march, their robes making a scratchy noise as they walked past us. This Irish minister was actually attempting to sing gospel! Thankfully, the woman clearly had roots in Gospel. She was belting it out and masking his lack of musical talent quite successfully. They made an odd couple—his tall, slim figure juxtaposed with her petite roundness and black skin. I suppressed hysterical giggles.

They reached the back of the church, where a crowd was gathered around two infants. The minister went about his business of dousing the screaming tots with water and in the end implored his audience to stand and sing hallelujah. Obediently, I stood, not knowing whether to laugh or cry. I was horrified that our feelings had been so callously disregarded. I wondered how those families were feeling. Happy to be celebrating new life during a time of sadness, or were they as appalled as I was at the inappropriateness of the occasion? Surely, a return phone call alerting us to the baptism would have been in order? I rolled my eyes toward the ceiling thinking, "Is this your way of telling me that you don't want a church funeral?" I suppressed a smirk as I imagined Arron's colorful reply.

I looked at Selena, who I knew eschewed religion of all types, despite her having spent a short time as a minister in England, and she looked as though she was going to spit bullets. With one glance at me, she got up and walked out. My mother looked at me with a quizzical look in her eyes that said, "Darling, are you sure this is an *Anglican* church?"

By the time the minister returned to the front of the church, the kids and I had joined Selena outside. On the cement steps, we all sat dejected, the door behind us firmly closed.

"Can you believe that?" Selena bristled. "That guy was an idiot! You did call and leave a message that we were all coming, right?"

"You'd think he would have called to tell us about the baptism," I whined. "You'd think he might have warned us."

"Mommy, I wanna go home!" Olivia whined in response.

"Home!" Carter mimicked.

"No one in his congregation directly affected? How does he even know that yet?" Selena demanded. "Surely someone in his congregation lost a friend or a relative! What an idiot! Fool!"

Fifteen minutes passed and the rest of our party had not yet emerged, clearly waiting politely until the service was over. The kids were jumping on me now and making too much noise. Suddenly, the large wooden door swung open and a woman appeared. She smiled as she handed the kids each a small teddy bear, and I managed a meek "Thank you" before she closed the door again. It was clear that I was going to have to find my own way to plan a funeral. Where I had expected to find refuge, I found only disregard.

Another week began and I struggled to maintain a routine. Waking up at seven. Showering. Unlocking the door. Collecting the bagels. Feeding the kids. But then the phone would start ringing and friends and neighbors would fill my living room, often armed with food dishes and generous hugs. The first difficult week had passed and now people felt more at ease about visiting. Nobody seemed to be back at work. Some people came out of curiosity, others looked at me like I was some kind of celebrity, and I imagined them telling their friends, "I know someone who was *directly* affected." One of my neighbors stood at my door, tears flowing down her cheeks. "I wasn't able to come before now, I'm so sorry."

I felt special in a fragile sort of way and was aware for the first time in my life that I needed to be taken care of. I was uncertain of every step I took. There was a look that others gave me that said, "Oh, you poor thing." Those looks made me feel that I would be excused for crying in public or looking puffy or askew and that I would be cared for. I would be excused for any weakness that I might display. But it was awful being pitied. Those looks were a constant reminder of the nightmare that my life had become. Many of my visitors had been merely acquaintances before and I stood frozen as some grabbed me in messy embraces, sobbing into my shoulder. I patted backs absently, saying nothing. They seemed to cry, not only for me, but for themselves and for the country. Perhaps they needed to share with me their fear that they could just as easily have been in my place.

I sat on the couch and received them, colleagues from Arron's company, and from mine, or parents of the kids' friends. Through the living room window one day, I could see a neighbor weeding my garden. Another neighbor brought us coffee and tea like a servant. I was like a public mourning post where people came for support. Or perhaps I was like an ancient Greek Oracle, whom people visited to make their offerings. They brought food and looked to me for some kind of prophetic wisdom that I was unable to provide. I imagined them looking to me for some kind of explanation of how such a terrible thing could have happened, and why. I felt like the antithesis of an oracle. Prophet and icon were unfamiliar roles for me. They left me feeling helpless. Normally *I* comforted. *I* consoled. *I* listened. *I* empathized. I wanted to offer support to the people around me who were grieving. I wanted to offer wisdom to those who sought my guidance. Instead I stood woodenly, a glazed look in my eye as I patted backs. I longed to find solace in their well-meaning attempts at comforting me. But I felt nothing. There were more awkward hugs at the door as I bid my visitors good-bye.

By now, the food had become as overwhelming as the hugs, so an organized neighbor taped a bright green sign-up sheet to my kitchen cabinet where names were scrawled in various colors of ink, in different handwriting: breakfast, lunch, dinner. Each day someone would call to find out how many they needed to cook for. I rarely knew. Each day the count was different, with out-of-town friends and family coming and going. My table was usually full and a large wicker toy box had become a permanent bench. Meal times forced a kind of routine. Occasionally I ate, out of obligation and to ease my shakes. I mostly ate the soups. They were salty, warm, and nourishing, the only food that didn't taste like cardboard. Carrot was my favorite and I must have told someone that, because we received pots and pots of carrot soup. It was always eaten, rarely left over. Perhaps the orange cheered us. Fran, my neighbor from across the street, brought huge bowls of fruit salad, another favorite.

"You're getting so thin!" I began to hear, even though barely a week had passed since my diet changed so dramatically. I knew my clothes didn't fit the same way, but I was surprised that I had lost enough weight for people to notice. I was hardly anorexic. I began to respond with dark humor. "Yes! It's this great new diet I'm on! The lose-a-husband diet plan! Works like a charm!" Faces fell.

Wine became my salve. It was poured for me, often starting at around 5:00 PM, my family's usual time for a festive cocktail hour. My glass was always full. Initially, it calmed the tiny panicky tremors that plagued my body, as though my heart was beating one too many times a minute. For a while, I could feel my frozen demeanor crack a little, and I felt almost normal. The wine settled me, eased my numbness, allowed me to taste my dinner. The effect of the wine, however, always diminished too quickly, leaving me feeling thick and tired.

At bedtime, the tremors would begin again, revived by the wine coursing through my immobile, prone body. I toyed with the brown bottle of tiny white pills on my bedside table, antisomethings given to me by a doctor friend. I had sat obediently in her passenger seat like an elderly patient as we drove to the pharmacy.

"I probably won't take any," I had said as she handed me the bag. I was certain they were addictive.

"They will calm you down at night and help you sleep."

One night, the jitters were overwhelming. My heart began to beat too fast. I took my first pill and felt like Alice drinking a potion from a cup labeled "Drink me." First, I felt too small for my body, and then too big. But my mind stopped racing. The jitters subsided. I could cope. I fell asleep almost immediately for the first time in a week. Each night, I took one, and sleeping did become easier. Still, I worried that when the bottle was empty, I wouldn't be able to sleep without the pills, so I decided to reserve them for only the really bad jittery nights. When the supply was gone, I would not renew it. I would learn to live with the jitters.

One morning, I felt brave, and the desire to do something physical was intense. I missed my kickboxing classes, so I pulled on my workout clothes, and with my mother determined to accompany me, we headed to Master Cho's dojo, the gym where I had been taking classes for over a year. My mother stood behind me in the class, trying to keep up while I tried not to notice that all eyes were on me. It felt good to kick at myself in the mirror. I imagined faceless terrorists and punched and kicked them hard. Afterward, my classmates proudly handed me two gigantic gift baskets full of toys for the kids. Women stood around my mother and me, and one by one, grasped my hand, and whispered, "Sorry for your loss" or "If there is anything I can do. . . ." I wanted to run away. I had thought that I would be anonymous in this class, like I always had been. Master Ricky offered Olivia, who had been taking tae kwon do classes, a full scholarship to the school. "All the way to a black belt!" Ricky's thick black hair flopped as he described his generous offer in Korean-clipped English. "And a scholarship! For college! From Master Cho!" I was stunned. I tried not to let the tears come.

We got home and I parked behind Arron's truck. I touched it as I walked down the drive. "Come home," I said. "Come home."

Lying in bed one night at 4:00 AM, semi-awake, I realized that Arron had been gone almost ten days. I wished him into bed with me. I imagined running my hands down his body, remembering every freckle, every bump, every curve as though he were still alive. I imagined again what he must have endured that day, his fear, his anger, his remorse all played out over the course of only a few terrifying minutes, the way a passenger might in a crashing airplane. I thought of his regrets: that we had never taken the weekend away from the kids that I had been nagging him about, that he hadn't spent more time with the kids, that we hadn't made love more often.

Abruptly, the hall light turned on. I kept my bedroom door open at night to hear the kids, so my bedroom was suddenly flooded in light. I sat bolt upright and listened, thinking that Olivia might have woken up to go to the bathroom since the light switch was just outside her room, though it would have been unusual for her to turn that light on. But there were no sounds of a stumbling midnight bathroom excursion. I got up to take a look, but when I peeked into Olivia's room, she had the flung-armed look of a child who had been asleep for hours.

As I stood awash in the yellowish glow of the hallway, I had the overwhelming sense that the light was part of Arron's ghostly communication. His message was clear: "I am gone, Bird. I have died."

My fantasies of air pockets, hospitals, and amnesia suddenly seemed silly. There was clarity to the moment that made his death seem final. For just a second, I imagined I could feel his presence swirling around me. The air seemed heavier and smelled slightly sweet, like honey. With my entire hand, I decisively pushed the light switch into its downward position. Its heavy click made me flinch.

I was alone in the dark.

[4]

NOT QUITE NORMAL

September had once been a month full of celebrations: my birthday and our wedding anniversary fell within the same week. This year, I was dreading my birthday, the first of the two events, wrapped up tight as I was in my cocoon of grief.

On past birthdays, Arron had taken me out for my favorite meal, sushi. I spent the two weeks leading up to the day reminding him of the date. He made special plans to be home early. I hired the babysitter. We snuck out for a few hours alone, held hands, drank saki, and discussed our day. We looked into each other's eyes and smiled. He always gave me a single red rose. It was a simple celebration.

Now, I wondered how I might be able to pretend that this day had never existed; that I did not exist. Unexpectedly, a big celebration of my birthday planned by my family helped me to feel joy for the first time in eleven days. My mother and Olivia secretly collaborated all day. They pulled shut the dining-room doors that morning and Olivia taped up a sign that read in a child's handwriting: "Momy, do not come in!!!" I heard the sounds of scraping chairs, giggling, and clinking dishes all morning.

Then I was given a respite from all the people in my house when my mother took everyone out on a secret mission, leaving me alone in the house for the first time. I wandered the empty, lonely rooms (avoiding the dining room per Olivia's orders), crying freely as I glanced in the direction of photos of my once-whole family. I stepped around the many bouquets of sickly yellow flowers that dominated every surface and had even made their way to the floor, lining the walls. My sobs were frustratingly short-lived. I wanted to feel cleansed the way you sometimes do after a heavy cry, but these tears felt stuck and left me feeling bleary and unfocused. Finally, exhausted by my fruitless effort to cry, I avoided my loneliness by succumbing to a nap.

Later, the house was again alive with action. I changed into a bizarrely sexy red tank top and black skirt at the prompting of my sister. Olivia and Carter told me to sit on the couch while the final preparations were made. Carter was already in his jammies, and Olivia was all dressed up in her favorite denim skirt. I heard movement and whispered conversation from behind the closed dining-room doors. The kids snuck out and Olivia said, "Mommy, close your eyes tight!" They each grabbed one of my hands and led me to the door, and when Olivia said "Okay, ready!" the doors slid open and I was presented with their day's work.

I was awestruck. They had taken all the white roses from our funeral bouquets and tied them upside down along ribbons strung between the chandelier and the walls of the dining room. The room, which had been oppressive as a result of all the dying bouquets, was now beautiful. A huge platter of sushi sat in the center of the table. My mother, Selena, Jill and Dan, Matt, Olivia, and Carter looked at me with excitement in their eyes; each was anxious to see my look of surprise, anxious to make me happy for just a little while.

I felt light with giddiness for a second, like I might drift away. I was shocked to feel an emotion, to feel anything at all. I had been an automaton for eleven days, and I had just felt a chink in the armor that protected me from sensation. Like a muscle that had atrophied, my emotions felt weak from disuse. They tired me quickly. I felt guilty for having joyful thoughts, as though they might erase my memories of Arron. As we ate, I looked around the room at each person. I felt grateful for each one who loved me so much.

Olivia and Carter presented me with a birthday present of a multicolored plastic beaded necklace, which I immediately tied around my neck. The shiny fuchsia, blue, and yellow beads clashed with my blood-red top, rendering its sexiness clownlike. In another life, I would not have put the necklace on. I would have made appropriate oohs and aahhs and then tucked it away, so that it wouldn't interfere with my vanity. Now, I wanted to please them, make them happy, mop away their sadness.

For the moment, Olivia had lost her look of constant concern, a look that made her seem so much older than her six years. I loved seeing her eyes light up, hearing her giggles, so much like her father's. Carter was wearing a ring of chocolate ice cream around his mouth and a dot on his nose from licking off his plate. There were long drips of chocolate down his white summer pajamas. I ached for these two wonderful children. They were thrilled with the celebration, such a break from the sadness that had engulfed the house. They were small, warm pieces of Arron. I gathered them up then and hugged them close. Tears formed for a second, but I swallowed them away.

The rest of my family then presented me with their gifts. My mother gave me a silver necklace; it seemed full of hope. My sister gave me some beautiful pearl earrings, like small eggs; they promised new beginnings. Each gift was meaningful, and thoughtful. But the most precious gift of all was the homemade plastic necklace, and the way it had made me smile. It represented all that I had.

I had received a call a few days before my birthday from Janet, a child psychologist. I assumed that Olivia's school had given her my number, but later she told me that she had seen my name in the local paper, looked me up, and called. "I had this sense that you might need to talk with someone. It was a matter of following what felt deeply right, though it was strictly against the 'rules,'" she said.

I called her back right away. I was indeed desperate for someone objective to talk to. I needed guidance with the kids, and someone to talk to about grief. My friends and family were grieving, too, and were too emotionally attached to Arron, the kids, and me to be of any help. Janet arranged to meet me at home shortly after my birthday, and also to meet the children. She arrived at the door, a small, dark-haired woman in her sixties, with soft brown eyes that crinkled in sympathy as she clasped my hand.

"I'm Janet," she said simply.

I ushered her into my living room. The kids were sequestered in our basement rec room with Martha and Selena.

"So, how are you holding up?" she asked.

"Fine." I began to cry. I was so relieved to have someone safe to cry with. I immediately trusted her and knew she would understand my tears and empathize with my trauma while remaining neutral at the same time. She was a professional and would know what to do with the emotions that were overwhelming me, causing me to retreat within myself, crying only when I was alone.

"I'm just fine," I repeated, fat tears rolling down my cheeks. I was overwhelmed with emotions that I didn't know how to begin describing.

"I'm numb. I don't really know how I feel. I was walking the dog today and met a couple of old ladies in the park. They were making a fuss over Harley and I blurted out that Harley had just lost her master in the World Trade Center. I shocked them and then felt terrible because I hated seeing the pity in their eyes. Yet I seem to need to tell every stranger I meet about my tragedy."

"That's very normal for someone who has endured a trauma. It will take time. How do you think the kids are doing?" she asked.

"I don't know. Olivia hasn't cried very much. She doesn't want to be seen as a sad person. Carter doesn't talk a whole lot yet, but he seems to understand. He says things like 'No more Daddy now,'

'Only Mommy now,' 'Daddy angel.'" Janet's eyes welled up slightly. I began folding a tissue in my hand, nervously, tears falling into my lap.

"Sorry," I said.

"Why are you sorry?" she asked.

"I feel bad for making you sad."

"I see where Olivia gets it now. Abby, this is what I do. I am here to help you, if you want it."

"Would we come to see you all together?" I asked, changing the discussion to one of logistics.

"No, I would prefer to see each of you separately."

"Even Carter?"

"I might see him a bit, but he is pretty little right now. Certainly down the road if we think it will help him. We'll take it slow. I have lots of toys and they can come to my office and play in my playroom."

"They would like that, I think."

I talked to Janet a little about the trouble I was having trying to convince Olivia to go back to school, the tears, the stomach aches, her long silences. "She keeps telling me how mean her teacher is," I explained.

"It's going to be tough. But you just have to be confident and know that getting her back into her routine is the best thing for her. Don't accept her excuses. Tummy aches, tired, hungry, whatever. Just persevere."

"Alright," I said, feeling emboldened.

Olivia and Carter peeked out from the basement stairs. Shyly, they ran over to me, Carter burying his head in my lap as he sneaked furtive glances at Janet. Olivia began her silly act of dancing around and giggling and talking gibberish in a baby voice.

"Hi!" Janet said. "I'm Janet. You must be Olivia and you must be Carter. Your mommy has told me all about you!" she gushed.

"You wanna see my turtle?" Olivia asked.

"Of course!" Janet responded.

Olivia dragged a big stuffed turtle over toward Janet's feet and then took a running jump, landing right in the middle of its soft green shell.

"Wow! That's a great turtle!" Janet enthused. Carter ran over to his toy basket and picked out a big red truck.

"Druck!" he said, handing it to Janet.

"Thank you, Carter," she said quietly as she took it.

I smiled. "You just passed the test, I think." Janet smiled her all-knowing smile.

I was grateful to have Janet enter our lives and almost audibly breathed a sigh of relief.

A few days later, on Janet's advice, I began to get Olivia ready for her first day of school since September 11.

"I don't wanna go!" Olivia wailed.

"Sweetie, it's been two weeks since you've been to school and you're missing too much," I responded, trying to sound calm, as Janet had recommended.

"I have a tummy ache!"

"It'll go away. You're nervous. I know it's scary going back to school."

"Everybody's going to look at me!" Olivia shared my own fear. I, too, had sequestered myself indoors, afraid I might burst into tears suddenly, or that something terrible might happen, a car crash or a kidnapping. I took rare walks with the dog, pushing Carter to the park in the stroller, but I preferred to stay home, only seeing the people who visited me.

"They might," I said. "But who cares. Just be yourself and you'll be fine." I was trying to sound nonchalant, trying to convince myself of this wisdom. A big part of me wanted to keep her home forever. We each had a new-found fear of being separated from one another. She feared I wouldn't come home some day, just like Daddy, and I needed her close, so I could watch over her, and keep her safe. I learned from Janet that she needed to get back into her own routine, that we both had to set our fears aside.

"C'mon, Livy, it will be easier than you think," Selena cajoled.

"Got your lunch?" I asked cheerfully as I opened the door for her, with Carter perched on my hip.

"Yes, but I won't be able to eat it . . ." she said sulkily as she stalked onto the porch. We walked together, Olivia, Selena, me with Carter, into the sunny September day, so similar to another sunny day a lifetime ago. As we got near the school bus stop, Selena looked up.

"Look, Livy!" she exclaimed. "Two butterflies following each other!" Olivia looked up and I thought I saw a smile. The need for signs from Arron was overwhelming, and butterflies always seemed to appear just when we needed them most. They comforted us all, making us feel somehow that he was close.

"They're following you to school. They're telling you it's going to be okay," I said, sounding slightly manic to my own ears.

"Maybe," Olivia grumbled.

We got to the bus stop and waited. I gave Olivia a hug as the bus pulled up.

"I don't want to go . . ." Olivia said but sounded resigned.

She stepped onto the bus, lips pursed. "Bye, sweetie!" I yelled too loudly, so she could hear me through the closed windows. I waved like a maniac, but really I wanted to run after the bus and take her home. What if she never returned?

For a while, each day was the same. To get out of going to school, Olivia complained of stomach aches, or a sore throat, or a sore nose. I struggled not to relent and let her stay home, even though her face was pale, her eyes sad. I hadn't seen her laugh in ages.

Several days later, I spoke with the school's guidance counselor, who assured me that Olivia was doing great. Her teacher was allowing her to visit either the guidance counselor or the school nurse whenever she needed a break from the overwhelming chaos of the classroom. When the school nurse called, at least once a day, I asked her to give Olivia a hug and let her rest a bit before sending her back to class. After some time passed, the school nurse and I agreed that a phone call home each time Olivia arrived in her office was no longer necessary.

Even though Olivia was only in first grade, the homework she got was extensive and ridiculous. I could barely manage it, so I didn't see how she possibly could. Each night her homework sessions ended in tears of frustration. "Everyday Math," a new math system that the school was using, became the bane of my existence. Fractions in first grade? Geometry? Olivia struggled with reading as well. She read Bs as Ds or vice versa. She missed small words like "of" and "the" altogether. Selena, our last remaining houseguest, was no more successful in helping Olivia. She complained bitterly about the homework, which didn't help my cause. When Olivia's tears began, I put the homework away, making her cry even harder, knowing that I, too, was frustrated and had reached my own melting point.

Getting to spend a moment alone with Olivia was also a challenge, as Carter demanded every ounce of attention I had. He refused to let me out of his sight and insisted on sitting on my lap everywhere we went. Olivia howled in frustration at any kind of noise that Carter made: "I can't concentrate!" We spiraled downward. The stomach aches continued. But I kept sending her to school. We kept trying to do the homework.

Olivia began visiting Janet's playroom. Janet told me how Olivia built huge towers out of blocks and knocked them down. A "bad guy" action figure, a small black-cloaked toy, alternately killed and was killed in her play sessions. He was crushed by falling blocks or else rescued from the tops of the block towers. In Janet, Olivia seemed to have found a person she could talk to about grief, sadness, missing Daddy, and bad guys all without worrying about upsetting me. She told me nothing about her sessions with Janet, but I began to notice small changes even after the first session.

One day, during a rare moment that I didn't have Carter on my lap crawling all over me, Olivia walked up to me. "Mommy, I need a hug." I was surprised. She had never before asked for a hug. I probably had not been very good about giving her hugs since 9/11. On the few instances that I had tried, she had squiggled out of my grasp, or allowed me to kiss only the top of her head. Whenever she did come and cuddle with me, Carter immediately became jealous, hitting her or pushing his way onto my lap, disrupting the moment. Although Janet had not mentioned it, I knew that she was teaching Olivia to ask for what she needed, and I was grateful.

"Come here," I said, grabbing her into a bear hug until she squealed.

"I know that sometimes I don't always give you the attention you need. A lot of that is because Carter is still so little and needs lots of my attention. You often seem like you don't need my hugs, but I know you really do sometimes. I want you to know that anytime you ask, I will try and give you what you need. Okay?"

"Okay, Mama." I hugged her tight, putting my arm under her legs and holding her like an infant, making her giggle.

Baby steps for us both.

I felt as though I had lived a lifetime without Arron. I wanted things to be normal again. I wanted his calm logic to help me with Olivia's school woes and Carter's clinginess. I wanted to see a smile on Olivia's face as she climbed the steps of the school bus, and to see Carter bouncing around on his father's shoulders instead of clinging to my leg.

Our eleventh wedding anniversary on Saturday, September 29, was fast approaching. I didn't know how to celebrate the day. The couple that we once were seemed to be a stranger to me now, characters in a romantic novel.

The newlyweds cannot stop smiling. Their faces ache. The night is magical and also slightly frightening in its magnitude. A day they will never forget. They see the affirmation of their love in the faces of their wedding guests. Gleeful, giddy. The guests know they are witnessing true love. The air is electric with good feelings.

Later the couple is in their hotel room, sipping champagne, already slightly drunk, though too tired to feel it. Their feet ache from dancing, their cheeks from over-smiling. They try to frown, but the smiles erupt despite them. They fall into bed and sleep in each other's arms, waiting for the light of dawn to consummate their love.

The tears cascaded down my cheeks as I thought of that happy couple. Now there was just me, alone.

My father and Sheilagh came for the weekend of my anniversary, knowing that my house was now empty of guests. Selena had returned home for a few days, the first time in three weeks. I was surprised by how quiet the house seemed without her constant chatter and her penchant for swinging the kids around the kitchen by their arms while they squealed and the dog barked. I relaxed in the long comfortable silences created by my father and Sheilagh, as they read books at our kitchen table and talked quietly while the kids played with toys in the other room. It was the calm before the storm of Arron's memorial service, just a week away.

I hadn't realized how much my full house had contributed to my feeling out of control. I had endured weeks of the jitters, jumping at loud noises, and feeling overwhelmed, thinking these feelings were a part of my grief. But now I could see that what I had thought was a safe haven full of people who cared about me had actually been the cause of my feeling besieged. My parents remained themselves, clinging to the routines I had grown up with: they still smoked too much, drank coffee, read for hours at a time while their cigarettes burned into long cylindrical remains in the ashtray. They also were able to hide their grief, possibly sensing my need for a grief-free environment, or else because they feared their own emotions. I wished I could know their secret.

The day before my anniversary was busy. In the morning,

Sheilagh and I sat on our haunches, gardening. I dug listlessly in the earth, pulling weeds without strength—vigorous roots held their ground. The tiny pine trees that Arron had dug up and brought back from our recent trip to my grandfather's cabin in Quebec were now dying. They needed attention, water, mulch. But Arron was dead, and I let the baby trees die with him.

Sheilagh planted bulbs along the stone wall that Arron had built. He is immortalized in a photograph, bending over the half-built wall holding a rock, wearing black shorts and a weight belt over his white T-shirt, his knobby-kneed elk-legs long and skinny compared with his broad shoulders and wide arms. He was proud of his garden, our garden. It was filled with flowers, shrubs, and trees that we had argued over, dug a hole for, heaved the root ball into, shoveled dirt over, and painstakingly watered. We had developed an addiction to nurseries. I teased him about our garden looking like the garden of a home adjacent to a nursery—its tiny postcard-stamp-size lot filled with one of every species of tree and shrub that the nursery sold. This spring, Arron would miss seeing our garden bloom.

That evening, my father and I did our customary dance around the kitchen, chopping, stirring, adding to each other's spices. I had not cooked since before September 11. I couldn't eat the dinner that we made, but the preparation felt wonderful. Normal.

The next day, our anniversary, was anything but ordinary. Arron and I normally spent our anniversary holding hands across a table at a romantic restaurant, smiling at each other, alone as if for the first time. We exchanged cards with handwritten notes promising back rubs or foot rubs, our only gifts to one another.

But today a limo came to pick up Sheilagh, my father, the kids, and me, to take us to the Canadian Embassy in New York, where Prime Minister Jean Chrétien was meeting with the Canadian 9/11 families. I wanted to meet the families, too. I longed for another widow to talk to, as I knew none. I wondered if there would be another widow with young children. I hoped. I wanted affirmation that I was following the widow rules, handling the kids correctly. I wanted to find someone with whom I could exchange stories, who would understand the same language of death, who would become an ally. I had imagined finding a widow-mom and becoming good friends, our kids playing together, sharing future Father's Days, taking kid-friendly vacations together, bound forever in our mutual catastrophes. I also wanted to see how the other widows handled the pressure of being the representative of a 9/11 death.

From the loop of highway that led into the Lincoln Tunnel we could see the still-smouldering World Trade Center. We pulled up too early to a nondescript building near Rockefeller Plaza. Killing time in a coffee shop next door, the kids filled their faces with Krispy Kreme doughnuts. It was like feeding them speed.

We arrived in the basement of the building through security turnstiles and found crayons and paper, cookies and candies neatly arranged on a low coffee table for the kids. Two other children, just slightly younger than Carter and Olivia, spilled into the room.

"Do you live nearby?" I asked their mother, anxious for a friend. She told me her name was Kimmy.

"Yes. I'm in New Jersey."

"Me, too!" I was excited. "We should get together!"

"Well, actually I'm going to be moving back to Quebec on the first of November," Kimmy said. I was crushed. A friend found and then lost. I was also shocked. I could barely get out of bed in the morning. I couldn't imagine organizing a move. Kimmy explained that she and her husband had built a house there and had been planning to move back anyway. My fantasy of meeting a fellow widow was gone.

"We will have to find a way to stay in touch," I said, trying not to sound too disappointed. Soon we were each chasing our sugar-charged boys around the room.

I stood with my dad and Sheilagh near the kids' craft table, watching Olivia color with crayons. Carter was like a whirling dervish. One minute he was coloring, the next reaching for me to pick him up, and the next jumping down and running across the room with me chasing after him. The din was getting louder as each family spoke to politicians and consulate staff, their nervousness diminishing with new familiarity. Suddenly, the room hushed as Jean Chrétien entered. His eyes darted around, avoiding eye contact with everyone. I felt sorry for him. This must be a terrible part of the job, having to express condolences to all of us, being watched, trying to look sincere. He glided to the first family on his left, and hushed introductions and cursory handshakes were exchanged. There were no hugs, no sad looks, just a man doing his job, one he obviously didn't relish. We met Stockwell Day, the leader of Canada's Official Opposition, briefly shook hands, exchanged names, avoided talk of the tragedy.

Joe Clark, who had for a short time been the prime minister of Canada, was suddenly standing in front of my father and Sheilagh and me, looking slightly more dignified than all the old caricatures had made him seem. Carter, again perched on my hip, was struggling to wriggle out of my grasp and run around, still high on sugar. I could not let him go, as I knew he might knock someone over.

"Hi. I'm Joe Clark," he said simply. We each shook his hand.

"I'm so sorry for your loss," he said.

"Thank you," I replied. I was becoming well versed at this exchange.

"So do you live in New York?"

"No, New Jersey." By now, Carter was getting mad, pushing against me with his tiny hands. He was at the age when he would sometimes hit me or grab my cheeks when he didn't get his way. The Krispy Kremes had definitely been a bad idea.

"And who is this?" Joe Clark bent down a little to say hello to Carter, obviously trying to distract him. Before I could stop him, Carter raised his hand and slapped Clark across the face. There was a stunned silence, punctuated by a flash as my father took the picture he had been poised to take of Clark, whose face turned bright red.

"Carter, no! No hitting! I am *so*, *so* sorry! Oh gosh, Carter! That was very bad! You say sorry to Mr. Clark right now!"

"It's fine," Clark said graciously. Perhaps this hadn't been his first run-in with a two-year-old.

"Down, down, down!" Carter yelled. I lost my grasp and he jumped from my arms to the floor, where my father caught him and tried unsuccessfully to hold him.

The Right Honorable Joe Clark slunk off to greet other families, no doubt avoiding small children.

What had at the outset been an anticipated excursion suddenly came crashing down around me. I had hoped to avoid thinking about Arron and our wedding anniversary by hiding myself behind my stoic, Jackie Kennedyesque widowhood. I thought getting dressed up and taking a limo to the Canadian consulate to meet the prime minister would distract me from the day. Instead, I was stuck in this tomblike basement room frozen with embarrassment at losing control over Carter, despairing at the surrealism of my new world. I wanted to escape, but we still had to meet the prime minister. I chased Carter once again across the room and brought him back, holding him tight between my legs despite his loud protests. Mr. Chrétien finally made his way over to us, no doubt wary of my wild child. I shook hands awkwardly with this gruff man. He offered a perfunctory "Sorry for your loss" in his gravelly French accent. We posed woodenly beside him for a photo. I barely managed to subdue the squirming Carter as our moment was captured on film for posterity. Mr. Chrétien hurried back to the refuge of a child-free couple.

At last Chrétien left the room, signaling the end of the event. I found Kimmy and hugged her good-bye, as Carter tugged me out the door. "Let's keep in touch!" I pleaded. In the limo, Carter mercifully fell asleep.

That night over dinner, I thought again of Arron and whispered "Happy Anniversary" under my breath, as if he could hear me.

47

Later, alone in my room, I looked at a greeting card that I had given Arron on our tenth anniversary, which he had framed. The title of the image was "La Belle Dame sans Merci" for John Keats's poem ("The Beautiful Lady Without Mercy"). An armored prince, hands outstretched, tilts his head upward so he can stare into the eyes of his silken-haired lady as she leans toward him from atop her horse. She is poised for a kiss, presumably to thank him for rescuing her. The card was cut apart, showing what I wrote a lifetime ago, taped securely to the back of the frame:

To my knight in shining "amour" who will be so evermore . . .
I never say thank you for being my hero.
I love you.
La Belle Dame sans Merci
(otherwise known as Bird)

The next day, a Sunday, I took my parents and the kids to Eagle Rock Reservation, a large park and woods overlooking Manhattan, where Arron, the kids, and I used to walk Harley. The buildings still smouldered in the distance. Carter pointed toward them: "Daddy there? Daddy angel now?" A cliff wall had become a makeshift memorial. I was touched by its poignancy—its simple poems of grief and tiny U.S. flags flapping in the wind, but also repelled by it. This same collection of memorabilia seemed to follow me everywhere I went: handwritten notes in ziplocked bags pinned to walls, often with photos of loved ones, reminiscent of the missing-person posters that they had replaced; soggy stuffed animals; candles long burned out. I had come to have a love-hate relationship with these memorials because of the way they always made me gasp inwardly, as if experiencing Arron's death for the first time.

Later that afternoon, my father and Sheilagh returned to Toronto. I hugged them as they stood beside the car, unable to find a way to thank them for providing me with what had felt like an almost-normal weekend.

Although I wished they could stay longer, I was excited to finally be alone in my own house, if only for a few days. I felt emboldened to attempt cooking dinner again for my shrunken family, despite my lack of appetite. The next day, I decided to venture out and make my first expedition to the grocery store since Arron's death. Perhaps it would rekindle in me an interest in food. As I drove into the parking lot of the A&P, I felt like myself again. Maybe I would roast a chicken, some potatoes, a veggie. I would put whatever meal the neighbors delivered tonight into the freezer. I would eat with the kids, like the times Arron was away on a business trip.

The shopping cart felt unfamiliar and huge. I stepped uncertainly through the doors and was immediately taken aback by the store's Fourth of July decor. Flags hung from the ceiling, small ones on sticks poked out from between the stacks of produce, flag-inspired fabric formed a swag around the bins holding sale items. I should have been used to the patriotic displays, but here in my regular grocery store in early October they seemed to be placed specifically for me. For a moment, I wanted to run away, tired of these constant reminders, but I was still high on my new-found independence and so I pretended it was July.

Four years of shopping at the same store took over and I walked along in autopilot. First, the produce. Apples look good. A salad would be nice, pick out a head of lettuce, some grape tomatoes, some broccoli for the kids. On to the dairy section: milk, yogurt, butter . . . I hummed along to a popular 80s hit playing over the loudspeakers. I felt normal! On to the canned soup . . . chicken noodle for Carter, clam chowder for me. Next the junk food aisle.

Ruffles. I'd better get a bag for Arron . . . I froze, then put it back slowly. Tears sprang to my eyes. Shit. "Clean up in aisle two," I thought as I wiped my tears on my sleeve. A woman with a cart scurried past me, pretending not to notice. I turned into the chips, hiding. I had visions of Arron eating his chips: walking in the door after work, still in his suit as he grabbed the bag and stuffed a huge handful into his mouth; standing in his tool belt, with a beer and an open bag while he took a break from building our deck last summer; sitting watching a football game on TV, flinging chips to Harley, who jumped into the air to retrieve them.

Hiding behind sunglasses, I carried on, past the low-cholesterol mayonnaise that I used to buy for him; past his favorite brand of razors; past his favorite brand of coffee, past the chocolate ice cream and chocolate syrup ("avec sauce!" was always his singsong refrain). I tried to concentrate on the task at hand. Diapers for Carter. Frozen waffles for Olivia. Chicken fingers.

As I stood waiting to pay, I noticed a placard: "Ask to donate to the 9/11 families." I would be donating to myself. I wanted to laugh and cry at the same time. I swallowed the lump in my throat and adjusted the sunglasses on my nose, tears dripping under them, down my cheeks. The lady ahead of me was writing a check, taking too long. I began to panic. About to sob, I needed to escape, so I distracted myself by bagging my own groceries, practically throwing things into the bags. Using a debit card, I paid quickly. "Have a nice day!" the cashier sang at me.

I ran the cart to the car and threw the bags into the back and got in quickly before the full flood of tears began. I sat for several minutes, letting the tears come, and then let out a scream of frustration. Just when things seemed to be feeling normal, I was ricocheted back into grief. I drove home through my tears and put away the groceries, seeing that I had bought too much. The apples would rot in the bowl. The chicken would remain frozen for months. I looked at the empty space on the top of the fridge where the chips used to reside, the only perceivable indication that my life had changed forever.

SINGING NUNS

I was wholly unprepared to plan a funeral, let alone my husband's. Death happened to other people. I was thirty-six years old and the only real losses in my life had been the deaths of my grandmothers. Ironically, I had attended the funeral of one of Arron's best friends on September 7. Tim died suddenly in Brussels of an apparent heart attack at the age of forty-two. Arron didn't go to Tim's funeral, and I was angry that he had not made more of an effort to be there. He cited a sales meeting with a big client as his excuse, and I tried to be understanding. He had just started at Encompys, a struggling start-up, and the meeting could result in significant new business for the company. But I was dismayed that he could allow work to keep him from such an important event. Later, I wondered if he didn't go to Tim's funeral because of some innate forewarning.

Tim always made the two-hour trek to see us whenever he visited his family in Pennsylvania. He brought treats for the kids and was full of jokes, smiles, and laughs. He was truly a man who worked to live and whose friends meant the world to him. Though he lived alone, Tim always maintained a three-bedroom apartment in Brussels, so that people could visit him. Arron had bonded with Tim while living with him in Brussels for a few weeks while he ironed out the details of a new job in London. I had been desperate to leave Brussels and so had spent those weeks living with Selena in Toronto, working as a temp. Tim used to call Arron and have Arron's secretary interrupt important meetings with "Mr. Armitage Shanks on the line for you, Mr. Dack." Only Arron and Tim knew that Armitage Shanks was the brand name of a British toilet.

Tim's memorial service reflected his vivacious personality and was full of laughs rather than tears. It was the first time I had heard the term "Celebration of Life" used to describe a funeral. I came home to Arron after the service preaching the message of living your life to the fullest and appreciating the people around you. Tim's death woke us both up to the idea that each day might be our last.

That spring and summer had been difficult for Arron and me. He was unhappy in his job and was enduring the slow process of interviewing for the one at Encompys. In the meantime, I was laid off from my own job as a web project manager at Audible.com, a company that sold downloadable audio books, adding to the pressure he was feeling. Even after he began the new job, with renewed enthusiasm, the distance between us seemed to grow. Suddenly he was traveling too much and working long hours, while pressuring me to find a new job. Only three weeks before 9/11, I had to drive seven hours on my own to my grandfather's cottage in Quebec with two small kids and a dog when one of his business trips interrupted our plans. He had staggered out to the car in his bathrobe, hungover, to say good-bye, after I had loaded the car with all our bags by myself. I had been furious and had pulled abruptly out of the driveway with barely a wave. How ironic. It seemed now that I would always have to do the drive alone.

But when he joined us a week later in Montreal, we each seemed to have had a change of heart. I was excited when he walked toward us at the Dorval airport, and I could tell he was as well. Our mutual resentment of one another seemed to have vanished and we spent a happy week together with the kids.

The weekend between Tim's funeral and September 11 was

full of living. Arron and I held hands as we walked to the park. I actually stood and looked at our house and our kids and Arron and said to myself, "I'm so lucky! I have it all." That Saturday, perhaps prompted by the effect of Tim's memorial service, Arron and I snuck into our bedroom while the kids watched a video and we made love quickly, furtively. It had been the first time in a long time. Little did I imagine that it would be our last, or that I would later rummage through garbage pails with his mother to collect the forensic evidence of our deed.

I was resolved to celebrate Arron's life, too, rather than mourn it. I wanted to remember him the way he really was, happy, and silly, and alive. A church funeral was out of the question. My experience with the Gospel-singing minister and my unease inside churches made that clear. Also, Selena, who was part of the planning, was vehemently against a church funeral, and I felt her wishes were important, too.

It was time for plan B. But I had no plan B. There were no books called *How to Plan a Celebration of Life*. There was very little information on this touchy subject of death at all. What was the etiquette when there is no body, no ashes, no physical evidence of any death? I was desperate for a rule book.

Finally my brilliant sister, Jill, had the idea of calling Dan's aunt, who is a Franciscan nun in Philadelphia. "Aunt Nora" had spoken at Jill and Dan's wedding, and her sentiments were beautiful and heartfelt, impressing both Arron and me. As a nun, she advised large companies on ethics issues, shattering our image of what a nun is and does. After my call, she dropped everything and drove for two hours the very next day to reach us.

Aunt Nora sat with Selena and me and patiently walked us through funeral planning 101. We told her some of the things we wanted, such as having my friend Jocelyn sing "Honeysuckle Rose," which Arron had sung to me at our wedding after Jocelyn had recited the lyrics to him over the phone from London. The song had become synonymous with our marriage, and Arron had hummed it to me often. "When you're passin' by, flowers droop and sigh. . . ." Selena asked to read a poem. I hoped to allow anybody who wanted to speak the chance to do so. Aunt Nora helped me to select the eulogizers. She added her own religious touches, of course, a prayer and a hymn, and Selena's lips pursed slightly until Nora suggested I select family members to read them.

Next I decided on a date: Monday, October 8, Columbus Day, and Canadian Thanksgiving. Selena was not happy with the date. "All our friends will have to miss their Thanksgiving!" I knew it was going to be difficult for our Canadian friends and family to miss their turkey, but it was a significant day to Arron and me. Wherever we were living in the world, we always celebrated Canadian Thanksgiving. Bruce and Jacquie had begun visiting us wherever we were, bringing tiny Lego toys that we would assemble after dinner. It seemed appropriate and important to keep the tradition, so that every Thanksgiving, we could always think of Arron, happy, full of red wine and turkey, lying on the couch in what we called a "turkey coma," moaning about his over-full stomach.

Nora went home and printed up a program with Arron's picture on the front. She told me that she would bring two of her fellow nuns to play some music. I was infinitely relieved. I had a plan, a direction, a mission.

I ordered a tent and got a permit from the county to pitch it at Eagle Rock Reservation. I ordered 350 chairs, not knowing how many people might come. I had been hearing about other 9/11 memorials where over 1,000 people attended and was glad we had only lived in the area for four years.

Robert, another of Arron's close childhood friends, was a filmmaker in Toronto and agreed to put together a montage of photos and music for the reception. I spent a day poring through all our photo albums, crying at every picture. Arron at age fourteen, smiling coyly in a school photograph, his blondish hair long and straight, tucked neatly behind his ears, his cheeks a lovely pink;

Arron smiling broadly into the camera as I plant a big kiss on his cheek; Arron, bending over, legs wide apart as he hammers nails into a deck at my grandfather's cottage, Carter holding a hammer beside him. It is one of the last pictures taken of him. I felt both comforted and anguished as I ran my finger over each one, as if trying to feel Arron or bring him magically back to life.

I spent another day listening to all of our music, finding his favorite songs, weeping as I read lyrics I had never listened to carefully before. I was stunned to realize that so many of his favorite songs dealt with death or dying. One of the songs was eerily called "Perfect Blue Buildings."

The day of the service was beautiful and sunny, but windy and unseasonably cold. The kids and I arrived on our own, as Selena had decided to attend a morning memorial service arranged by Accenture, the parent to Encompys. Accenture had lost several of its consultants in the collapse and would be honoring them as well as the three from Encompys. I had shied away from what I worried might become a media event, as Mayor Rudy Guiliani was scheduled to speak. I also couldn't imagine attending two memorials in one day.

As I walked toward the tent, averting my eyes from the lower Manhattan skyline, I was surprised to hear music. I looked over to see two women singing and playing guitar. Both were dressed very casually, one wearing jeans, the other in a skirt with long graying blonde hair, pinching out high soprano notes. Their appearance contrasted with their solemn demeanor. "They must be the singing nuns," I thought.

And then my giggling started. The nuns seemed to have stepped out of an episode of *Saturday Night Live*. I thought of sister "Pat" and "the Church Lady" and my giggles turned to snorts. I remembered Sally Field playing her guitar in that gargantuan airplane-wing hat she wore in the TV show *The Flying Nun*, and I was lost to more laughter.

Soon I was swallowing my sobs, my eyes tearing.

The last thing I expected during my husband's memorial service was to be wracked with a severe case of giggles. I hoped that if I hid my face in my hands, people would think I was crying. Although there were tears in my eyes from suppressing my laughter, it didn't feel sad. It felt hysterical. By now, Selena had arrived and taken her seat beside me. She looked at me quizzically. I managed to say through my chortles "singing nuns," and within a moment, she was as overcome as I was. I kicked her under the seat but we set each other off in a downward spiral of uncontrolled laughter. I bit my lip until I tasted blood. This was unseemly. Carter sat on my lap and kept twisting around to see what I was doing, annoyed that I was burying my face into his back to wipe my tears on his jacket.

I imagined Arron sitting beside me. He would have been giggling, too, except that his would have been audible, and contagious, making the whole audience laugh with him. He wouldn't have been trying to hide it. He used to embarrass me in movie theaters by guffawing loudly at inappropriate times, loud enough that people often stared or shushed us. I missed him terribly then, imagining the things he would have been whispering only to me under his breath. "Singing nuns at my funeral? Nice touch, Bird!" I imagined myself discreetly reprimanding him with my eyes, so that he would say loudly, "What!?" I loved those nuns for providing me with hysterical laughter. It was so much more satisfying than crying. I felt lighter, and truer than I had in the weeks it had taken me to plan this service. I felt like Arron was with me as I giggled and wept my way through it.

Partway through the service, Jocelyn got up to sing "Honeysuckle Rose." She had warned me that she couldn't really sing, though I had imagined that she was just being humble. But true to her word, she sang the lyrics in many different keys and octaves. I could see people looking around at each other, wondering if this was some sort of joke. Her off-key notes, combined with her choked-back emotions, made it a horrendous performance. I laughed, openly this time, and cried simultaneously during her song, tears once again running down my face, and loved her ten times over for performing this small miracle for me.

As she stepped off the podium, she looked at me with a sheep-ish grin. I laughed and said loudly, "You were *awful*! Thank you!" Everyone under Arron's tent released a surprised chuckle, and the air became electric with positively charged energy. I was satisfied. I had captured Arron in a way that he would have wanted to be remembered.

Later, many of the people from the service made the fifteen-minute drive from Eagle Rock Reservation to a lovely Tudor manor house in the woods of New Jersey. The reception room was large with two arched wooden doors on either end that were now shut against the world. The floors were well-worn terra cotta tile. Sunlight skulked into the room through haphazardly drawn burgundy curtains that covered the beautiful leaded windows. About two hundred people were there, the same number that had attended our wedding eleven years earlier. This room's Gothic features had similar qualities to the hall where we held our wedding reception at the University of Toronto. Many people who had attended our wedding now stood with tears in their eyes.

Someone dimmed the lights so we could watch the photo pres-entation that Robert had put together. I clung to my glass of red wine, gazing into it to avoid the sideways glances of the other mourners. I could feel their compassion. I watched my tears drip and then ripple the wine's surface, unable to look up and see the photos of my happy, laughing, alive husband. Hearing his favorite music was unbearable. No one could comfort me at this moment. My mother hovered closely. She wanted to embrace me, but I didn't want to be touched. She moved toward me, finally succeed-ing in putting her arm around me, and I slithered away too quickly, surprised that I didn't want her consolation.

Carter alternated between clinging to my skirt and hanging from my hip. My shoulders and back ached from the effort of lifting him up and down. Occasionally, he darted across the room to my twenty-one-year-old brother. Matt looked almost grateful as he stepped out of the room into the hallway to chase after Carter, just as photos of himself as a ten-year-old boy posing with Arron appeared on the screen. More tears came as I thought of what Matt had lost. A big brother. A friend. A mentor.

Olivia stood at the front of the room with two other little girls, a friend from school and our next-door neighbor. I could hear the occasional giggle as they watched the pictures, and I could hear the odd snippet of dialogue.

"Your Daddy looks like a girl in that one."

"Is that you or Carter?"

There was a photo of Olivia as a naked two-year-old, appearing to float in midair as she is supported by Arron's strong hand. He stands on one leg, with his other leg kicked back up into the air at a similar angle to Olivia's, and they are twin superheroes sailing through the imagined sky. Olivia emitted a combined laugh and sob when she saw the photo. Fresh tears streamed down my cheeks. The photo had embarrassed her and I heard her whine across the room, "Mommeeeeee!" The large group laughed for a moment, but then the photo changed and the silent pall once again settled over the crowd.

After the photos, people got up one by one to talk about Arron, but the sound was low and the room was still dark and I was unable to hear them as I met and chatted with each person at the reception. Occasionally, the crowd would laugh, and I'd turn around but by then I'd missed the joke. I wished I had thought to have someone record the speeches.

The reception ended and I was still greeting people on the curb outside the manor after nightfall, Carter whining at me to go home. Olivia had gone ahead with a friend.

I drove home alone, Carter strapped into his car seat in the back. When we walked into the house, I was amazed to see an entire Thanksgiving dinner neatly arranged on my dining-room table. My neighbors, so thoughtful knowing that so many Canadians were missing the holiday with their own families, had prepared a feast. There was a huge turkey, cornbread, mashed potatoes, sweet potatoes, Brussels sprouts, and cranberry sauce. People were lined up with paper plates and the turkey was already half gone.

I wanted to cry with gratitude. When I asked how they had all gotten into the house, given that I had the only key, someone pointed to the living room window, where the lock was now torn from its mooring. Little Ed, one of our neighbors, had broken in. "I'll fix it later," he said sheepishly.

I was exhausted. I didn't know how I was going to make it through dinner. I sat on the couch, pushing turkey around on a plate and wishing I could go up to bed. My head throbbed and I wondered when everyone might leave, if I would be too tired to cry or if the dam was about to break, shattering my carefully built veneer of calm. Slowly people began to drift away, and Selena and I began cleaning up, putting dishes in the dishwasher, wrapping things in plastic. I was a zombie working without thought. At one point I found a package that had been delivered earlier in the day. I recognized it as a bag I had ordered for Selena's birthday, a lifetime ago. She opened it in mock excitement and hugged me. "Oh wonderful!" she exclaimed, although she knew it had been coming. I turned to see my mother scowling.

My relationship with my mother had become tenuous since 9/11. She couldn't seem to see that I needed Selena to be my connection to Arron. I needed her tough English demeanor, her no-nonsense approach to grieving. Selena was plain in her grief. She cried when she was sad and was able to communicate her feelings clearly. My mother, on the other hand, seemed at a loss for words when she tried to comfort me, something that I was not used to from her. She drank too much wine, making her voice slightly too loud and her neediness too apparent. I did not realize the wedge that Selena was driving between us, wittingly or not, and it would be a long time before I truly understood this to be a contributing factor in our faltering relationship.

After my mother retreated upstairs to bed, Selena and I continued to clean the counters, ignoring the good-byes of our last guests. I walked out onto the back porch, shivering in the cold air, and waved goodnight to the posse of Arron's Toronto friends, now congregated on the garage deck. I could not see faces clearly, just tiny orange embers, and I smiled, wondering what was being smoked. Then I said goodnight to the stragglers—Selena, Matt, and a couple of the neighbors.

When I walked into my bedroom I found my mother in my bed.

"Mom, you need to go upstairs to your own bed." My voice was flat.

"Oh, sweetie . . ." she held her arms up, rolling toward me.

"What are you doing?" My voice was angry now as I helped her up. She sat on the edge of the bed, crying.

"I want to be here for you! I want you to be able to talk to me! I'm your mother!"

"I know, Mom, but I'm tired. I need to go to sleep now and so do you. We can talk in the morning." I seethed. "Just go to bed now, okay?"

When I lay down, my bed was still warm. I was too tired to be angry. My eyes were heavy as I thought of Arron. *So?* I wondered. *Did you approve? Did I do good? I didn't expect your old girlfriend to be so nice. Maybe she was nice to me because I'm the widow. But I don't want to be the widow. You were supposed to be here. This should have been someone else's funeral. How could you leave me?* Tears filled my ears and I rolled over and screamed into my pillow, hoping that no one could hear me.

[6]

THE FINAL NAIL

When my grandmother died, many years before, it was several days before my family was able to plan the memorial service for her, and to me those days felt strange, as though we were all caught in limbo between life and death. After her service it was a relief knowing that she had been given a proper farewell, that her death was absolute. Arron's service had had the same effect on me now. Over the course of several weeks, he had gone from late to missing with the possibility of being rescued, to missing with no hope of being recovered, to finally presumed dead. But despite the memorial service, he still wasn't *officially* dead.

Perhaps for this reason, on the Friday following the service, *10/12/01* Selena and I made a pilgrimage to the new Family Assistance Center at Pier 94 in Manhattan for our first tour of Ground Zero. We felt ready to see Arron's final resting place for ourselves. Although I considered taking the kids with us, I opted not to. It seemed too early, too gory. Also, I knew that a day at the Family Assistance Center would be grueling for kids.

While there, we also planned to apply for Arron's death certificate. I would need it to claim life insurance and begin the process of settling Arron's estate. Selena seemed reluctant. She still held out hope that Arron might be found.

Arriving at the Family Assistance Center, we stood in the middle of a cavernous building the size of four football fields. The Armory now seemed minuscule in comparison. The place was swarming with people, some seemingly invigorated by the excitement, others weeping quietly, consoled by family. Many of us clutched folders filled with original documents: birth certificates, marriage certificates, bills, proofs of residency, P-numbers. Volunteers sat behind large tables covered with file folders and forms, under the glare of stadium lights. In one corner massage chairs were filled. Kids played in a tiny area filled with brightly colored Little Tykes toys. Big plastic insulated barrels filled with iced soda and water were stationed at regular intervals. A mini food court was arranged at one end of the building. It was like a convention of grievers.

To get to Ground Zero, we were shown to a private room to wait for a small ferry that shuttled people at regular intervals from Pier 94 to lower Manhattan along the Hudson River. The room was like the chapel in a hospital. A dozen others sat quietly in chairs, facing forward, as if there was an altar at the front of the room. We were invited to take flowers and teddy bears from a display off to the side, so Selena and I walked over to it. "Carnations," I said quietly. I had never liked carnations. They seemed like the default flower, cheap and plentiful. Selena helped me create a bouquet of all-white flowers and then I grabbed a red one, to represent the single red rose that Arron used to give me on special occasions. We took two teddy bears to give the kids later. After ten minutes, we were led in a small procession across a huge industrial loading dock to the ferry.

The cold breeze tousled my hair as the ferry made its way down the river. It was a beautiful October day and I watched the boat's white wake against the deep black-purple of the Hudson. The cool air seemed to wake me up momentarily and I realized that I had spent the morning in a daze. I did not want to feel anything. Too many Red Cross people, and Oklahoma-bombing family members who had volunteered to help the 9/11 families, hovered nearby, ready at any moment to supply us with tissues. I wondered if we were meant to engage them in conversation as though we were on a pleasure cruise.

"Look at that!" Selena said suddenly. A butterfly was following the boat. The unlikelihood of seeing that butterfly following us was surely a sign from Arron. We weren't alone in this excursion and I was glad for it.

Manhattan was on our left side. We began to see devastation. A hole gaped in the glass dome of the Winter Garden, as though a giant metal spear had pierced it from above. Twisted girders of steel hung precariously out of the shorn-off corner of another building above it. But in the little marina near where we docked, several little sailboats bobbed perfectly in the water as if nothing was amiss.

As we disembarked into the eerie silence, I picked up my things and noticed that the red carnation I had added to my all-white bouquet was now missing. The blank faces of family members and volunteers didn't reveal who might have taken it. I noticed one of the Red Cross volunteers carrying a single red carnation and followed her, eyeing what I was certain was my flower, but she walked ahead, oblivious to my glares.

Other family members, Red Cross workers, and Oklahoma-bombing family members walked alongside Selena and me as we moved in single file between the damaged buildings on a dusty path laid over with plywood. We crossed a deserted street. Police seemed to be everywhere, which was odd, as there were no cars or other people around. At an intersection, the traffic lights swung around uselessly in the wind above us, changing at their normal timed intervals, but we crossed the intersection diagonally, ignoring them. We were led to a wooden platform looking very much like someone's backyard deck. I clung to the railing tightly, wondering if its smoothness was a result of all the people who had come before me, also gripping it too tightly.

Bulldozers in the vast expanse of destruction looked like Tonka toys atop huge smouldering piles of rubble, their headlights shining through the yellow-brown light. It was almost like a winter scene, with fresh snow newly fallen in a quiet dusk. But the snow here was a dank, brown dust mixed with ashes, and though it was a bright sunny day, the sky had an ochre haze that hovered low to the ground. The smell was stifling: a mixture of wet concrete, plaster dust, smoke, and burnt flesh. It was a smell I will never forget. It took me a long time to get my bearings and to imagine where Arron's tower had been. Not a single chair, desk, computer, or anything else was recognizable amid the rubble. I watched a bulldozer, balanced precariously atop one of the gray mountains. It moved back and forth awkwardly, bumpily, then its huge shovel rose up and dropped heavily to take a giant bite out of the pile beneath it. Be careful! I thought. Don't hurt him! Irrational. Moronic. I wondered if they had even reached a level where Arron might be. Perhaps he was in the area that was still smouldering. I spoke to him angrily in my mind: "What were you doing here? What *are* you doing here? Where are you? Why am I here? Damn you!"

I wanted to stay there and never leave.

I wanted to run away as fast as I could go.

I was finally *with* him. I hadn't realized that this had been the goal of my visit to Ground Zero. This was the place where he had died. I felt him watching me and wondered what that was like for him. Did he feel the same disdain for this place that I was now feeling? Did he feel sad for me, standing here gripping the railing with white fingers, his mother beside me looking grim-faced? I wondered when the bulldozers would uncover their treasure: Arron's body or even just a memento of him—his tie or his ring, some evidence of his existence.

After five minutes at most, I was told it was time to leave. A party of dignitaries was set to arrive and we had to clear the way. I was angry that I was being made to leave. Didn't they realize how long it had taken me to get there? I had endured so much pain to finally reach this place. "I can't believe this!" Selena hissed to me, loud enough for others to hear.

A policewoman and a Red Cross worker ushered our group along. I pried my hands off the wooden railing and forced myself to take a step. We marched like convicts into the dust and away from the one place that made sense, at least to me. The one place that brought me comfort in all its ugliness.

I blinked back my tears as I bid Arron farewell and followed the others. I wished that I could have walked up to that bulldozer and touched the ashes and dust beneath it. I wanted desperately to hold the dust in my hands, to bathe in it, to breathe it, to weep into it, to mingle my tears with his.

Instead we were led into a narrow alley lined in wire fencing now hung with posters and banners and weathered stuffed animals. This was where we were meant to lay our flowers and our mementos, but the area made my skin crawl. I shoved the flowers into a corner and turned to Selena. "Let's get outta here!"

We arrived back at Pier 94 to a large group of men in dark suits standing on the dock. One of the Red Cross workers whispered, "Those are all U.S. Senators waiting for our ferry. They're the reason they cut our trip short. They're going to tour Ground Zero now." She seemed awed.

Neither Selena nor I smiled at them as we walked by.

We made our way to the food court and ate a sandwich while we waited for Kathleen from Encompys. She was meeting us to help me apply for Arron's death certificate. Kathleen had already helped us determine which floor and tower Arron had been in, had navigated charities, and gotten us a free insertion of Arron's obituary in the *New York Times*. A slightly plump woman, with the efficiency of a bulldog, she had a way of bustling around in her gray flannel suits that made her seem the epitome of competence.

We all sat in a tiny curtained room with two city-appointed lawyers who looked young enough to still be in high school.

Kathleen handed them a letter confirming Arron's presence at the World Trade Center on the morning of September 11. They took a statement from me about Arron's phone call that morning. Without a body, these were all they had to prove his death. They took copies of our documents, birth and marriage certificates.

"I think we have everything we need. You will receive the certificates via FedEx in seven to ten days," the young lawyer said.

With a handshake, Arron was officially dead.

[PART TWO]

THE WHITENING

In privacy, where no one saw me,
Nor did I see one thing,
I had no light or guide
But the fire that burned inside my chest.

"The Dark Night" by St. John of the Cross

7

THE CLEANSING WINDS OF ANGER

I set out one beautiful sunny late-October day to mow the lawn, feeling more alive than I had in weeks. I was having a "good day," one where I felt like I could actually manage my life. The kids were out playing in the yard with their friends. It seemed like a perfect day to give the lawn one of its final trims before winter frost set in. All of my out-of-town family and friends had departed following Arron's memorial service two weeks earlier, returning me again to a large, empty house, now my responsibility alone to maintain.

I used to mow the lawn, when Arron was alive, but it seemed easier then. He once took a photograph of me pushing the huge mulching mower, in a bathing suit and shorts, wearing big work boots that exposed my muscular legs. I look strong, capable of handling the large, unwieldy Honda mower that was typical of everything that Arron bought—well built and overly powerful.

Our property was treacherous for maneuvering the heavy machine. The garden was a myriad of narrow-gated stone pathways, sloped terrain, rounded edges, and kids' toys. The amount of yard work was dizzying. The lawn typically took an hour to mow, but today I embraced the task. It would prove me capable again after weeks of feeling feeble, cloistered inside my stale house amidst dying funeral bouquets.

I took a deep breath and pulled the starter handle. Hard. The string attached to it was longer than I had anticipated, and my hand flung wildly into the air above my head, so that I lost my grip. The handle whipped out of my hand and smacked me hard on the side of my head as it retracted.

"Shit!" I yelled.

The engine barely sputtered. The blow brought tears to my eyes. "Damn! This is all your fault!" I screamed to the air, hoping my voice would reach Arron. "This is your stupid job!"

I was shocked by how quickly anger shattered my rosy day. I grabbed the lawn mower handle again, wishing I could rip it right off its string. I pulled, harder this time, wrenching my arm. My knuckles caught against the top of a small screw sticking out of the side of the mower, tearing skin across my knuckles. Bleeding and bruised, I kicked the mower over onto its side, pain shooting through my foot. "Damn!" I crumpled to the ground in tears. "I hate you! I hate this life! I want my old life back!"

The mower was lying beside me, useless. I was full of self-pity. I hated Arron for dying, for being in the building on that day. I hated that he had taken that new job. Why couldn't he have just stayed in his old one? He would be alive now if he had. I hated myself—I couldn't handle anything alone. I groped for someone to be angry at, yelling at the sky: "Damn you for leaving us! Damn that building! Damn Osama! Damn American Airlines! Damn Encompys! Damn Honda lawn mowers! Damn this house! Damn my life!"

I was shocked when I first heard a friend describe Arron as being "murdered." Murder happened in crime shows, with guns. I still thought of what happened to Arron as akin to a natural disaster, like a hurricane. If I acknowledged that an individual was responsible for Arron's death, I would have a responsibility to avenge him in some way. But revenge implied being angry—anger that, until that moment, I had denied. I hated realizing, as I sat on the ground beside my tipped-over lawn mower, that in fact, despite myself, I had become an angry widow. And now I was going to have to pay someone to mow the lawn.

I was vaguely aware of Elisabeth Kübler-Ross's stages of loss—denial, anger, bargaining, depression, and acceptance—but I loathed the idea of fitting a pattern. My grief felt different, unique only to me, not a life process that everyone goes through. It seemed ridiculous that everyone should follow these common steps. Surely grieving was as individual as fingerprints. I was determined to grieve my way, without anger.

Since Arron's death, I had begun to be aware of other, more public 9/11 widows and was surprised at the fervor with which they threw themselves into causes in support of surviving family members—fighting for the fair distribution of money from charities, or brandishing huge framed photos of sons and husbands as they sat in meetings with pursed lips, unhappy with the empty words and lack of accountability from politicians. Those "other" widows were also fighting to maintain sacred ground at the Ground Zero site, to ensure better building safety, and to get our loved ones' remains out of a dumpsite called "Freshkills." I admired their courage and their tenacity. I relied on them to be my voice. I wondered where they found their strength—perhaps in the community of similar voices and experiences that eluded me. I felt alone in my grief.

I wondered if these angry outlets soothed and healed those widows and family members, or if their causes perpetuated their grieving. Their anger frightened me with its intensity and sureness. I feared that if I succumbed to it, I would be lost to bitterness and unable to cope with the new complications in my life of children, home, dog, family, neighbors, and grief.

And yet I longed to connect to the community that these widows represented. They supported each other and had become friends. I still knew none of the 9/11 widows, other than Kimmy from the consulate. I wanted to know if their anger helped them, if their common mission to address the lack of policies and inadequacies that had conspired to create the buildings' collapse was a good outlet for their grief. I wondered if they felt as guilty as I did receiving money from charities. I wondered if they knew how to act when someone cried on their shoulder and they heard the words "Sorry for your loss" for the hundredth time. Did they tell their tragedies to strangers in the park? Kick the lawn mower? Did they fall asleep feeling the hole of their missing loved ones in the pits of their stomachs?

With Janet's help, I assembled ten local families who had lost either husbands or children in the World Trade Center. We met in a hall, where chafing dishes of donated pasta lined tables. We wrote out tags that bore our names and the names of our lost loved one. We were all still so numb; everyone seemed to walk around in a daze. There was no real excitement or emotion from anyone in the room, and yet there was a palpable sense of relief at our having found each other. We were in a safe environment and felt free to talk matter-of-factly about some of the horrible aspects of a 9/11 death that we were unable to share with other people: finding bodies, DNA tests, our last phone calls with our loved ones. We lamented over those phone calls. We exchanged stories that we had heard from other widows about their last contact.

"One widow I met told me her husband was also at Windows on the World and that he called and told her how hot and smoky it was up there," said Liz, a feisty blonde whose husband had helped numerous people escape the burning North Tower by running them down the stairs. He had not expected the building to collapse.

I latched onto these statements, as they gave me clues to Arron's last moments, adding fuel to my haunted thoughts. As we stood eating our lasagna and salad from paper plates, our conversations centered on the question of remains. "Has your husband been recovered?" I asked Jennifer, a statuesque widow with no children. It was a carefully constructed question because rarely was a whole body found. You couldn't ask, "Was your husband's body found?" because you would then have to endure the response that in fact only his pinkie finger was. I had to brace for the answer and was relieved when she said "no."

Later, I was talking with Laurie, who spoke very quickly, as though buzzed on coffee. She could barely stand still. "I heard the Red Cross was going to be giving out a second gift," she said. "Have you applied yet? You really should. Also, I was at the Family Assistance Center last week and the Buddhists are giving out checks for $1,000. You should apply." I knew she wanted to help me as much as I wanted to help her, but I couldn't help feeling that she had an underlying motive, as though we were in some kind of secret competition to determine who was most adept at working the system, who had got the highest charitable payout.

I looked around the room at all of these disparate people. We had nothing in common. Jennifer and Liz had no children and were slightly older than I was. Laurie, who did have children, seemed unreachable and neither of us had the emotional capacity to forge a friendship. We all came from different walks of life, and yet tragedy had brought us together. I had thought that our connection would be immediate and certain because of this, but our loved ones' common fate was not enough to bind us. Or perhaps we were all just too raw to be of any help to one another. Our reactions to our grief were indeed as different as our fingerprints and finding our few common experiences was more difficult than I had expected. I stood among these women feeling glad that I had found a community and yet lost and isolated within it.

I left that evening feeling more dismayed than when I had arrived. Surely we wanted to talk about our loss, losing our husbands? "Do you miss him?" I had longed to ask. "How are you coping?" But these questions seemed too personal to ask strangers. I wanted to connect with others who could understand a 9/11 loss, and with those who could understand the humanness of my loss, but for some reason, the 9/11 loss overshadowed the human one.

The very fact that we had been in one room together had high-lighted this anomaly.

Every time we turned on the TV and saw the burning build-ings, we were reminded that this was an entire country's loss and not just a single human one. Those TV images prevented me from separating 9/11 from Arron's death. I could be sunk in the aspects of *his* death and my loss, the loneliness, the sadness, the grief, but the images of burning buildings instantly reminded me that the loss was greater than this. That day marked a worldwide loss of innocence. It sparked a sense of fear in people that hadn't existed before. In that context, Arron became very small, and my grief even smaller. I was left feeling as though I didn't deserve to grieve for Arron, which had me desperate to mourn him as an individual. News headlines flashed "Since September 11 . . ." but never did those articles mention Arron's name. A toxic 9/11 cloud overshad-owed my human grief and prolonged it. It was what separated a 9/11 death from a non-9/11 one.

That night, mingling in the hall, we had each hidden behind our tangible losses, discussing last moments and exchanging horror-movie talk about bodies, or chitchatting about where we might receive the latest charitable donation, afraid to discuss our emotions. It was as though each of these women was a kite flying high in the air, and I was incapable of pulling even one back down to earth long enough to make a deeper human connection. Perhaps I was expecting too much. I was seeking support, the kind they were unable to give me, the kind I was unable to give them.

My meeting with the other widows started me thinking about my own financial situation. Like many couples, Arron and I had had a contentious relationship with money. Our arguments were often instigated during Christmas, when it was up to me to purchase all presents, decorations, food. Before I would head out for one of my dreaded Christmas shopping sprees, Arron would grill me. "What is your budget for each person this year?"

"The same as it always is, fifty dollars."

"Okay, well, just make sure you stick to it. I know you always spend more, especially on your family."

At this point, the steam would escape from my ears. "I know, I know." I would try to keep my voice calm. "You're feeling righteous again because there is only you and your mother, whereas I have my whole family. Well, you know what? My family is your family now, so money has to be spent on them for Christmas presents. Sorry. If you want to come with me and help, then you can keep tabs on my spending."

Although I would have liked his help, he always refused. In retaliation, the real budget I spent on each person (including him and his mother) was closer to one hundred dollars.

I hated these spending discussions. If it wasn't about Christmas presents, it was about the paperback books I was fond of buying, or a new tube of lipstick. Since combining our bank accounts when Olivia was born, I had gradually reached a point where I resented his frugalness and found ways to hide my expenditures. I paid the VISA bill. I used cash when I shopped. I hated hiding things from him but it was easier than being confronted by him. I think in his mind I was a shopaholic with a Platinum card, buying myself thousand-dollar wardrobes. But nothing could have been further from the truth. Most of my wardrobe was from the local Gap, and I bought my underwear at the A&P. Guilt followed my more costly clothing and home decor purchases. I tried to stick to classic styles that I knew would last, reasoning that although expensive at the outset, they made sense amortized over time. But Arron still disapproved. He understood the idea of quality, but only when it came to things he purchased for himself. He bought only the best Brooks Brothers suits, and Florsheim shoes. He could spend more in one outing at Home Depot than I did on the entire Christmas shopping put together. If I complained about his hypocrisy, he would retaliate with "I need these things for work," or "The Home Depot stuff is for the house. We can write it off on our taxes."

After his death I questioned what good it had done him to be so tight with money. Although his frugalness had ensured financial security for the kids and me while he was alive, I don't think we were his motivation. Most likely he saved for himself. "I don't want to work for someone else *forever*, Bird," he would say. He was driven by jealousy of people who worked in his industry, finance. "I could be making a *lot* more money. . . . If I were a. . . ." A what? I wondered. A stockbroker? An investment banker? Dead?

Arron's life insurance policy, which we had purchased shortly before his death, paid out only a few weeks after the Towers fell. It scared me to think that we almost didn't have that policy. After sneaking a few cigarettes during a late night booze-fest with his work buddies, he had failed the blood test that would have proven him to be a nonsmoker with the first insurance company. Only many months of nagging on my part had prompted him to take out a more expensive policy, and this time he didn't smoke before the blood test. We had only paid a year's worth of premiums.

Although Arron had only worked there for two months, Encompys sent another life insurance check, via a visiting financial advisor named Jennifer, one of the insurance company's "survivor support" team. "I can help you to plan for the future, plan what to do with the money that you now have," she said. She asked questions about my financial standings, and as she sat at my dining-room table, I ran upstairs to Arron's office, looking for the financial statements that he had kept in a three-ring binder.

Jennifer studied the documents. "He did a lot of investing on his own," she noted.

"Yes, he had an ETrade account. I'm not even sure what he invested in. It was sort of a hobby of his. The rest we have in mutual funds and in the investment property we own."

"He did a good job, but now you'll have to consider your options more carefully. You seem pretty savvy compared to a lot of the widows I see."

"Really, why?"

"Many have never used a checkbook and have no idea of the state of their financial affairs."

But of the widows I had met many had filed applications to several charities and some were trying to settle their husbands' estates. At least I had already met with an estate lawyer and applied for my Surrogate Certificate, proving that I was the "executrix" of Arron's estate, a word that conjured up noirish images. I met my prim lawyer that day at the Newark Courthouse, an old, classic building whose beautiful marble interiors were juxtaposed with grimy hallways and stark fluorescent lighting. After appearing in front of a judge who confirmed my identity and verified Arron's death certificate, we walked over to a local bonding office, which smelled of cigarettes and was cluttered with stacks of boxes and file folders spilling their contents onto an oily gray carpet. I handed a check for one thousand dollars to a woman with big blonde hair and curiously long nails, looking like she had just walked off the set of *The Sopranos*, and watched, fascinated, as she clicked the check between her nails and placed it on the table and then somehow managed to type my receipt. She handed it to me, smiling. "Here, hon. You'll need to keep this in case anyone makes a claim on your husband's estate."

Still, sitting with Jennifer, I felt anything but confident. The financial future of my family was a constant worry. My own income potential was a third of Arron's. I had begun to prepare myself for the very real prospect that I would have to sell my house, move to a less expensive neighborhood, scale back our lives.

"What I really need to know is how long this money will last. I know it seems like a lot, but how do I tell? Do you think I'll need to move to somewhere less expensive?"

"Well, the general wisdom is not to make any major changes for two years, if you can help it. I'll do some different scenarios for you, which will help you to see where you stand."

Jennifer helped me figure out my cash flow. Social Security death benefits, Worker's Compensation, investment property. I gave her a rough estimate of our monthly expenses: real estate taxes, utilities, nanny, food, car. She helped me figure out ones I hadn't thought of: summer camps when the kids got bigger, more life insurance for me, therapists. Our expenses had already changed in the past month. No more of Arron's commuting expenses, work lunches, expensive suits, cell phone bills. They were replaced with babysitters, therapy sessions with Janet, and handymen fees. Jennifer provided me with investment tips, such as diversifying among the five asset categories: cash, bonds, large company stock, small company stock, and foreign stock. She recommended a percentage breakdown for each. She also suggested investing in education accounts and Roth IRAs (individual retirement accounts). She told me to get a will drafted. But she was unable to tell me what I wanted to know: Was what I had enough?

Jennifer's report was the first I heard of something called the "September 11th Victim Compensation Fund." Apparently, I was eligible for a claim under an act that had been passed by President Bush and Congress. I would have to waive my right to sue the airlines, the World Trade Center, or anyone else. Any amount awarded from the fund would be reduced by any collateral benefits that I received, such as life insurance and death benefits and Social Security payments. The application process was supposed to be easy, with very few forms to fill out. I was skeptical. What would this fund give me? Would it make up for the years of Arron's lost income? Would I have enough then? I was also hopeful. Perhaps we would be okay after all.

Despite Jennifer's advice about what to do with the money her company had just given me, it was overwhelming and so I did nothing. Instead I visited Gene, the financial guy at our local Chase branch, and bought a nice, safe low-interest certificate of deposit with the insurance money.

"You know," said Gene, "this money could be invested with the bank so that you could earn more from it. . . ."

Our friends Rachel and William invited the kids and me over for a late fall barbecue. Arron and I had become friends with them through our children, though we hadn't spent much social time together, other than at the playground or an occasional impromptu Friday night dinner where we shared music and commiserated over parenting issues. Still, they had become close friends over the four years we had lived in Montclair.

During dinner, as I sat with them on their back deck, watching the kids play in the yard, and drinking homemade margaritas, William took a deep breath. "So, Abby. Several of our friends have been asking me how they might be able to send you money. You know, for the kids."

"They want to send me money? But why?" I could feel the heat of a blush spread across my face.

"Well, I guess they want to help. I think you'll need to set up a special account at the bank, a trust. I'll print up a flyer letting people know that checks should be written to the trust and sent directly to the bank."

"Gosh!" I was taken aback. "A trust?"

I hadn't realized that this was what people did for the bereaved. Checks and food.

Checks began to arrive daily. Some were for $10, or $100, but a few were for as much as $1,000 or more. We received quilts from strangers and a banner made by schoolchildren in Manitoba. We got boxes of condolence cards from Sunday school students. I had ordered some preprinted thank-you cards and sent one to each friend, acquaintance, and stranger who sent me a condolence note, a quilt, or a check. Strangely, thanking people for sending money was easier than I had imagined. A quick scrawl at the bottom of each stiff card: "Greatly appreciated," "For the future of the kids. . . ." The notes for close friends were the ones I was unable to write. How could I thank someone for the priceless gift of simply being there, for allowing me to cry unabated in their living room, for taking my kids to Toys "R" Us, for bringing lemon gelato over at ten on a Tuesday night. I worried often that I was not grateful enough and would never be able to reciprocate.

A state of gratitude and its accompanying humbleness followed me everywhere. I constantly thanked people. I hoped I was doing it gracefully, but it was a difficult state to maintain. There was something about being humble that felt weak. I equated it with being an invalid. I was helpless and needed people to send checks. This was not a mode of living that I was accustomed to. I was the lone eight-year-old who took a half-hour streetcar ride to school each day, proud of her independence. I was the seventeen-year-old who drove alone across Canada just six months after obtaining her driver's licence. I could paint a room like a pro painter, I wrangled websites. I did not need checks from strangers. And yet, I deposited them into what was now known as the C. Arron Dack Memorial Trust Fund. It would be for the kids' college, I reasoned. I signed the back of each check feeling small and needy and helpless.

Each day the mail came, it was like winning some sort of macabre sweepstakes. The checks for the kids' fund were augmented by others: three months of mortgage payments from the New Jersey Association of Realtors, periodic checks from the New York WTC Relief Fund, the September 11th Fund, the Salvation Army, the United Way. With each check I felt more and more unworthy. I was a charity case. I received gift cards to Safeway, Toys "R" Us, Wal-Mart. Were food stamps next?

"What if Arron had simply died in a car accident?" I asked Jill over the phone one night. "What if I was just a regular widow? Was Arron's death so different? I don't deserve to get all this money."

"Arron's death *was* different," she insisted. But I failed to see how. Arron was dead. Dead was dead. Did the fact that I didn't get to say good-bye make the difference, as though a final good-bye might offer me some kind of closure? All sudden death was difficult, I reasoned. What I failed to understand was the impact the collapse of the towers had on the rest of the world. Everyone wanted to help. People donated money to charities, who were obligated to make sure the money was given to the intended recipients. But I wanted to give the money away. I thought of all the widows who received nothing and had to struggle to raise their children. I imagined myself having to work, having to move, having no resources for a good therapist. The money seemed tainted, like blood money. There was also a certain irony in being the recipient of money Arron had so greatly desired. It was like being paid by the devil. Yet, the money came from people who cared, or were haunted by the event, who felt for me.

I was sick of feeling guilty about accepting the money. The guilt made me angry at Arron, something that seemed to have a firm hold of me. Yet being mad at him made him seem alive again, because I was able to attribute to him a tangible emotion that I could feel in my neck and shoulders, my jaw, and in the crease between my eyebrows. I could only hope my anger would ultimately be akin to a cleansing wind, sweeping away my grief.

8

EVERYDAY HERO

My mother decided to visit us for a few days over Halloween, her first opportunity to visit without the distraction of other houseguests. We needed to reconnect with one another. In our phone calls my mother sounded desperate: "I just want to be your mother. . . . I want you to need me." She was threatened by my apparent disregard for her motherly ministrations. I dreaded having to deal with her insecurity, and her need for me to need her, which I couldn't meet and found suffocating. Her trip would coincide with New York City's first public memorial for the victims of 9/11, which I wanted to attend. My previous trips to Ground Zero and the Family Assistance Centers had created a bond between Selena and me, as if we were warriors who had fought side by side. I hoped that some time alone with my mother at the memorial might somehow bridge the gap between us and repair our mother-daughter bond.

The day after her arrival, I took my mother shopping in downtown Montclair. In the window of one of my favorite stores was the frame to a beautiful queen-size bed. It was covered in soft, mushroom-colored fabric and had a sturdy body of kiln-dried wood. It was a floor model and so was on sale. "It's beautiful," my mother encouraged. "I think you should go for it."

Bedtime had always been the one time of day that Arron and

I were certain to see each other. He went to bed at ten and was up at six. He whimpered at me to come to bed, even when I didn't feel like sleeping. He complained when I kept the light on to read. One year for my birthday I was insulted by his gift of a clip-on book light. "Is this for you or for me?" I asked, disappointed. One night, after a fight, I threw the book light and it broke. I was happy. I had to turn the overhead light on again to read. He would sigh heavily at me until I turned it off and rolled over to clutch his hand.

The bed was a familiar piece of our family life—of Arron and me and then Olivia and Carter. It held our joys, our illnesses, our lovemaking, our fights. The bed held our history, and now that history was just that. Moments in time. Moments that we could never get back.

Without Arron, our bed felt huge and cold. I slept hugging the edge, as though the middle were a vast sea, a place I could fall into and drown. I could not keep warm in the bed, no matter how many blankets I piled on top of me. I fell asleep with my right arm flung across the bed, my hand clutching the space where Arron's hand had been. I crunched pillows between my knees, imagining his warm torso in their place.

One rainy day in London in March 1994, four years after we had married, Arron and I climbed into our VW Rabbit and drove to the IKEA off the ring road. We had just moved into our little row house on Prothero Road and didn't have a bed. We bounced on mattresses lined up under the bright warehouse lights. Our house had narrow stairwells, and having once sawn the boxspring of a queen-size mattress in half so it would fit up the narrow stairs of our Toronto apartment, we knew better. IKEA was used to narrow European stairwells and sold their king-size beds as two twins, providing a thick roll-up mattress that fitted over the top of both beds, making a large one. We tied the twins together onto the top of the VW and drove home to grunt them up the stairs to the bedroom. The rolled-up topping fit perfectly, and I made our bed using our wedding sheets and duvet. We snuggled in the center that night, warm for the first time in a month since we had moved in.

Our first bundle of joy came only a few months later, furry and yellow with a wet black nose and long pale eyelashes. Harley whined beside our bed that first night, until we relented and pulled her up into the blankets with us. We awoke to a telltale wet spot on the bed and spent the following weeks training her that the bed would not be her domain. I would fall asleep near the edge of the bed, stroking her as she lay on the floor beside us.

The bed became our wrestling ring when we needed to vent our frustrations. We jumped on each other, holding down arms or legs. Arron always won, often by pinning me to the bed and covering me in kisses. The wrestling became more gentle on the day that I took a pregnancy test and discovered that a visit to Florida for Brent and Marie's wedding had resulted in an extra special souvenir.

In January 1995, Arron's job moved us from London to Boston. We spent a frantic few months painting and renovating, getting the London house ready to sell, although we had only spent a short ten months there. Arron was still painting the floor on his way out the door as we left for the airport, dropping the wet brush into the trash bin outside before hopping into the taxi.

We found ourselves in an almost empty house by the water in Hingham, Massachusetts, a short drive south of Boston. Our twin-mattress-king finally arrived from London and by June a little girl was taking up a space between Arron and me, bundled tightly in her green flannel blanket. We folded our bodies around her protectively, our feet and noses touching, watching her sleep.

Our bed moved two more times until it finally found a more permanent home in Montclair, New Jersey, and in August 1999, we were once again encircling a small baby, this time a boy.

But by the spring of 2001, I was feeling alone in my side of the bed, unable to warm the spot despite Arron's mute presence.

We were at a low point in our marriage. My getting laid off from work just made matters worse.

"God, I am so jealous that you got laid off," Arron said one day as we emptied the dishwasher.

"Why?" I was astonished.

"I would love to have a few months off to do nothing. I am so tired of working."

I let his implication of my idleness slide. I understood how he was feeling. He had worked hard for so many years. I never understood where he got his energy. "Then take a few months off. Take a year off. We could move somewhere less expensive. We could change our lifestyle. Why do you always feel the need to work so hard?" The vague prospect of changing our lives excited me. The rat race of living in one of the most expensive areas in the country and his long hours and endless traveling was exhausting us both. I was convinced we could change how we lived and be happier.

But I also knew his ambition to start his own company. It was what drove him to work as hard as he did. Lately Arron had been unhappy that he had not yet made partner at Capital Markets Company, a financial consulting firm that he had been working with for almost two years. He was close to securing a new job with Encompys, but the process was slow and the uncertainty was making him irritable.

"I want to get a smaller bed," I declared to Arron one night as I turned down the sheets.

"Why?" Arron asked, climbing into his side of the bed.

"Because a king-size bed is a marriage wrecker. We wind up sleeping miles apart," I whined. I was aware that I was grasping at him. The bed had become my life raft as the distance between us these past few months had grown wider and wider, like a flooded river. Nothing pleased him and I seemed to just exasperate him, especially if I suggested spending money on frivolous things such as beds. He seemed to resent his financial obligations, worrying incessantly about money.

"It's good, though, when the kids jump in the bed with us." Arron seemed compelled to defend it.

"Yeah, but you know how much of a sleep-Nazi I am. The kids are never there for long." I tried to keep myself from whining. "I think we should get a queen-size." I was forceful now and not a bit whiny. "I want to sleep closer to you."

"When you get a job, Bird, then you can get a new bed." To Arron the bed was not an issue. Replacing it would be costly. He couldn't see that it was my plea to get us back on track.

We had never gotten around to buying a new bed, and now, albeit posthumously, I wanted to close the gap.

That October afternoon, with my mother's encouragement, I finally bought the bed that I had once hoped would save Arron and me. I spent the next day on the computer researching mattresses and my mother and I found ourselves at Macy's that afternoon bouncing on them. It was a crash course in mattress-speak. Pillowtop, posturpedic, coil ratios, foam. I found the Sealy that had gotten the good online reviews. The following day my new mattress was delivered, and that night I nestled into my new bed, finally content. I felt closer to both Arron and my mother in one fell swoop.

The 9/11 memorial was to take place near Ground Zero on October 29, 2001. I was determined to attend. Arron's memorial a few weeks earlier had confirmed his death for me. Now I wanted his death to be acknowledged on a larger scale, as though an official public memorial might make everything seem more real. I wanted Arron to be represented by his family, to stand out from the crowd of victims. I also wanted an excuse to return to Ground Zero, to see the bulldozers on their diminished piles of Trade Center rubble, perhaps getting a little closer to Arron.

On the day of the memorial, we drove to a parking area where hundreds of buses lined up to take us into the city. We settled onto one of them and awaited our departure, silent, deep in our own thoughts. I did the math in my head. Each 9/11 family was allowed to bring two people, a potential of about 9,000 people, crammed into the narrow streets of lower Manhattan. I dreaded crowds.

Coming out of the Holland Tunnel, our convoy of buses made its way into lower Manhattan, where we got off and walked several blocks down West Street to the memorial site, past shops and restaurants that were still closed. Each of us was given a large laminated ID card that hung on a metal chain, which was supposed to be worn around our necks. I felt like I was wearing a badge of death and put it in my purse until we were asked for it. As we entered the gated area where the memorial was to be held, Red Cross workers handed us little white plastic bags containing tissues, a face mask, Aspirin, a bottle of water, a granola bar, and, inexplicably, an ATT long-distance phone card. The bags frightened me. It was as though we were being given rations, in preparation for another disaster.

For a few moments I lost sight of my mother and panicked the way I had once when I was five years old, holding my mother's hand on an escalator only to look up and realize it was a stranger's hand that I was holding. But then I saw her, straining her neck to see over the heads of some people who had come between us.

Everyone around me wore the same numb look of grief that I wore. We all looked pale and zombie-like, as though we couldn't quite focus our eyes. Like sheep, we were herded into a street that was lined with folding chairs, walled off by police barricades. Throngs of people were pushing forward, trying to get closer to the makeshift stage that was set up farther down the street, closer to the Ground Zero site, but we stepped into a row of chairs where we were unable to actually see the pit or the pile of rubble that had been the buildings. We were happy just to find empty seats and escape the crowd.

The air was damp and putrid, despite the warm sun. It smelled like wet plaster and cement and gave off acidic fumes that stung our eyes and nostrils. Many people donned their masks but I decided against it. I wanted to remember the smell, to inhale what Arron might have smelled, to breathe him. The smell reminded me of last year's kitchen renovation, and Arron. He was trying to tear down the old ceiling one Saturday afternoon, when I came down the back stairway to find him hanging from what looked like a chain-link fence that was embedded in the kitchen ceiling. Chunks of ancient plaster lay all over the floor. More large pieces still clung to the wire mesh. Arron's upper arms were covered in scratches and cuts from its sharp edges. The ceiling was built at a time when ceilings were made to last one hundred years or more, and his weight did not budge it at all.

"Why don't you use a crowbar?" I'd asked, laughing.

"Because that wouldn't be any fun!" He'd grinned at me, his knees almost touching the floor as he hung.

But the smell here wasn't kitchen plaster dust. This smell contained death. I hated my need to remember it.

I looked to my left and realized that we were sitting next to the wrought-iron fence of St. Paul's Chapel, a beautiful Gothic stone building that had miraculously weathered the attacks unscathed. I could see a tiny patch of green lawn and several very old, blackened gravestones. I had often admired this church and its beautiful graveyard on visits to see Arron when he worked on Wall Street. It was a lush secret sanctuary in the middle of all the bustle and cement of the city. To my right I was shocked to see one of the last remaining World Trade Center buildings, charred and black. At the street level was a grimy Borders bookstore, dirty posters barely visible through the soot-blackened windows. It looked like a bombed-out city in the Middle East or some other war-torn area.

Watching thousands of people find their seats in the middle of these long, narrow streets, I suddenly felt extremely vulnerable. The terrorists might strike us here, as we sat exposed, with no way of escaping. I was jumpy and my palms were sweaty. My heart seemed to beat too quickly. I worried about the kids becoming orphaned. My fears were irrational, but I also knew that I wasn't alone in feeling them. Fear was evident in the furrowed brows of those around me. I tried to comfort myself with logic, telling myself that the odds of something tragic happening to me a second time were remote, but I didn't really believe it.

I looked at my mom and could tell in the tense line of her mouth when she tried to smile that she, too, was frightened, probably more so, given that this was her first exposure to the devastation that had once been a thriving downtown business district. She had the Canadian perception that the United States was a more dangerous place; more guns, more violence, more terror. At this moment, I couldn't disagree with her.

A woman began singing a haunting rendition of "Amazing Grace," a hymn that had become synonymous with a 9/11 death. Her voice echoed among the ruins. Somehow, amid the destruction, the music instilled peace. We were all here to bid our farewells. The air was full of the presence of those who had died, heavy like the smell. Arron was among them, near me, in the smell, in the dust, in the music. I clasped my mother's hand, glad she was with me, knowing she felt the moment, too.

Various dignitaries stood up to speak, but we could only hear their voices, not their words. The Archbishop of New York, an imam, a rabbi. More music filled the air. The service ended with a fire bell ringing, the only sound in the eerie silence of thousands of people. It was a fire department tradition to ring the bell during the memorials of fallen firefighters, the last fire bell that they would hear. A hero's farewell. I felt like an imposter witnessing a private ritual, one I had no business seeing. Yet I found the resonance of the bell cathartic, lulling me with its long tones. I was glad I had come to sit here amid this frightening destruction, with thousands of others, and for a few minutes I felt the magnitude of what had happened. Suddenly the collapse of the towers felt real, not just an image seen in replay over and over on TV. For a moment, I was able to see past my personal loss to the larger picture and see the ripple effect that this event had had on the rest of the world. I was again reminded that this was bigger than just Arron, than just me.

After the service, we slowly made our way out through the crowds, anxious to find our bus and escape the smell and the dust and the city. This time I had no remorse leaving the site. I couldn't carry the world's grief on my shoulders. The fear I had felt at the memorial was not a cathartic sojourn with my dead husband. I didn't want to think of him being there, clinging like a leaf to a charred piece of cement. This place represented an absence of life, and I wanted his spirit to be alive, happy, and near those he loved.

We took our seats on the bus heavily and silently. It was only when our bus rolled into the depths of the Holland Tunnel that my mother and I were able to speak again.

"I saw Larry last week," she said, breaking our silence. Larry was my stepfather, who left my mother for a friend of mine ten years earlier.

"Oh. How did that go?"

"He makes me so nervous! I wish I could just say what I need to say to him. He gets all patronizing with me. He keeps insisting that he has no money and makes it sound like I'm demanding too much from him."

"Why? Do you need more money?"

"Well, I'm getting the same amount as I always got, but things are more expensive now."

"Has Larry never increased your alimony since the divorce?"

"No." The lighting inside the Holland Tunnel created a moiré effect against my mother's face.

"So, he has given you the same amount for over ten years? Did you not have a clause in the divorce stating that the amount needs to go up for cost of living increases?"

"I don't know . . ." she trailed off. We popped into bright sunlight, which momentarily blinded us.

In trying to avoid delving into the emotion of the day, we had unexpectedly found our diversion. But I was shocked at my mother's revelations. "Are you kidding me?"

"Well, I do have some savings . . ." she said defensively. She flicked her platinum hair and turned to look out the bus window at the spidery black iron bridges that were so ubiquitous in Newark. I knew I had struck a nerve.

"Besides the alimony, does he owe you anything else?"

"Well . . . um . . . actually he still owes me my share of the house after we sold it. . . ." She almost flinched as she looked at me.

"What!?" I nearly shouted, oblivious to the other passengers. I could feel my shoulders hunch into my ears with tension. She looked sheepish, like a little girl being caught stealing cookies.

"Mom, this is crazy. You need to get a good lawyer. You have rights. Why do you let him walk all over you like this? Can't you see that by not fighting for what is rightfully yours you are giving him power over you?" I sounded like Arron.

"I know, sweetie. You're right," she squeaked.

Larry's treatment of my mother incensed me. He had treated us all badly, and I resented him for it. At that moment, I needed to be angry with someone, and he was a perfect target. When Larry had left my mother for my friend, someone twenty years younger than him, I had been unable to accept the relationship. Our lunches together ended. His phone calls stopped. He had been in my life since I was eight years old and now old loss was catching up with me.

"So, do you know a hotshot lawyer?" I asked. My vengeance was spilling out of me, unstoppable. I realized I was also angry with my mother, for allowing herself to become defenseless in Larry's presence.

"I think my friend got a really great settlement. She told me her lawyer was amazing."

"Hire him," I said decisively. My anger burned through a life-time of fears that had sometimes prevented me from telling my mother the truth for fear of hurting her feelings. I wanted my mother back. I needed her. I blamed Larry for her inability to be strong for me now. I was determined to fight for her. I hoped she would take my advice. I shut my eyes, exasperated and tired.

The bus was taking us to a new Family Assistance Center, one exclusively for New Jersey families, which had been set up in the old terminal building near the Statue of Liberty. This lovely building had been a train terminal at the turn of the century, where immigrants, after being processed at Ellis Island, began their lives in America. It was also the place where our new lives were being processed, but this was not the life in America that I had yearned for.

The bus dropped my mother and me off at the building's entrance. The sun was setting in tones of copper and streaks of lavender, and we had a perfect view of Ground Zero from across the Hudson River. Except for the broken glass dome of the Winter Garden in the background, the incomplete skyline was almost beautiful. My mother asked someone to take our picture. I stood against the coral-reef sunset, war-torn buildings across a river, feeling like an old woman with a crooked smile pasted onto her face.

We entered into a makeshift arrangement of tents and booths. Parts of the building were open to the elements, giving the place the feel of an open-air market. We huddled in line, trying to stay warm, to wait for food. We were starving. We had left the house at 10:00 AM and it was now 5:00 PM There had been no time or place to buy lunch and we had long ago eaten the granola bar and drunk the water that the Red Cross had so graciously provided. We were told the line for receiving an urn of rubble from Ground Zero was inside, but we were in no hurry to go through that process and decided to get something to eat first.

As we ate our pasta salad, my mother began talking with another woman around her own age who explained that her pregnant daughter and son-in-law had both been lost. My mother was visibly shaken. It could have been worse. She could have lost the kids and me as well. She could have lost our entire family. I was thinking that perhaps that would have been better. Arron, the kids, and I would at least be together. We wouldn't have to be living our lives alone, without him. The thought was peaceful, though I was a little spooked by it. Did I really just wish us all dead? We continued our meal in silence after the woman and her husband walked off to claim their urns. I wondered if they would get two or three. I stood up feeling incredibly sad and close to tears.

Only one family member was permitted into the area where uniformed soldiers were handing out the urns, so my mother agreed to wait for me. In line I filled out a form and stated Arron's P-number, while someone with a huge book rifled through the pages looking for his name. The book was cumbersome, like something I imagined St. Peter referring to at the pearly gates, yet another reminder of how many people had died.

I watched others collecting their urns full of Ground Zero dust. Each person was instructed to hold out both arms so they could be handed an American flag that was folded into a triangle form. One hand under, one hand over. I busied my mind by trying to remember the name of those folded flags—triangle? Tri something. Maybe tricorne? Trifold?

Then it was my turn. I sucked in my breath as an official-looking man introduced himself as a New Jersey politician and shook my hand. He expressed his condolences, and I began to feel overwhelmed. I bit the inside of my cheek trying to keep my composure. "Breathe," I commanded myself. I swallowed several times to hold back the tears that had been threatening all day. He was begging me with his eyes not to cry.

He handed me a dark blue cardboard box that was supposed to represent my husband. I understood that now. This was supposed to be Arron. It was an attempt to replace the body that I did not have, might never have. I wanted to run and throw the box away, deny its significance. But now I was turned toward a soldier.

There was a little ceremony—one hand under, one hand over as the flag was placed between my shaking palms. We exchanged a firm, bone-crushing handshake. There was a touch-of-the-cap salute. I almost expected to hear the loud crack of twenty-one guns. As the soldier saluted me, my eyes welled up with tears. I tried to get angry with myself, chastise myself for the tears, but they came anyway, defiant. I was caught off guard by the significance of this ceremony. It was an American ceremony, like the ones I had seen in movies, and it was beautiful in both its simplicity and its grandeur. It was a hero's farewell, like those reserved for police officers and firefighters and soldiers. Arron, my British-Canadian husband, had unwittingly become an American hero.

I wanted my everyday hero back. The one who, donning his weight belt, constructed a twenty-foot-long dry-fit stone wall in our garden; who unscrewed the training wheels of Olivia's bike and had her riding on two wheels within half an hour; the one who hoisted Carter into his big red truck for a Saturday morning trip to Home Depot, teaching him the names of tools as they cruised the aisles.

Finally, arms full of my hero's treasures, I was herded toward a wall of clergymen. They stood around, many wearing robes, awaiting their next victim with solemn faces. Quick, what is my faith? I couldn't remember. Someone was waiting for my answer, so I blurted, "Anglican." Door number three. My prize was a kindly, portly white-haired gentleman who clasped my free hand. I wanted to shake him off and run. I felt my crooked smile glued to my face once again. I had no idea what to say to this man, who was trying to offer me his words of kindness and faith. I willed him not to use the word "God." Something about it in this context scared me. It felt false, idly used, useless. God didn't belong here. *I* didn't belong here.

"He's with God now," my minister was saying.

"Tell God to give him back then." I wanted to say it but didn't.

"Thanks," I mumbled instead.

I was desperate to find my mother and go home but I managed to walk away in as graceful a gait as I could muster. I clutched my "souvenirs" and headed for the door, happy to escape.

When we got home, I opened the cardboard box with my mother and kids as witnesses. Inside was a blue velvet bag with a card that read "September 11th, 2001. In Loving Remembrance." Inside the bag was a cherry-colored wooden urn about the size of a grapefruit with 9-11-01 carved on its side. There was a gold plate in the bottom of the box that I supposed was meant to be engraved with Arron's name and nailed to the bottom of the urn, but I knew I would never get it engraved or nailed. I shook the urn and heard the muffled sound of the dust inside. It was a disappointing sound. I wanted to hear a more substantial noise, with weight, the way I remembered the urn of Arron's beloved dog Kaylee, whose ashes we sprinkled onto Round Lake near Arron's cottage when we first started dating. That urn was heavy and when Arron opened it, it contained bone fragments mixed with a pound or more of dust. It rattled when it shook, and it took us a long time to sprinkle the dust onto the lake. The dust spread in a wide gray swath around our boat before disappearing into the water. There was not enough dust in this urn to represent a dog, let alone a whole person. I didn't know what to do with it, so I simply placed it on the table. The kids shook it but were also unimpressed.

"What is it?" Olivia asked.

"It's dust from the building," I replied.

"Why do we need it?" she asked. I stared at it for a while, as if the urn itself might provide some meaning.

"Because that's where your father died," was all I could think to say.

Our urn resides now, still in its box, on a bookshelf collecting dust. The folded flag is packed away in a green Rubbermaid box along with letters from prime ministers, presidents, and princes, magazines and newspapers devoted to 9/11 coverage, cards of condolence, quilts made by strangers, and banners made by schoolchildren. I keep them packed away, preferring to remember Arron's everyday heroism in the smiling, laughing pictures of him that I keep around the house.

9

WORKING WIDOW

A few days before my mother's arrival, I had had a visit from my old boss at Audible, Rob, who showed up at my house bearing Chinese food. He wondered if I wanted to come back to work. I was surprised. Did he want me back based on my merit, or was he asking me because he felt sorry for me? Audible had been incredibly supportive of me during the previous two months, with many of my colleagues coming by to see me. They had even pooled their money and donated a large sum to the kids' trust fund. Of the many checks that I received for the fund, Audible's was the most substantial.

"Rob, I'm not sure I could do a very good job right now, but I'm flattered that you've asked me back. I'm surprised actually, given that I was laid off."

"It was crazy that you got laid off. It was a mistake. You were and still are very valuable to the company. We need you to come back."

"Gosh, I don't know what to say." I was pleased, but I still wondered about Rob's motivations. I would be useless as an employee. Surely he knew that.

"The job will be really easy. Just one project. We need you to help us come up with a wireless phone interface. AT&T is about to launch their GPS service and we want to begin testing Audible on some GPS-equipped phones. You will be working directly with me and the job will be only three days a week. It should be really easy for you."

In my old role as Web Project Manager, I had worked on upwards of fifteen projects at once. The job required incredible concentration and organization, something I felt incapable of now. I was still so fragile and I still cried unexpectedly. It seemed impossible, and I worried how the kids might be affected. I told Rob that I needed to think about it.

When I told my mother about Rob's visit, she was not enthusiastic about the idea of my going back to work. "It seems a little soon. Are you sure that you're ready, sweetie?"

"I don't know," I said. "It does seem a little scary right now, I have to admit."

"What about the kids?" she asked.

"Well, I'm paying Martha a full-time salary. I don't think it would change their routines too much." I was on the defensive but was beginning to see the pros and cons more clearly.

I called my sister the next day. "Would it be nuts for me to go back to work so soon?" I asked her.

"No, not at all. I think it could be good for you. It'll get you out of the house and into a routine." I was grateful for her wisdom. I had been filling long days wandering around the house, crying, looking at widow websites and feeling lost. Working would give me something besides Arron and 9/11 to think about. It would give me a safe place to be every day and people to talk to. At least I knew Audible, so it would be better than trying to get a brand-new job. People at Audible cared about me and they would be tolerant of me if I stumbled.

I was also worried about money and medical insurance. I had received some money from Arron's life insurance, but I was still uncertain about our future in the house and in Montclair, an expensive town to live in. A paycheck, even a small one, would provide me with a certain peace of mind. Arron's company would be paying our medical benefits for the next three years, but it would be good to have a fallback. In the volatile financial market, Encompys was on tenuous ground.

I had kept on Martha even after I was laid off, in anticipation of working again, thinking my unemployment would be temporary. She cared for Carter when he wasn't in preschool and was there when Olivia came home from school. She kept the house tidy, did the laundry, and fed the kids. My life was set up to be a working mom, yet I worried that long days away from my kids might be too difficult for them and for me. With Janet, I determined that as long as I was happy, the kids would be happy, too. I wasn't sure if this old working mom's mantra would hold true for me and my grieving kids, but I decided that I would give work a try. I could always quit if it didn't pan out. I accepted the offer and on November 5, 2001, I was once again sitting at a beige desk at Audible.com in Wayne, New Jersey.

My first day back at work was a strange foray into public life. I woke up that morning nervous, uncertain of what to wear. I had never been nervous working at Audible before, even on my very first day. After being tucked away for two long months in my house with only minimal contact with people other than my family and closest friends, I feared how people at work were going to treat me. I still felt the weight, whenever I stepped in public, of what felt like others' reverence toward me, or pity, or fear. I found I could classify people into three categories: Those who empathized with me and who always managed to say just the right thing; those who didn't really understand, but tried anyway—they were usually the ones who said, "I'm sorry for your loss"; and those who didn't get it at all and just tried to avoid me altogether. How was I supposed to respond to "How *are* you?" That look of desperation in someone's eyes, willing me to tell them everything was fine. But it was not fine and it would never be fine. Could they see it in the dullness in my eyes? Audible wouldn't be any different.

I managed to spend my first day with very little contact with others. My new office was located on a side of the building where there were fewer people, so it was quiet. Many of the people I used to hang around with had either been laid off with me or had resigned during the shake-up, so my old social patterns were forced to shift. I hid in my office and only said hello to people in the kitchen when I got my tea.

In the following weeks, I would occasionally go out for lunch with someone, but more often, I would buy a sandwich and eat it alone in my office, something I had rarely done before. The job required minimal interaction with others in the company, and I mostly worked with two Russian programmers whose English was heavily accented and who were even more reclusive than I was. Their offices were just down from mine, and I spent a lot of time listening to them arguing in Russian.

I really didn't have enough work to keep me busy, which was perfect as it allowed me to spend time dealing with all the 9/11 paperwork I was bombarded with, mostly from charities. Applying to each one entailed photocopying piles of documents and mailing. I began lugging a heavy, accordion-style file folder that contained originals of all of our personal documents: birth certificates, mar-riage certificate, death certificate, Surrogate's certificate (proving my status as the executrix of Arron's estate), and so on. I had to change our car registration, take care of bills that hadn't been paid since August, and remove Arron's name from all our house-hold accounts. I had to roll over his airline miles and his 401(k)s. One of the services provided for 9/11 families was a credit check on Arron's name to ensure his identity hadn't been stolen. I then had to fill out all the paperwork to ensure that he was removed from the credit rating company's lists.

My days off centered around appointments related to my "estate" paperwork: meeting with the bank (it took a year to have Arron's name completely removed from our accounts); meeting with the lawyer to set up a trust for the children; going to the courthouse in Newark to obtain a Surrogate's certificate; buying appliances at Sears for our rental property; and heading to the

New Jersey Family Assistance Center to meet with the Red Cross or some other charity. I was thankful to have a flexible job that allowed me the time and resources to do many of these tasks. Audible was patient with me, allowing me the time I needed to ease back into working. I was hardly the ideal employee.

Sometimes as I worked on my computer, I was overcome with thoughts about Arron—remembering him driving his truck to my office to pick me up during a snowstorm, or the thrill I used to get on the rare instances when I got an e-mail from "Arron Dack" listed in my inbox. I often had to stop what I was doing and turn my back to my office door while I cried. I learned not to wear mascara at work. I kept a big box of tissues on my desk. My friends often corresponded with me via e-mail, and many of my replies were difficult. "Today I am very sad and there is nothing I can do about it," or "I just can't seem to stop missing him," I wrote with tears dripping down my face. It was a relief to be in a sparsely populated part of the office. I hated the thought of people seeing me cry all the time, although everyone probably knew anyway.

Often, I completely forgot what I was supposed to be doing, my hands still on the keyboard as I stared blankly out the window, my head full of cotton, empty. My phone was silent. I could see trees from my window. They had turned color and were dead-looking. The sky was the color of steel. I knew I was at work and should be doing something work-related, but I had no idea what that might be. I forgot to do simple tasks. It took me hours to complete things that used to take me mere minutes. I worked hard during conference calls, concentrating on what was being said, and forced myself to make notes so I wouldn't later forget conversations.

Over time, my self-esteem began to erode and I felt incapable of doing a job I had once loved and excelled at. Once, I was on top of the world. I could awe my colleagues with how much I could accomplish, with speed, efficiency, even glee. I was proud of all that I achieved and wanted that feeling back again. But that person was gone, had died in those buildings that day. Instead it was a new me, staring, not sure which task to begin or end, whom to call. Partly, there was too little to do, not enough really to warrant a three-day workweek. But I had no control over my wandering mind and knew that I could not complete more than was expected of me. I couldn't help feeling disappointed in myself. I was not doing the job well, at least not by my standards, and I was dismayed.

And yet working provided me with some structure to my weeks. I could escape the melee of the kids and bask in the quiet of the office. I could avoid the tomb that my house had become with Arron's dusty shoes still awaiting his return, his summer jackets hanging on the hook, but making no sense now that winter had arrived, his handwritten budgets still tacked to the bulletin board. Now, I put Olivia on the school bus, pried a sobbing Carter from my leg, and escaped to the office. I enjoyed my enforced routine. I arrived at my office, hid my purse in my drawer, walked to the kitchen and made my tea from the red spout of the water cooler, tried hard to make small talk with whoever was there. Happy voices: "How *are* you?" Then I snuck off to my sanctuary to stare out the window. I hoped this was the right thing to be doing, going to work. I kept repeating the mantra: "Happy mothers mean happy kids."

But was I happy? I worried about Carter's mental health on my workdays when he would clamp himself to my leg, wailing "Don't go, Mama!" Olivia gave me great big hugs when I got home, as though I had been gone for days. Martha made them early dinners, so I was left to fend for myself, making dinners of popcorn or cereal. The kids seemed sadder than they used to, and one night Olivia asked, "Why do you have to work, Mama?" I didn't have an answer beyond, "It's just something I know I need to do right now." I felt like the frozen, gray-steel winter sky I saw from my office window.

Within a week of my first day back at work, on November 11, there would be a second celebration of Arron's life. When Selena had called and suggested the date it had made sense. Remembrance Day: elevens. The numbers of the date September 11—9 + 1 + 1—totalled 11. September 11 was eleven days before my thirty-sixth birthday; our eleventh wedding anniversary was a week later; the flight numbers of the planes that hit the buildings were all divisible by 11; every time I looked at the clock it read 9:11. November 11 seemed significant. It would fall on a Sunday, an easy day to attend a memorial, and it meant I wouldn't have to take a day off during my first week back at work.

I was glad that Selena was planning this event. Now that I was working, I was tired and I had no interest in organizing a second one, but I was glad we were having one. Many people from our lives in Toronto had been unable to attend the New Jersey memorial. I also knew it was important to Selena to plan something meaningful to her, something from a mother's perspective, rather than a wife's.

I was surprised, however, to find that I was annoyed when Selena used a number of my memories of Arron in her plans. She asked about flowers. I suggested daisies, remembering an almost two-year-old Olivia triumphantly holding a bouquet of daisies that Arron had just given her for Valentine's Day, and a photo of him with Carter, daisies behind their ears. Despite daisies being difficult to find and expensive at that time of year, Selena persevered and ordered huge bouquets of them for the tables. She had wanted my opinion about where to hold the memorial. She had been thinking of the music room at Hart House, the University of Toronto's student center, where Arron and I were married. Did I think this was a good idea? "Of course," I said. "It's perfect!" Because, for me, it was. She asked me for a poem Arron had written as a teenager, whose first lines I had painted on Olivia's headboard. She wanted to print it onto cards as keepsakes.

I knew Selena added these things out of respect for me and for Arron, but I wondered where her own memories of her son were. Surely, she, too, must have a special flower, a poem. Although she wanted to honor me as the wife, she also seemed to struggle with her role after Arron's death. I sensed in her a need for acknowledgment for her loss. In public, she seemed to hug me a little too tight, or suddenly scoop the kids up like props as if to declare, "Look at me, I am the mother! I am important, too!" Perhaps because I was younger, had kids, and was Arron's wife, more public sympathy was directed at me. Society seemed to think losing an adult son was less difficult than losing a husband, the father of small children. But grief and loss could not be measured. I sensed Selena's displacement, and I hoped that in planning this celebration for Arron, among her friends, she would have her chance to publicly mourn him on her own terms. The irony was that I was glad that Selena would be hosting this memorial instead of me, to take a turn being the one to hold the pain, the memories, absorbing others' sadness, being the lightning rod for everyone else's grief.

I realized too late that there was a price to pay for relinquishing my memories and my grief to Selena. I looked at the baskets of bookmarks and cards with Arron's poem printed on them, wishing I had thought of using it for the New Jersey memorial. I realized that I was unhappy that the daisies and the music room, a part of Arron and me together, had been usurped. I didn't want my memory of these things tarnished by death, but it was too late for that now. I had already made the suggestions.

The kids and I traveled to Toronto with Kathleen, whose help I was constantly grateful for. She had organized our flights and hotel rooms, with Encompys footing the bill. I looked forward to staying in a hotel with her, rather than staying with family. It was easier to tolerate Kathleen's brisk, no-nonsense demeanor than the messy, unpredictable emotions of my friends and family.

At the memorial, I sat cross-legged on the floor of the music room at Hart House, a room that was stopped in time, looking much as it had the night of our wedding reception on September 29, 1990. Large leather chairs were scattered around the spacious room, sand-colored stone fireplaces flanked each end of the room, and overflowing bookcases dotted institutional-green walls. Carter burrowed into my lap. I was wearing a long fuchsia dress, which felt odd, despite the black turtleneck I had pulled over it to hide its original purpose as a long, slinky evening dress. I was tired of wearing black, and I wanted to wear a color and a dress that Arron would have loved me in. He had oohed and aahhed appropriately when I had paraded around the bedroom in it. The dress was stretchy and clung to me now as I sat cross-legged, making me feel at once too comfortable and too sexy. I was happy to be at eye level among all the children who came to the service, so I could avoid their parents' stares.

I stared into my wine, remembering this same day a month ago. The same pictures and music. I wiped my tears on my sleeve, not wanting to get up, but someone had been watching me and handed me a tissue. The "celebration" photo and music montage elicited the same agony from me as it had the first time in New Jersey. I was anticipating a new addition to the montage: a movie put together by Robert, Arron's childhood friend who had created the photo montage. He filmed the movie at Arron's stag party, a weekend spent at their friend Mike's cottage on the French River the week before we were married. I knew it would be funny and it didn't disappoint. The movie depicted the debauchery of that weekend, an edited version that Robert dubbed *Raising Heck*. There were shots of the interior of the cabin with every surface covered in beer cans or bottles of alcohol. There was a drug-induced game of golf and a morning-after scene of hungover awakenings. There were some poignant shots of Arron telling his friends in all sincerity that he wouldn't move after he got married and that he wouldn't change. I wanted to go back to that time, be those people who would not move or change and who would remain forever in Toronto, safe and alive.

The humor was a relief as Arron came alive on the screen. But his infamous giggle wrenched me. I had forgotten how it sounded.

The movie elicited old memories: How he used to rub his leg when he woke up; the twinkle in his eye as he made one of his typical nonsensical jokes, comparing a fish with entropy. His giggle could be heard even off-camera. I laughed, but with a bit too much hilarity.

The movie set the tone for all the speakers who came next. Every story about Arron was funny. A beautiful brunette stood up and I felt a momentary pang of jealousy. Sheilagh was smitten with Arron in ninth grade. She told stories of how he used to flick chewed-up bits of pen at her and about their walks home together.

Sometimes after school, we'd walk from Wellesley up Yonge Street, passing through the seedy top part of the strip. While other fourteen-year-old boys might have been drawn to one of the many pinball arcades, with Arron you were more likely to find yourself traipsing through a supermarket, where he'd urge you to join him in "fondling vegetables." He was on the lookout for the forlorn or the misshapen; fruit was also of interest, particularly anything exotic or hairy. Points would be awarded for finding the most "depressing" turnip, the "cheekiest" melon, or the "froggiest" zucchini. This could be a challenge, because "frogginess" was a mysterious quality that only Arron truly understood. I soon figured out that it wasn't an attribute or a flaw, just a quality he instantly recognized in people or things that delighted him.

Her stories of Arron made me laugh and weep. She remembered him with such detail, a detail that seemed to elude me, despite all of the years that I was with him. I envied her words and loved them at the same time.

There were many more stories about Arron told by his close friends, and friends I had never met. Selena stood up and recited Mary Elizabeth Frye's bereavement poem "Do Not Stand at My

Grave and Weep." As she stood at the front of the room, Olivia got up and took her place beside her grandmother and clasped her hand. Selena barely maintained her composure.

After the speeches and stories, the crowd thinned a little, though I had a sensation of it undulating around me. Waves of people came to hold my hand. Old friends seemed to fade in and out in front of me. Many of the people I was excited to see, not having seen them in over ten years, but I was being pulled in many different directions and satisfying visits with everyone were impossible. I began to grow tired. My facial muscles hurt, as they had hurt eleven years before on our wedding day.

Much later, Bruce and Jacquie took us to a small gathering that Selena had arranged at the apartment of a friend. It was nice to be cocooned among Arron's friends as we talked about the memorial and about Arron, and they were taking special care of me: helping me with the kids and taking time to play with them. I hoped that someday they could tell the kids their stories about him, stories that I felt unable to recite, unable to remember through my grief. But it felt strange to be with Arron's friends without him. We all expected him to walk through the door.

We awoke on Monday in the hotel, prepared to take an early afternoon flight back to Newark, in time for me to get back to work the next day. The kids spent some time in Kathleen's room, jumping on the beds and eating her Altoids, her new nickname. As we were packing to leave, Kathleen got a phone call from the office. They told her to put on the TV. There had been a plane crash in New York. We stood watching the coverage on CNN, propelled back to the morning of September 11. It was happening all over again. A fiery New York neighborhood. Grounded flights. Talk of debris and terrorism. A chill ran through my body. I began barking at the kids to stay quiet. Carter began to cry. Olivia became silent.

We called the airline. There were no flights going into New York while they determined whether this was a terrorist act or not.

For the first time since this long nightmare began, I felt panicked, remembering that morning all over again: The waiting and not knowing, the fear that someone else I loved might not come home. I was glad my kids were with me and that we were in Canada. My stomach began to knot, my throat got dry. Kathleen was in a panic of her own, one played out in her take-charge attitude.

"I don't think we should try and fly out today," she said, her face pinched.

"I can't believe this is happening. Not again," I said, squeezing my hands into fists.

We went through all of the scenarios: Waiting to see if we could get on our flight; waiting until the next day and trying to get on another flight; renting a car and driving.

"I think driving would be better than sitting around an airport all day. At least we would get home," she said. I saw her reasoning. Suddenly, driving seemed like a really great idea.

"There is no way I want to get on a plane now," I said. Kathleen agreed but soon discovered that none of the rental agencies would allow us to take a car across the border. I felt trapped in my own hometown. I called my dad, thinking that we might need a place to stay that night, explaining the situation.

"I can drive you to Buffalo," he said, making it sound like a quick half-hour trip rather than the three hours that it actually was.

So my dad drove us to Buffalo. He seemed almost jovial as he drove and I was grateful for his calmness. Perhaps he, too, was glad we were not flying. At the Buffalo Niagara airport's Hertz dealership, we transferred our things to a red Ford Taurus and began our journey along the sprawling freeways of New York State. Kathleen drove, her knuckles white, staring straight ahead. I entertained the kids, unsuccessfully, my mind distracted. Each time I turned around, pain shot through the knot that had formed in my neck. Their bickering and crying and whining punctuated the day. The statistics said that being in a car was less safe than being in a plane.

Was that true on this day? As a passenger, not in control of the car, I began to fear the car even more than the airplane.

Late in the day, we arrived to an Arron-less home, tired and grumpy, but alive. I wanted the drama to end. I wanted to curl up in my bed alone. But after a fitful sleep, I was once again waking at seven to Carter's morning demand: "I want chocolate milk!" I gave him his sippy-cup of Ovaltine and warm milk, toasted Olivia a waffle, made her lunch, and got her onto the bus by 8:10. Martha arrived at 8:30 to care for Carter and take him to nursery school at 9:00, and I slunk out the door and into the car to make my way to work. Yesterday's dead husband, memorials, plane crashes, and stressful car rides were forgotten for the time being. Just another day in my strange new life as a working widow.

[10]

SERPENT RISING

By early November, my body had become a barometer of my grief. My vigorous twice-weekly kickboxing classes left me feeling stiff and sore. After my trip to Toronto, my neck ached to the point where I was unable to turn my head to the right without a sharp pain. Turning to the left was impossible. I could no longer raise my left arm high enough to push open a door. I often had headaches. Each ailment compounded my grief, and my grief compounded my aches and pains. My shoulders felt as though they had caved in around my body and I felt like a feeble old lady, hunched and miserable.

Janet saw me cringe one day as I took a seat on her couch. Ever protective of me, she was dismayed by my near disability and told me about Maureen, a craniosacral therapist. "Your pain is part of your grief," Janet said. I didn't really know what she meant or what a craniosacral therapist was, but I was willing to try anything to feel better. I called Maureen the moment I got home.

I had no idea what to expect when I got to Maureen's office later that afternoon. Ethereal, chanting music was playing and the faint, honey-sweet smell of incense filled the air. Pinned to the walls were diagrams of the human body traced with bright red and blue lines indicating various body systems and labeled in foreign alphabets. I was nervous about the new-age setting, but willing, desperate even, to let her help me. Maureen was a small woman with no makeup and graying long hair pulled into a ponytail, but despite the gray she looked to be only about thirty-five. She wore a big fleecy pullover over black yoga leggings, revealing her slim, muscular legs.

"Come on in!" she said cheerfully. "I have something for you—a book that my boyfriend wrote. It might help you." She handed me a pink book with a bright orange sunset on the cover titled *Awakening from Grief: Finding the Way Back to Joy*, by John Welshons. "It's my present to you."

"Gosh. Thanks." I was touched by her thoughtfulness. I tucked it into my bag and tried not to be judgmental of the cheesy title and cover. Maybe I would even read it, I thought.

"I was not surprised when you told me over the phone that your pain was mostly on your left side," she said, as I lay down, fully clothed, on the sheet-covered massage table that took up most of the room.

"Really? Why?" I asked.

"All the issues you seem to be experiencing indicate that your heart meridian is probably involved. This meridian can affect the left arm, shoulder, elbow, into the outer edge of the forearm and out to the pinkie finger. Given what you told me about your husband, it makes sense. Broken heart."

I was astonished. It seemed so simple. My body was collapsing in around my heart, protectively, causing me physical pain. Broken heart. I had a diagnosis. Grief was a powerful force and I was beginning to see that it didn't just manifest in one's mind but also in one's body.

Maureen started slowly sliding her hands between my back and the table, touching what I assumed were my acupressure points: a spot below each of my shoulder blades; under my hips, what she called my "sacrum"; the back of my skull, my temples. I relaxed into her touch. Something in me filled, became less empty. Long-buried memories of being held seemed to seep up from some forgotten place. It had been so long since I had been touched that I hadn't realized I'd craved it. I realized then how much I had missed Arron's touch, even just holding his hand.

Maureen's touch was so light that I couldn't help wondering how it was possible for anything to be happening. But as I began to relax an odd thing started to happen. As she pressed one place on my body, I would feel pain or pressure in another part. Pressure on the sides of my calf muscles resulted in an ache in my jaw, neck, or shoulder. Maureen began pulling my left arm over to the right side of my body and something in the back of my neck changed: a release. A tension eased.

When she was done, I sat up feeling slightly dizzy. It seemed like she had done nothing, and yet my body felt fuzzy, cloudy, heavy. My head ached all over again.

"It's normal to feel slightly shaky after a session. Your body is reorganizing itself and it can be very disorienting," she soothed. "Try and take it easy for a few hours. You might also feel very emotional over the next couple of days."

In the ensuing weeks, Maureen continued to work on my left shoulder, delving into the many layers of pain and emotion accumulated there. Her small hands were powerful and got extremely hot as she worked. The thick muscle along the left side of my vertebrae felt like a writhing snake in her hands. Many times, I was desperate for her to work my muscles hard to relieve what felt like a deep itch, and without my even telling her, she would begin to work the serpent in my neck and shoulder with incredible force. Within three sessions I could open doors again and the rope of sinew that had crisscrossed my collarbone began to disappear. I felt taller. Sometimes when she worked, hot tears would slide down my cheeks inexplicably. I felt lighter and more optimistic when each appointment ended.

During my sessions, I often found myself in a deeply relaxed meditative state. As I lay on the table, I felt peaceful and calm. When I concentrated on what my body was feeling and doing, I felt as though the physical parts of me—skin, muscle, and bone—

were becoming more in tune with my emotional and mental sides. I felt myself floating, as though I were suspended in midair by strings. It felt strange and wonderful. I felt more whole, more aware of each ache or twinge in my body and how it connected to what I was thinking or feeling. If I listened to my body, I started to see that it could tell me more about how I was feeling. An ache in my left shoulder signaled frustration and anger, but a sharp pain over my right kidney often accompanied sadness.

As I lay on Maureen's table, I imagined that a great light was shining through the top of my head down to my feet, its beam perfectly straight now that my body and mind had aligned. I could feel the blood pulsing through my body. It seemed to hum. Something in me was changing, but I had no idea what it was and was barely conscious of how curious I was about it.

My friend Jacquie called me from Toronto one day, carefully broaching the idea of psychics. "So Bruce and I went to see a psychic the other day. The woman who did the reading was pretty amazing," she began. "Some stuff about you and Arron came up at the end of our session."

Jacquie told me that the psychic had described me as "feeling very lost," as "holding onto Arron through fear," and as "being cold and difficult for Arron to deal with right now." I couldn't help feeling slightly panicked. Did he really think I was cold? Unapproachable? I felt as though I had let him down somehow. The psychic also mentioned a "little boy who could see Arron" and a "nightgown." The reading continued along this vein with references to the roses in our garden and to a ring he might have given me. I was shocked by the line "He really loved her and didn't say this as often as he should have," because I knew that was how he felt.

But the psychic's description of Arron was what I found most incredible, as it described him perfectly. "He was a tall man, very statuesque, very intelligent, very driven, but with a great sense of humor. There was a loveliness to his sense of humor and a kind-ness. He could be quite sarcastic sometimes, as he is saying, 'a real bastard.' But he's okay. In life he would never have believed in someone like me." The phrase "a real bastard" was one he often used to describe himself, especially after successfully launching one of the devilish practical jokes he often played on his work-mates. I found myself smiling, and wanting more.

"It's funny," I said. "Here I am all worried about him in the afterlife and he's worried about me. I'm kind of insulted that he doesn't have more faith in me."

When I got off the phone, I sat for a long time thinking about what I had just heard. How could I be cold? Now, I wanted to prove him wrong. With this psychic's words, I felt I had crawled a little closer to Arron, and I wanted to dig deeper. Maureen was helping me to find an inner calm and I was discovering new aspects of myself, seeking new ideas. I hoped I was opening up to him.

After that, while lying on Maureen's table in my quiet state, watching colored lights dance behind my closed eyes, listening to myself breathe, and pushing away all the worried thoughts of the day, I imagined Arron could finally hear me. The thoughts I allowed into my mind were only for his ears: "I miss you," "Are you all right?" Maureen taught a yoga class that also provided me with this same opportunity for quieting my mind through long downward dog poses and meditations at the end of each class.

I had to believe that Arron still existed on some level and that we could touch, because I was unwilling to believe that our con-nection was lost forever and frightened of the possibility of noth-ingness after you die. Being able to reach him in some way, even in death, kept me crawling out of bed every day.

Arron and I had been happy people. We laughed a lot. We had many good friends and we lived what many would call a moral life, raising our children to be the kind, caring citizens we hoped we were. Our morality didn't come from church or a religion. God didn't really exist for us or perhaps we didn't exist for God.

We didn't pray. Yet uncharacteristically, in the summer of 2001, I had had notions of getting the kids christened, which Arron thought was insane.

"We don't even go to church!" he exclaimed when I broached the idea.

"Well, perhaps we should," I said defensively, confused by my own request.

I told myself it was because I wanted the kids to know a religion, a sense of belonging, something I never had. But the truth was, for about six months before 9/11, I had been haunted by strange premonitions involving the kids: car accidents, kidnappings, falling from high places. I would lie awake at night with my hand on my bedside table so I could "touch wood" in an effort to neutralize my negative thoughts. Christening our children felt like a kind of protection, a godly force shield that would keep them from harm. I began to nag Arron to make a will so the kids' future would be secure if we died. Foreboding followed me like a shadow. If only I had known that it was Arron's life and not our children's that lay on the line. Perhaps if I had, I could have convinced Arron to stay home that day.

My true spiritual mettle was put to the test the day the buildings fell. Being so abruptly and horrifically ripped from life, as Arron had been, could not possibly result in a calm afterlife. I worried that he was like the husband in the movie *Ghost*, stuck on earth, unable to move into a spirit world, determined to wreak his revenge. He communicates with his wife through a psychic to help him avenge his death. His ghost was stuck in a physical plane until he could accomplish his task. I worried that Arron was also stuck, wanting revenge for his death, and I worried about his spiritual well-being. I imagined Arron like a trapped bird, crashing around inside the chimney, unable to escape the darkness, desperate to find light. I longed to find him a better place in my mind, one where he was relaxed, sipping a martini while wearing a toga and sandals, his legs visible beneath. I needed to imagine him raising his glass to me and smiling his contented, languid smile.

Maureen's bodywork, combined with Janet's weekly sessions of grief therapy, where I was allowed to cry and wallow safely, became akin to my religion, and they were my gurus, guiding me to live again. I began to relish the catharsis of crying on Maureen's table or on Janet's couch, folding my tissues into squares.

Over time I became more self-aware. I started to make decisions by listening to my body in the moment, through my gut, rather than allowing my mind to plan ahead. The decisions could be as banal as what to have for supper or as important as whom to invest our money with, but I followed them almost blindly.

I was becoming more honest with myself about what I wanted and needed and worried less what other people thought of my decisions, no longer fearing the consequences if I was wrong.

I also began to notice tiny coincidences: being told about a great financial adviser just as I needed one, Arron's favorite song playing on the radio just as I was thinking of him, knowing who was on the phone before answering, or discovering a book that discussed the exact topics on spirituality or death that I had been wondering about. I thought now of Arron's apparent influence when his mother and I had found the perfect spot for his memorial service, the Tudor manor in the middle of New Jersey. As Selena and I had driven down the long wooded driveway, we had looked at each other. "This place is perfect," she said. It was as if there was a blinking neon hand with its finger pointing toward the place, flashing to us the signal "Go here, Bird, this is the place I want." Perhaps I sought coincidences, but they felt like breadcrumbs along a path, and I was more than ready to follow them.

I found other ways to tune into Arron's frequency. Walking Harley, I practiced the meditation that Maureen had taught me. I emptied my mind as I walked, concentrating on the sound of my breathing. I tried to notice the leaves dancing along the path beside me, the sound of ice on the puddles cracking as I stepped on them, or the sound of a woodpecker in a nearby tree. I thought of Arron walking beside me, like we often had in this park, and tried to have conversations with him. A bird chirping nearby or the wind rustling the leaves overhead became his responses to my questions.

At times, Arron's presence became almost tangible. In my office at Audible one day, a few weeks after returning, it smelled like there was something burning. I went next door.

"Steve, do you smell smoke?"

"No . . . I hope the place isn't burning down!" he mocked.

A few days later I noticed the smoke again, this time in my bedroom. I figured a neighbor had a fire going. I noticed it again a week later in the living room. Again I assumed a nearby fireplace was the source. A couple of weeks later I smelled it again at the office. Finally, one day, I walked into the bedroom and was puzzled by the faint woody smell of smoke yet again.

"Again?" I said out loud to no one. "That's so weird."

And then it dawned on me. Arron.

"Eeeewww! Smoke? Is this your way of communicating with me? Why smoke? That's just creepy! Why didn't you choose another smell, one that wouldn't make me think of 9/11? Mothballs, or lemons." I must have sounded like a crazy person, talking to no one, and shuddering. The smell wasn't like the Ground Zero smoke, which smelled of wet plaster, cement, and the sickly sweetness of death. It was definitely a friendlier smell, like that from a fireplace.

When Arron used to make fires at home, the room would fill with smoke, and our eyes would begin to tear. We would prop open the front door until we were shivering, still wiping our eyes.

"This damn fireplace won't draw!" he would say as he crumpled more newspaper to add to the smouldering fire, making matters worse.

"It's a great fire, honey! You really have it going now! Did you forget to open the damper again, though?" I would enthuse. He would turn and glare at me.

"Oh my God!" I said to the air now. "This is your joke! Even as a ghost you're joking around!"

And so I was happily haunted by a smell of smoke, mostly when I entered our bedroom. To me the odor, though initially disturbing, conveyed Arron's presence. I grew to be increasingly comforted by its signal, like butterflies and lights turning on, telling me that he was near. I took to chatting with the smell. "Is the smoke smell your way of telling me that you don't like my outfit?" or "Hi, honey. I had another rough day without you today."

I found myself reading the book that Maureen gave me, *Awakening from Grief*, despite my initial superficial reaction to its cover, and it became a turning point for me, allowing me to see for the first time that grief could have a potentially positive outcome. By telling stories about other people facing death and then dying and the experiences of those grieving them, John helped his readers to overcome the fear of death. Learning the intimate details of other people's circumstances helped me to realize that death was a natural part of life. I realized that I had spent my life fearing loss, fearing death, perhaps as a result of my parents' divorce when I was eight. As a kid, I breezed through all the changes in my life easily, deferring dealing with my emotions. But early in my marriage, I began to have separation anxiety whenever I was away from Arron, and more recently I had had visions of violent traumas happening to the kids. Now, with death so close, I was forced to face it.

As I read the book, I realized that Arron's death had weakened my own fear. Perhaps my so-called communications with him were all in my head, but I was surviving his death. I was learning to live without him. I now knew that all of us had the ability to cope with loss in our lives, and that we learned from our losses. I liked to think that there was more living after you died, that death wasn't just an endless black hole. But even if it was, knowing that I had lived a life filled with successes and mistakes, knowing that I had loved and was loved by others, was enough to allay my fears of dying.

I began to see the opportunity that grief could give me: freedom from fear. With that freedom, I no longer feared making wrong decisions and I cared less what other people thought of me or my choices. I realized that I had spent my life doing things for other people, getting the right job, being a good wife and mother. Now, the possibilities for my life seemed to have opened wide. I could move to Paris if I wanted, take up skydiving. I could become a writer. I could see the carrot of diminished grief dangling before me; saw that the intensity of my present grief might eventually result in a fresh, positive perspective on life. I was already becoming more open to new ideas, seeking the advice of people and books that I might have normally avoided, deciding they were too "new age" or "touchy-feely."

I talked to Diane, my neighbor, about my spiritual exploration and my interest in psychics since Jacquie's reading with the Toronto psychic. I knew Diane was a good person to talk to about these things. She was wise and pursued her interest in everything from psychics and astrology to numerology to alternative medicines. She was one person I could trust not to laugh at me. She recommended I read her stash of books by the well-known TV psychic Sylvia Browne. I was a little skeptical. Sylvia Browne was not the type of person I imagined a psychic to be. On the surface, she seemed crass and rooted in earthly pursuits, out to make a buck. She hardly embodied the ethereal image I had of a genuine psychic. I imagined a tiny, middle European gypsy-type woman, quiet, soulful, yet powerful. But I delved into those books like a hungry wolf, desperate for information about Arron. Her words offered me what I didn't know I was seeking: a detailed description of heaven.

She described buildings and great halls, and homes and people (souls) with an authority that I found compelling. Her visual descriptions of these places matched my juvenile ideas of them and provided for me a setting in which to place Arron and a way of understanding why tragedy might have befallen us. I was slightly embarrassed to be embracing this form of spirituality, as it seemed naive and simplistic. But it suited the baby steps I had begun taking toward understanding my own beliefs. Her words comforted me and I felt calmer when I began to imagine Arron being cared for by "spirit guides," being "cocooned" as he moved back into the spirit world.

Dwelling on Arron's fate, I kept asking two questions: Did we guide our own fate, or was fate preordained by some higher being? It seemed to be Arron's fate to have been in those towers on that particular day. There were abundant stories of people who were and weren't in the buildings on 9/11. A man who worked in the World Trade Center for twenty years played golf that day, avoiding the tragedy; another WTC long-timer, a neighbor, ran late because his cleaning ladies lost their key to his house; a chef at the Windows on the World restaurant broke his glasses early that morning and dashed to the basement mall to have them repaired and so was spared. Many, like Arron, were there just for the day, having a breakfast meeting or making a delivery. Did each person who was caught in the towers decide that morning to embrace his or her own fate, and die? The idea was ludicrous.

Preordained fate seemed to make more sense. Nice, clean, out of our hands. God's will. But I wasn't even sure I believed in God. If he didn't exist, then who was making the decisions and why Arron? Why all those people? Why that day? I hated the cliché that "God had a plan for them." I hated thinking that God had anything to do with that day whatsoever.

Browne offered a new take on fate: the notion that we each created our own fate before arriving on this earth. It was like a combo-pack solution to my dilemma: fate that is both self-guided *and* predetermined, though individually, rather than by God. To ascend the spiritual ladder toward nirvana, we choose to exist on earth to feel emotions and encounter trials that the spirit realm is unable to offer. Before our birth, we create for ourselves a "life path" for our time on earth. We choose the people who will enter our lives as guides and teachers, we choose our parents, we even choose our own exit points, a total of five points during the span of our lives where we have the option of exiting earth if we feel that we have learned what we have come to earth to learn.

I was immediately caught up in the romance of Arron and I having preselected each other as mates. Imagining him choosing his moment of demise almost made me laugh, knowing that he would have wanted to find the most dramatic end available, keeping true to his maverick, larger-than-life character. "Bring it on!" I could almost hear him saying. Still, I questioned what spiritual lesson he could have mastered to feel ready to part this earth. Perhaps the nature of his demise had itself been the lesson: life needed to be lived and not spent at work. Life was not all about making money. Life was about those that you love. Life was short.

Arron had lived his life as if he was trying to cram a lifetime into a few short years. He was fanatical about saving money. He made huge demands on himself, setting elaborate goals that he wanted to meet before he turned forty. Work out more, spend more time with family, earn $500,000 a year or start a business, purchase another investment property, spend more time with friends, write a book. He worked jobs for no longer than two years, growing bored once he mastered the skills required. I wondered, looking back, if all these things added up to his unconsciously knowing that he would die young.

Arron lived by the mantra "If you don't like your life, then change it." He welcomed change and I'm sure if we had ever really had a discussion on fate, he would have declared himself the master of his own.

The logical, rational part of my brain admonished me for believing Browne's simplistic, clichéd rhetoric, but since I had already questioned the more accepted forms of religion, and since I wanted to know where Arron had ended up, I was open to the beliefs of someone who sees dead people.

I resolved to keep an open mind and the psychic babble made me feel better. I wanted to talk to dead people, too. I wanted Arron to see me, to be able to see him in his afterlife. I longed to feel the smoothness in the shape of his back or hip, feel the slope of his nose and inhale him into my lungs as I would a cool, fragrant spring morning. Slowly, I began to remember the things that grief had forced me to suppress: the twinkle in his eye and the guffaw of his infectious laugh. I spoke with him silently and listened for his imagined whispers. "There is so much for you to learn, Bird," I would hear him say in the birds' songs as I walked in the woods. "It's beautiful here" or "You are doing an amazing job with the kids—I am proud of you, Bird." These conversations with Arron propelled me toward the next day, and I put one foot in front of the other.

Every person I met, every book I read seemed to have ideas that I could learn from. With the phrase "Life's too short" continually rolling off my tongue, I delved into new areas of thinking—spirituality, fate, death, and afterlife—that I had never thought much about before. I became more spontaneous—buying a bed, taking a job, booking a vacation—no longer rooted to the status quo. Life was in a state of flux and I was learning to be flexible.

It was up to me to release myself from grief through the choices I made, and my outlook on life. I could feel my body unfurling, becoming less weighted down as sadness escaped from my tissues. I was learning that if I relaxed and allowed people to help me, in whatever form it might come, it would be possible to find happiness and pleasure again.

11

CHRISTMAS WITH A VENGEANCE

My spiritual discoveries of the late autumn fell by the wayside as Christmas approached, and I found myself again rooted in earthbound grief. It seemed that everyone wanted to celebrate the holidays with a vengeance in 2001, as if in an effort to keep fresh the feelings of charity and goodwill that had pervaded the months since September 11. Everyone around me seemed determined to make this a great Christmas, perhaps to help me through my grief, but the effort to make plans seemed urgent and I was inundated with dinner and party invitations. In every store I entered, smells of cinnamon and pine assaulted me, and old carols triggered memories: Arron and me wrapping gifts for the kids on Christmas Eve, while he ate the cookies and milk left for Santa; buying a tree in the dark from the pool club parking lot, and once home, watching him curse as he tried to fit it into the tree stand; Arron in his blue terrycloth bathrobe on Christmas morning, playing old bluesy Christmas tunes, while he drank a mimosa and wrestled with the packaging of a Barbie or Fisher-Price toy; Arron relaxing at my dad's place in Port Hope on Christmas day, reading the instructions to his latest gadget, eating shrimp, and drinking a beer. Each memory brought sadness.

I went overboard buying presents for the kids, for teachers, for neighbors. I had received so much kindness over the previous months that I felt compelled to return it in the form of Christmas gifts. I bought most presents on Amazon.com and had them delivered to my office. An accidental double click of the BUY button had sent two of everything. I sat alone in my bedroom at night, wrapping and crying.

date

On December 22, Arron would have turned forty. I wondered how we might have celebrated if he were alive to see this day. A fancy dinner? A weekend away? A big surprise party? I thought of the glee I would have had at sneaking one past him. He was terrible at surprises, always finding a way to spoil them. I felt sorry for myself knowing I would never get to try.

Selena had flown to New Jersey a few days earlier to help me drive the ten hours to Port Hope, where we would celebrate Christmas with my father and Sheilagh. It seemed fortuitous that Selena was with us on Arron's birthday, despite the added pressure of finding a way to celebrate that she, too, would find meaningful. His birthday coincided with a Christmas performance at Olivia's school, which seemed the perfect distraction.

I was last in the school's auditorium for Olivia's kindergarten performance the previous June. Arron and I had played the proud parents, waving madly from the balcony of the large auditorium each time we thought Olivia was looking our way. Now I sat with Selena and Janet, who had offered to come and help me with the kids. Carter sat in my lap, and we sat in the same balcony seats that Arron and I had used that June. I expected to see Arron make his way through the crowd, sweating, having run from the bus, tie loosened, relieved to be there just on time.

The show began and each class performed one section of the play, a celebration of different countries. We marveled at how cute all the kids were and strained to hear what they were saying and singing. Olivia's class appeared last, performing a Chinese dragon dance, an undulating line of kids traversing the stage in little hops and jumps. As part of the tail, Olivia didn't have any special role other than to sing and dance with the rest of her class, but I was proud of her for managing to keep herself together enough to perform after all she had been through and after missing so many rehearsals. All I could think of was how proud Arron, too, would have been of her and how loudly he would have clapped at the end, whooping and whistling through his fingers.

I felt both glad and ripped apart that night. It would have been a perfect birthday for Arron, watching Olivia dance. I tried to tell myself he was seeing it all, but it wasn't working. I wanted Arron to squeeze my hand. I wanted to be embarrassed by his loud whistles and whoops. I wanted to be near him and touch him. I held back tears as the auditorium erupted in a final applause.

We got home late, still not knowing how to celebrate Arron's birthday. I had bought a tiny ice-cream cake. Feigning joviality, I gathered the kids and Selena around the kitchen table so we could sing "Happy Birthday to Daddy." The kids sang happily while Selena and I held back tears and choked out the words to the song. I handed out the gooey slices of cake, the kids quickly licked off the icing, and it was over.

"Can we go play?" Olivia asked.

I was irritated that they hadn't understood the importance of the moment. I wanted it to last, to tell stories of Arron, to remember him again and again and never forget. But the kids had short attention spans and needed to go to bed. I needed to prepare for our early-morning departure, which included packing and wrapping presents. So I dropped the half-eaten cake unceremoniously into the garbage.

In Carter's room, my voice cracked as I sang his ritual lullabies and tears rolled down my face and fell off my chin silently. Nothing I did ever seemed to properly honor Arron.

There was the usual chaos as we spilled into my dad's house in Port Hope the next day, with Harley barking her excitement and the kids running around, finally freed from car seats. That night, I sat with my dad and Sheilagh, having a late dinner, drinking wine. It was an evening of relative normalcy. I had sat at this table many times, both before I met Arron and since, drinking wine, discussing politics and architecture, and these old, familiar patterns were calming. Except for the empty chair.

I wished Jill and Dan could have come this year, but by now Jill was almost seven months pregnant and air travel was not advised. But Jill would have jostled me with her silly humor. She was one of the few people who could always reduce me to tears of laughter. I longed for a good belly laugh now.

I was dreading Christmas, not really knowing what to expect from my emotions. I threw myself into making tourtière, a French-Canadian meat pie that was our Christmas Eve dinner tradition. With some help from Selena, I kept Carter busy and out of mischief, napped and fed, and the two days sped by quickly.

Suddenly Christmas Eve was upon us. We were invited to two parties, the first at the home of one of my father's friends. The couple's many grandchildren were tearing around in excitement. It was a fun, lively group but I was overwhelmed by the chaos. There is a movie effect where the main character is in full focus while those around him are moving and thus blurred. I felt as though I was in sharp focus while people I didn't know blurred past me. I made small talk hiding behind Carter's clinginess, not knowing what I said.

Soon everyone gathered in the living room, kids sitting on the floor, the seniors getting the more comfortable chairs, and everyone else either perched or standing. Smudged and crinkled song sheets were handed around and everyone began to sing carols. I wasn't in the mood. Everyone seemed so happy, oblivious to my sadness. I wanted desperately to leave and willed Carter to run out of the room, so I could chase him and escape. Instead, he toddled over to Olivia's spot on the floor and grabbed her song sheet, much to her annoyance. It seemed like ages before I saw my dad glancing around at our group to signal it was time to head to the next party.

At the next party, at a house named Blue Stone and lit only with candles, I could feel my fatigue taking root. The kids had eaten dinners of Christmas cookies and little else and were tired and overly excited. With Carter and Olivia following me, I wandered the historic house, impressed with its meticulous renovations, and tried to make small talk with some of my parents' friends, trying to catch the eye of my father or Sheilagh. I knew it had worked when I saw Sheilagh talk quietly into my dad's ear.

When we finally arrived home at 9:30 that night, I put the kids to bed and went downstairs for a late supper of tourtière, which I barely tasted. Afterward, I filled stockings, including ones for my dad, Sheilagh, and Selena, hoping they might provide a little fun the following day. Exhausted, I fell asleep instantly.

The next morning, the kids were up and had ripped open their stockings by seven-thirty and were wearing big red wax lips and silly glasses. Selena arrived early so as not to miss a thing. My dad and Sheilagh eventually awoke and my efforts to keep the kids from opening gifts were suddenly abandoned to mayhem. Packages spilled from under the tree in a wide radius, more than we had ever had before. Everyone, especially me, had gone overboard buying the kids gifts, as though more things could keep them from being sad. We all watched as Carter and Olivia ripped open wrapping, flinging the presents aside before ripping open some more. They seemed maniacal. I was embarrassed and told them half-heartedly to slow down, though I wasn't in the mood to enforce discipline. Not every Christmas was going to be this way. Everyone's attention seemed to be riveted on the kids, our exclamations overly joyous.

I sat on the couch and watched Olivia open a doll. She looked forlorn, as though she missed Arron, but said nothing. I could practically see him sitting there as he had in other years, struggling to open packages with a million twist ties and doll hair stitched to cardboard. I remembered his look of excitement, and his mirth, opening his own presents. He would become a child again as he helped the kids to play Santa, handing the presents to them, directing them to the correct recipient. Now I was directing the kids, coaxing them to slow down to let others open their presents before another was handed out; I was the one struggling with the sewn-in Barbie hair. I was missing that look of glee, and I felt as stiff as the doll, hemmed-in, tied with wires, unable to move.

My aunts and uncles and cousins began to arrive in the afternoon, each time to a new round of present opening. Usually I participated in the dinner preparation, but I had to keep Carter entertained while continuing to wrestle dolls and toys out of their plastic clamshell packages, insert batteries into toys, and pore over complex directions. Arron had always put the toys together. Arron had always taken the kids outside for a walk or a toboggan ride while I helped to cook; Arron had always played with the kids' toys more than the kids themselves had.

At dinner, everyone tried to be jovial, but we were all trying too hard. We pulled on each other's Christmas crackers until they snapped loudly, startling me. A small toy flew through the air and Carter dove under the table to fetch it. I donned the obligatory pink tissue-paper hat. Carter's ripped, and I averted his tears by trading. Sheilagh looked at us, annoyed at all the indulgences the kids had earned that day. I knew they were being spoiled, but I didn't care and didn't have the energy to do anything other than let them have what they wanted.

Dinner was served up, along with the usual conversations. Weather. What other family members were doing. Someone's latest project or silly work story. I tried to reminisce about Arron's propensity for charades, which this same group had played the previous year, but no one was in the mood for laughing and the conversation died. No one else had a story to tell about Arron.

Carter couldn't sit still and kept sliding off his chair so he could sit under the table. Olivia kicked him and he cried. I pulled him onto my lap, where he started playing with one of the cracker's pulls, trying to make it pop again. He pulled a little too hard and nearly knocked over a glass of wine, which I caught just in time. He cried for a minute when I grabbed his hand and then jumped down again so he could join Olivia under the table to look for another cracker toy that had dropped. He stood up and bonked his head on the underside of the table and began to wail again.

After dinner, the kids were restless, overtired, and cranky. It was time for Carter to go to bed, but I had been trying to be helpful by cleaning up. I calmed Carter down and gathered more plates from the table, but Sheilagh took the dishes from me and said, "Isn't it bedtime yet?" Her tone was overly sweet, one I knew well from my childhood. She spoke through gritted teeth. She was done with crying children and wanted them in bed. My carefully constructed facade cracked and I did everything I could to hold back my tears. We were all exhausted. I, too, longed for bedtime.

Angry and hurt by what felt like criticism, I got Carter ready for bed, glad to have escaped the noise below. I was crying, wishing I were home. Silenced by my tears, Carter crawled obediently into bed. I sat beside him and asked him what he wanted me to sing to him. The usual repertoire included "Brahms' Lullaby," "I Gave My Love a Cherry," and "Hush Little Baby."

"Heaven peace song," he immediately responded. It took me a second or two to place the song—"Silent Night," with the last line "sleep in heavenly peace." My eyes began to tear again, my throat constricted.

"Daddy heaven song," Carter said, as if reading my mind. Was this how he imagined Arron—sleeping in heaven? I did not remember having sung this song to him, even though it was Christmas, but somehow he had heard it and understood the words. Somehow he had connected the words "heaven peace" to Arron.

I began to choke out the words, which came back to me from years of Christmas caroling. At first my words were broken, but as I relaxed, my anger subsided, and I sang louder, enjoying it. We were in the "brown room" of my father's Victorian house, which he and Sheilagh had painstakingly restored to its original grandeur over the past ten years, and it was dark except for a night-light of plastic white tulips in the corner. There was a pile of unwrapped but mostly unopened toys near the bed. Outside the large window, the full moon shone brightly on the crisp snow that had fallen silently all day. Its blue light shone back into the room and I felt as though we were in its spotlight. It was so peaceful and beautiful.

Carter looked at me with his solemn little face and the song began to warm me, and I felt calmed by its cadence. "Silent night, holy night, all is calm, all is bright. . . ." It seemed to be describing the magical scene outside. The night indeed felt heaven-sent, holy. I sensed that Arron was with us, or had somehow conspired to create such a beautiful scene, and the thought comforted me. Carter fell asleep and as I kissed his forehead, I whispered both to Carter and to Arron, "Merry Christmas."

My mother, Margot, and my brother, Matt, were invited to spend Boxing Day afternoon at my father and Sheilagh's house. This was unprecedented. In the twenty-eight years since my parents' divorce, when I was eight, my mother had rarely been invited to my father's house. I knew that my father and my mother had, over the years, managed to overcome their animosity toward each other and become friends, but there had been virtually no contact between my mother and Sheilagh during my childhood and there was little now. In my strange emotional state, I felt like a child who can't bear to have two foods touching on her plate. I could not tolerate the stress of my parents' two worlds touching.

On Boxing Day morning, I felt the old childhood queasiness at the prospect of my mother being in the same house as my dad and Sheilagh. The left side of my neck already ached, and I had developed a headache. I snapped at the kids for yelling, running, and fighting. Carter demanded to be carried incessantly. Sheilagh's face looked drawn. I knew she was more nervous than

I was at the prospect of my mother coming. She was shy and found social situations extremely difficult. She was known to hide in upstairs bedrooms during parties. I shuffled the kids into another room and set them up with a video in an attempt to get some peace and quiet.

Selena called and I made plans to take the kids to her house for a visit, to give Sheilagh some quiet. I was still feeling annoyed at her, too, and was looking for an escape.

"I just need to know if Sheilagh wants me to bring mincemeat tarts over today," asked Selena. Since moving to Port Hope a few years ago, Selena had spent every Christmas Eve, Christmas Day, Christmas dinner, and Boxing Day with my dad and Sheilagh.

My father walked into the kitchen just as I asked Sheilagh the question and handed her the phone.

"No, no, no," my father said gruffly. "I don't think it would be a good idea for Selena to come this afternoon. It's going to be enough with Margot and Matt here." He really meant that having my mother and Matt here would be stressful enough for all of us, without adding Selena to the mix. Selena and my mother could get along, but the tension between them had grown in the past few months. My father's awareness of this was a surprise to me, something I thought I was alone in feeling. I was touched that he was now trying to ease my mother's visit, but I did not envy Sheilagh, who was now left with the nasty task of uninviting Selena. She shot me a flustered look.

"Uh, Selena, I think it would be easier if actually you didn't come over this afternoon." I cringed, knowing that Selena would feel offended. And now I was headed over to her house and would get an earful.

I arrived on Selena's doorstep in tears, overwhelmed with self-pity. I couldn't seem to appease Sheilagh and I knew Selena would be angry and hurt. I was trapped between my family, helpless and frustrated, without any emotional strength to calm myself down. I wanted to scream.

"I have to get out of here! I don't understand why Sheilagh is being so awful! Doesn't she see that I'm doing my best to control the kids? It's not like she's helping me with them at all."

"It's unbelievable how she's treating you. And me, too!" Selena said as we sat on her couch while Carter and Olivia watched another video. "Sheilagh *asked* me to come weeks ago. She was worried about your mother coming and wanted to have me there for moral support!" I understood her rage. It was a callous social gaffe.

Grief was changing my family's dynamics. No one was acting normally. Since Arron's death, my mother had become closer to my father, whereas Selena's footing with him now seemed tenuous. Sheilagh had gotten caught in the middle. I was no longer able to play the role of the buffer the way I always had, working desperately to calm frayed egos, acting as the go-between among disparate parties. My father was no longer the easygoing, let's-have-everyone-come-over party host. Sheilagh, in her shyness, was dependent on a carefully controlled social life and was becoming more stressed now that all her established social rules seemed to have changed. Selena could not empathize with anyone else's grief and in her fragile state took anyone's odd behavior personally. She wore the loss of her son plainly on her sleeve and seemed to revel in the attention that the people of Port Hope bestowed upon her. In contrast, my father and Sheilagh found this kind of attention abhorrent, and shied away from the notoriety that Arron's death had brought them. We all handled our emotions and the publicness of Arron's death differently, and each of us was trying to find sure footing where there was none. I wished Selena could understand that everyone was grieving for Arron in their own ways. Now my anger at Sheilagh was eclipsed by Selena's, and I found myself defending my father.

"I think it was my dad who didn't want you to come today, not Sheilagh. I think my father is stressed out about my mom coming."

"And how exactly am I going to make that worse?"

"I don't know," I said, though I did know. But I could no more explain to Selena the subtleties of my family's grief than I could explain the frankness of hers. Grief was causing us all to ignore the social rules of politeness. I was beginning to realize that my new, closer relationship with Selena had somehow hurt both my parents, who also wanted a role in helping me through grief, but I didn't know what to do about it. I simply had to take what I needed from each of them. It's hard to empathize with the pain of others when you yourself are in pain.

"Well, I can't understand why Sheilagh had to be so *rude*!" Selena said.

I was still in tears. My anger at Sheilagh, the stress of Christmas, and now the wrath of Selena were just too much to take. "Maybe I should leave. Head back to New Jersey tomorrow," I said bitterly.

"Anytime you want to go, I'm ready," Selena said. She seemed almost gleeful at the thought. I could tell it would make her day if I jumped back in the car and drove home. My plan had been to stay until the day after New Year's, but that now seemed an impossibly long time. Unfortunately, I had already made plans for various friends to visit us in Port Hope during the upcoming week. My friend Kim was set to drive from Montreal with her three-year-old daughter to spend New Year's with us. If I left now I would miss out on seeing all of them.

"I think you should leave," Selena was saying. "You can't stay there."

"I know, I know . . ." I managed.

"Of course I would be thrilled if you stayed here. . . ."

I was used to Selena's little hints and wondered if she knew how guilty they always made me feel. She wanted us all to stay in her tiny house, but I wouldn't be able to tolerate the crowding, and I needed a break from all the time we had spent together in the past few months. Staying with my father and Sheilagh was important to me, but I hadn't anticipated how emotional the visit would be. I was stuck, it seemed, between unyielding family members who had no idea of how their behaviors were affecting me. I raced between their homes, I tried my best to calm Selena's angry outbursts, I endured my father's silence and Sheilagh's backhanded suggestions. I wanted to be angry, to scream, but all that came out were more insidious tears.

"I know I can stay here . . ." I folded my tissues into tiny squares, overwhelmed with frustration by my inability to soothe everyone's hurt feelings, the way I used to.

An hour later, with my face washed and hoping that my eyes weren't too puffy, the kids and I were back at my father's greeting my mother and Matt. I was glad to see them and relieved for the excuse to flee from Selena's hurt and anger. The room was full of smiles and laughter and warmth. Matt swung Carter around by his arms while Olivia jumped on Matt's back. I could tell by his jovial mood that my father was genuinely happy that my mother and Matt were there. Matt, whose father was my stepfather, Larry, had visited Port Hope on other occasions and got along well with my father. They seemed to have a kind of father-son camaraderie. All of my childhood worries about my mother being in the same house as my father and Sheilagh vanished. Our mutual grief seemed to erode those old animosities. With my mother in the room, I remembered that it wasn't the first time that my two worlds had collided. Now I remembered the graduations and weddings of my sister and me. Those events seemed such a long time ago. My mother had been in this house only two years earlier, for my sister's wedding. How could I have forgotten that? Why did my old childhood fears surface this morning and not then?

Sheilagh didn't seem to feel the warmth of my parents' reunion in the living room. She spent a lot of time escaping to the kitchen, tidying dishes, bringing out more cookies, or sitting at the table, smoking. I felt sorry for her. She didn't seem comfortable with my father's obvious pleasure in my mother's presence. Perhaps she, too, was grieving. I tried to make amends for my earlier resentment toward her by helping her to clear dishes. I wished I could think of something to say, that I could tell her I was sorry—sorry for being angry with her; sorry that Arron died. But I was lost to my own pain.

As the afternoon wore on, everyone seemed to relax. Even Sheilagh began to enjoy herself, laughing at Matt's jokes. Dinner went smoothly, and after my mother and Matt left, my father, Sheilagh, and I sat at the kitchen table while they smoked another cigarette.

"Well, I think that went well!" my dad said, obviously pleased. He had managed to get everyone to be one big, happy family. If only that generosity and understanding had been extended to Selena. If only he could see how much more complicated my stay was to become in the wake of Selena's exile from this day.

I spent the rest of the week jostling the kids between my father's house, my mother's cottage, and Selena's house while also trying to visit with my own friends. I felt as though everyone wanted a piece of me, and once again I was overwhelmed trying to give everyone what I thought they wanted—a sense that they had helped me by spending time with me and the kids. I loved seeing my friends and yet I felt like a terminally ill patient, unable to take too many visitors at once. I needed quiet and serenity—something completely out of my reach. My conversations were constantly interrupted by demands for candy, cookies, bottles, carrying. I worked hard to keep the kids on their routine of naps and meal-times, living in a house of smokers where people didn't rise until 9:30 AM or eat dinner until 9:30 PM.

As the week wore on, I became tired and more stressed out and the kids seemed to feed off my fatigue. Carter cried more from napless days and clung more tightly to me, cranky and mis-erable. I gave in too often to his demands for candy canes off the tree, adding to his intensity. Olivia was growing bored with the videos that I had brought. She needed help with the various "art project" Christmas presents she had received, and Carter decided he was the perfect assistant, setting off bouts of yelling and wailing. Olivia could be lured outside to play in the snow, but Carter, hating his cold weather gear, guaranteed that I'd end up wrangling a screaming bundle of snowsuit with one arm while pushing a morose six-year-old on a swing in minus fifteen weather with the other.

Despite my struggles managing the dynamics of the house with the kids, there were moments of sweetness as well. Sheilagh patiently helped Olivia mix ingredients for cookies and pies, as she once did with Jill and me many years earlier. My father took Carter for a ride on the "tractor," a riding mower that was all Carter could talk about for weeks afterward. My father listened patiently to each of the kids when they hurriedly told him stories, often with Carter perched awkwardly on his lap. My dad would look to me blankly so I could translate. A childhood illness had made my father partially deaf and he relied on loud talkers and face-to-face conversations to be able to hear properly. He struggled to understand the gibberish of a two-year-old.

On New Year's Eve my friend Kim and her daughter Liane arrived to celebrate with us, while my father and Sheilagh spent the evening with friends. The kids played and fought, hyper from too much sugar from huge rainbow-colored lollipops, while Kim and I sat in the kitchen and drank red wine and tried to catch up as we fed and reprimanded and chased and coddled our kids. I met Kim in Verbier, Switzerland, when I was eighteen and she was twenty. I was unable to ski due to a nasty cut trying to slice a salami with my new Swiss Army knife and she had just sent her skis back to Canada with her sister. After two long days of drinking tea and talking, we decided to continue to drink tea together through France and Spain and finally Portugal over the following six weeks. Over the years, we had maintained our friendship despite months and sometimes years of not seeing or talking to one another. When I introduced Arron to Kim, they got along well and developed a mutual affinity for each other. Kim, like Arron, did not suffer fools. We had spent time with her over Labor Day weekend, so she had seen him only a week before he died. I knew how much she also missed Arron. Kim had recently divorced her husband, Dean, and this Christmas was difficult for both of us, our first as single mothers. We were struggling together.

At ten, we told the kids it was "time for New Year's" and had a celebration with them, drinking "champagne" from wine glasses and "cheers-ing" in the New Year before putting them all to bed.

We then had a melancholy celebration of our own. We reminisced about the New Year's that we had spent with our husbands three years earlier, in this same house. I had made beef bourguignon and we had toasted with expensive champagne. Arron and Dean got drunk and silly, but I had been pregnant with Carter, and Liane was only four months old, so Kim and I went to bed long before midnight. Our mutual losses were palpable now as we sat in the kitchen drinking another bottle of the same expensive champagne. I was glad we were alone together.

The next day I looked forward to getting home. Selena sat beside me in the car continuing our circular conversation. "Why did Phil and Sheilagh not want me to be there when Margot arrived?"

I gripped the steering wheel tighter and tighter. I didn't have any explanations that she was willing to hear and accept. "People behave badly when they're grieving." I didn't know what to say because all of my answers meant second-guessing my father, a person who was difficult to second-guess. The kids started fighting in the backseat.

"*Enough!*" Selena yelled. In the silence that followed, I felt myself getting sadder and my neck began to seize. The anger and fatigue of the trip was catching up with us all. We finally arrived home and Selena and I unloaded the car while the kids ran around the house rediscovering their toys and their rooms. I got the kids to bed and poured a glass of wine for Selena and myself. We avoided talking by turning on the TV. There was nothing left to say.

12

WEDNESDAY'S CHILDREN

After Selena left, I spent the next few weeks barking orders at the kids. I emptied the dishwasher feeling resentful that I had to do it alone. I yelled at them when they fought with each other. I had screaming temper tantrums at Carter, frustrated at his two-year-old insolence, carrying his writhing body upstairs and throwing him down onto his bed, where he half giggled and half sobbed. I slammed doors. I tried to hide in my bedroom, crying, but Carter always found me, whimpering and gesturing for me to pick him up. I felt claustrophobic in my own house.

"I need to be alone now!" I would bark at him.

"Up! Up!"

"No. Go find something to do!"

He would cry harder until I finally picked him up, roughly. He had learned to whine and cry to get what he needed and I had gotten into the bad habit of giving in to him too often. I was too fragile to do otherwise.

Olivia was still having trouble with her first grade homework and I was becoming exasperated with her. "This stuff is easy. I know you can do it if you just try," I begged.

"I can't!" she wailed. "I'm so stupid! I hate school!" She was hiccuping her sobs. I wanted to run out the door and never come back.

I was still angry about Christmas and my parents' apparent disregard for how their behavior affected the kids and me. I was convinced I wouldn't be angry with Carter and Olivia if Christmas had gone a little more smoothly. I was now contending with anger that I didn't know how to control or explain. I was taking my frustrations out on the kids. Again. I felt I was the worst mother in the world, screaming at my kids, who had just lost their father. How could I be so cruel?

In mid-January, one of the other Montclair widows told me about Comfort Zone Camp, a day-long bereavement camp for kids. This program had been in existence in Virginia for several years, the brainchild of a woman who had lost both parents at an early age, and after 9/11, volunteers from the camp began making pilgrimages to New York and New Jersey to hold one-day sessions for 9/11 kids. They were holding one only a block from our house, so I decided to take Olivia and Carter, thinking it might be good for them to meet other kids who had lost parents on September 11.

When we arrived, we were directed to the school's gymnasium, where a number of tables were set up with crafts. Adults, teens, and kids were playing a ball game in one corner, and we were greeted with huge hellos and smiles. Olivia hung by my side, shy at having so much attention directed at her. We made her a name tag. Carter was in his usual spot, aloof in my arms, drinking a bottle, holding his ear.

One of the volunteers came up to us. "Hello. Welcome. We're just doing some crafts. Olivia, would you like to decorate a box? You'll be able to use it to hold special things that belonged to your dad." I could tell Olivia was dazzled by the copious quantities of art supplies on the table. She tugged on my coat, pulling me to the table. We all sat down and both Olivia and Carter dove into the markers and glue and glitter and stickers. I smiled at some of the other mothers, who looked as awkward as I felt. After a half hour or so, an announcement was made that the parents were to meet in the library. Olivia had found a friend and was now content for me to leave, happily gluing and glittering and eating cookies.

I took Carter to the nursery and stayed with him for a few minutes, but the woman running the day care was experienced and she signaled for me to leave. Before he could cling to me and cry, she grabbed him and immediately began distracting him with cookies and toys. I could hear his wails as I followed other mothers toward the library.

Around thirty of us settled into our seats. All women. All 9/11 widows. This time they weren't just from Montclair. They were from all over the tristate area, New York, New Jersey, Connecticut. A panel of four volunteers sat at the front of the room, smiling at us as we sat down. Soon, the members of the panel began to tell their stories. A couple described losing their daughter in a car accident and how it had affected their other children. They talked about how helpful Comfort Zone had been in getting their kids to open up. Another woman had lost her husband four years earlier when he dropped dead of a heart attack during a jog in the park. I was fascinated by her—a widow, four years on, managing her life, albeit not always perfectly. She described how her three daughters still slept in her bed. I groaned inwardly. I struggled to keep Carter and Olivia in their own beds at night. She had given up and told us that her fourteen-year-old daughter was the worst culprit. I was shocked that bedtime visitations could continue into the teen years. This woman still seemed so sad after four years and I wondered if I would be, too. Still, she had not shriveled up the way I expected to at any moment.

After the panel, several 9/11 women stood up and told their stories, each giving the details of where her husband had been in the building, when and if her husband had called, and how she was managing their family alone. Boxes of tissues were passed around the room and I had to wipe away tears several times. We were all still so raw. Hearing others' stories brought our own grief to the forefront.

After lunch, we broke into smaller groups for more thorough discussions.

"I seem to be constantly angry with my kids," I said timidly at one point.

"Me, too!" resounded around the room. Heads nodded in agreement.

Our mediator, the mother of the car accident victim, commiserated. "That is very common. It's okay to be angry. And normal. You'll need to find ways to talk with your kids about it and also to find ways of getting your anger out. Exercise helps. Hitting pillows. Find an outlet and help your kids find an outlet, too."

Soon the afternoon was over and I felt exhausted, having spent the time swallowing back tears, worrying about Carter in the nursery, and trying to make friends with other widows who were as emotionally broken as I was. I hurried back to the nursery. Carter was playing quietly.

"He only cried for a while after you left," the caregiver said. Carter immediately clung to my neck.

We went into the other room, where Olivia was sitting with a group, a huge smile on her face. Cindy, Olivia's new big buddy, handed me a letter attached to a helium balloon: "Dear Daddy. I miss you. I hope you like heaven. Love Olivia."

The group gathered in the playground and let all the balloons go with a loud, vocal "whoosh," and then we moved back into the gymnasium to sing a tear-jerking rendition of "Lean on Me."

We walked home in a snowfall and I felt shaky and weak, as though my energy had bled out of me and I was running on fumes. We walked in the door and Olivia began to cry. "I miss Daddy!"

I wasn't ready. I didn't have the reserves. "I know, sweetie, I know." I could say nothing else. I tried to hug her as Carter clung to me stubbornly.

In time, her sobbing subsided and we had a quiet night and an easy bedtime. We were all tired. But the next day our anger was back. Olivia constantly yelled at Carter or burst into tears. Her complaints of stomach aches returned and getting her to school again became a challenge. One morning in particular, I was not sympathetic. "We have to go *now*!" I yelled, stomping my feet. Olivia cried while we were inside the house but swallowed her tears the moment we stepped outside. She refused to talk to me the entire way to the bus stop.

One day, shortly after Comfort Zone, Carter walked up to Olivia and, unprovoked, hit her on the head as she watched TV. Olivia cried great sobs at the injustice and I cringed at the noise. "You're okay," I said, impatiently. What I really wanted to say was "Get over it! Now. Stop crying."

But soon her sobs got louder and I realized that she was a child missing her father. I softened and held her close to me, hugging her. Carter walked over to us and pushed us apart, trying to crawl into my lap.

"I need to hug Olivia right now," I told him.

"No!" he yelled and pushed harder until Olivia fell off my lap. She looked at me for a moment, stunned, before bursting into ever-louder sobs. I picked up Olivia and tried to balance one child on each knee, but this did not appease Carter.

"Carter, I need to spend some time with Olivia right now. Why don't you sit here beside me?" My patience was ebbing. Carter wouldn't budge and grabbed my ear, his habitual soother.

"Carter, off. Now! This isn't fair to Olivia. Sometimes I need to be with her, too. I know you're jealous and I'll hug you in a minute." Now Olivia pushed Carter off my lap as her resolve against him strengthened with my reprimands.

"Nooooo!" Carter wailed, as loud as Olivia.

"I can't do this!" I yelled, getting up. Carter clung to me even more desperately, choking me, hanging from my neck like a thirty-pound necklace. I pulled his hands off me and walked into the kitchen, both kids sobbing behind me. Now I was crying, too, pulling at my own hair. Stuck. Lost. Not knowing what to do. Carter came into the kitchen and gestured for me to pick him up.

I was still crying, but I picked him up absently. In the living room, I heard the TV go on and Olivia's sobs subsided. Nothing was resolved.

Later that week, I lamented to Janet, "The kids and I just seem to be fighting all the time. I don't know what's going on!"

Even before I had finished the sentence, I realized exactly what was going on: postevent anger. In my more lucid moments I was able to see a pattern to my bouts of anger and frustration. Each memorial, each visit to Ground Zero or the Family Assistance Center, our anniversary, my birthday, Christmas, and now Comfort Zone Camp, all resulted in a fury. I braced myself to get through an event, and once it was over, I needed to discharge all that pent-up energy. The kids did the same. Exercise helped, but it wasn't enough. If I had had the insight, I would have installed a punching bag in the basement that we could all hit. Instead, I took my anger and frustrations out on Carter and Olivia, and they in turn took theirs out on each other, which then ricocheted back to me until we found ourselves in a dangerous spiral.

The simplicity of our being angry at Arron for not being with us at Christmas and our feeling post–Comfort Zone Camp upheaval seemed both obvious and ridiculous, but I was beginning to understand that grief was like a two-year-old child. Its behavior was often irrational. Grief demanded instant focus and it was persistent, not giving up until it got the attention it needed. Grief could erupt at the tiniest provocation and could leave a trail of debris a mile long. The good news was that once I had acknowledged my anger to Janet, it subsided and our house became a little more peaceful. But the peace was short-lived.

In the new year, Olivia was still having difficulty in school and it was still a struggle to get her to go. The school nurse and I had decided long ago to dispense with a phone call every time Olivia arrived in her office, as it happened so frequently. She explained that Olivia just seemed to be looking for assurance and some quiet time and once she had it, she would make her way back to class. I asked Olivia to try not to visit the nurse so often, unless it was a real emergency, and she agreed.

At home, her tantrums over homework continued and she refused to read. I bought her books of all sorts to try to pique her interest, and I read to her every night, but whenever I coaxed her to try reading on her own, she was tearful and resistant. My exasperation and the tension between us grew, and her refusals to go to school increased, though I persisted in sending her. Olivia was truly struggling with schoolwork and I started to wonder if perhaps she had some sort of learning disability. Whenever I managed to get her to read aloud, she had difficulty distinguishing letters and didn't see the small words such as "the," "of," and "an." She also had trouble following instructions. If I told her to get dressed, brush her teeth, and then grab her lunch, she would get panicky and teary and would complete only one of the tasks, or none at all. I learned to ask her to do only one thing at a time.

She was also having trouble sleeping. Her labored, noisy breathing at night worried me. At times, I was convinced that she had stopped breathing altogether. I learned from my friend Cornelia about her child's bout with sleep apnea. Her daughter had had her tonsils and adenoids removed the previous summer with wonderful results. She gave me the name of her doctor in Manhattan, who said Olivia had overly large tonsils and adenoids, which were beginning to make breathing difficult, especially at night, and her ears were compacted with wax, which was likely causing some hearing loss. He suggested that these issues were likely contributing to her troubles at school and recommended the same operation for Olivia. I was glad there was action we could take to help her and decided she should undergo the surgery, but I also worried that it would add to her woes.

Between grieving, her problems at school, and sleep trouble, Olivia was struggling hard. I felt guilty, convinced that I had let her down. Carter demanded most of my attention. Olivia was stoic and seemed not to need me. I allowed her to be independent, relieved that she didn't demand more of my time and energy. In fact, Olivia probably needed me more than she ever had.

At the end of January I went for a parent-teacher interview, to make up for one I had missed in the fall. I was curious to see if the teacher, too, noticed what I perceived as some real learning difficulties. She began to explain that Olivia was having trouble in class, mostly because she was missing a lot by going to the nurse so often. I was surprised. "I thought she wasn't going as often. Is she asking to go?"

"Sometimes. Olivia just needs a lot of attention. There are a lot of other kids who also demand my attention, so I tell her she can go to the nurse." I asked her if Olivia had been complaining of any illness, and the teacher started tapping her nose with her finger and said that Olivia sometimes complained that her nose hurt. What did that mean? A runny nose or cold I could understand, but how could her nose "hurt"? Clearly, Olivia was asking for some quick reassurance and comfort. What she got instead was a brisk brush-off to see the nurse. My child was missing school because this sad woman couldn't take a few minutes to give Olivia a kind word and a hug. I was appalled.

Awkwardly sitting on a tiny chair, my knees pressing against the table, I wanted to wail out loud. I wished Arron were beside me, giving this woman a piece of his mind. He would have questioned her further, made his anger obvious, stated it plainly. He would have fiercely defended Olivia, as I should be doing. But instead I could do nothing but fight back tears, knowing the teacher would assume that they were about my grief. They were, but I was also frustrated and angry that I couldn't stand up for Olivia against this teacher. The loss of her father meant the loss of her best advocate, her strongest supporter, her fiercest ally. I felt like I didn't have the strength to be any of these things for my daughter.

It was clear how hard Olivia was working to keep up with the other children, to be the same, when she was not. Olivia could not discuss her grief, and when she had difficult moments, she was dismissed. The school, despite having two students who had lost a father on 9/11, made it their policy not to discuss 9/11 with any of the children. Olivia was left to flounder in a vacuum where her feelings and the other children's feelings about that day, their fears or their sadness, were quietly swept under the carpet. When I had questioned the principal on this policy, back in September, she had told me that the children were too young to really understand what happened, especially given that the school taught only kindergarten and grades one and two.

"I strongly disagree," I told her. "These kids know that something is going on, and I think it's your responsibility to offer them an outlet for their fears. We're being sent quilts and cards made by kids from schools all over the country. Don't you think the fact that Olivia's own school isn't doing those things is confusing for her? Don't you think it would be cathartic for the kids to be doing something to help?"

"Well, actually, we have had a few parents call and ask specifically that we not discuss the issue in school."

"For that, I am truly sorry and I think that you are doing all the students a huge disservice," was all I could say. I was furious.

I thought of that conversation now, and finally, my anger began to take hold. I visualized Arron beside me, egging me on. "I think you need to stop sending her to the office so often. She just needs a little reassurance, a hug, a pat. That's all she's looking for."

"Fine. I can do that," the teacher said meekly.

Next I suggested that Olivia was struggling due to a learning problem. She looked at me quizzically. I gave her some of the examples I had seen of Olivia's difficulties, the mix-ups with b's and d's, 6's and 9's.

"I've noticed that, too, but I really just felt that she was having trouble from missing too much school," she said.

"You don't think those things are signs of a learning disability?" I wanted to shake this woman. Was she completely daft? Why was it up to me to tell her that Olivia might be having difficulties when it was clear that she had noticed problems as well? I began to see that I was going to have to fight hard to ensure that Olivia wasn't simply labeled a "grieving child" as a way of explaining away other serious issues.

Back in my car, the tears flowed freely. Arron, tonsils, now a potential learning disability. I wanted to call Arron, to hear his calm, rational voice saying, "It's okay, Bird. We'll figure it out. Olivia will be fine."

When I got home, I wrote a letter to the school's principal requesting that Olivia be evaluated, barely managing to refrain from writing about how I felt about her ridiculous closed-mouth 9/11 policy. From there, a whole formalized system kicked in.

The following week, I needed to tell Olivia that she was going to be pulled out of her class to take some tests. I did not want her panicking or stressing about it.

"So, Liv, you might find that you get taken out of class every now and then to play some games with a special teacher."

"Why?"

"Well, you know how you're kind of having a tough time reading and stuff? Well, they're going to try and figure out why."

"Is it because I'm stupid?" Olivia looked at me with sad eyes.

"No, sweetie, of course not. Everybody just learns in different ways, and we need to figure out how you learn so that your teachers can teach you better." I could tell she was thinking about this.

"Why don't any of the other kids need to play games like me?" Olivia always had a way of asking the tough questions. "It's because I'm stupid, right?"

"No. It's not, Liv. It's because you're really smart. Probably way smarter than a lot of other kids in your class. But something is making it harder for you to learn and we have to figure out why, okay?"

"Okay," she said, morosely.

"Come on. It'll be fun!" I tried to sound as upbeat as I could, but I knew I wasn't fooling her.

Over the next several weeks, I would hear snippets from Olivia about the testing. "I had to do one of those stupid tests today again."

"How did it go?" Again I tried to sound light.

"Fine. I guess."

In February, Olivia's school had a weeklong break, and I decided that the warmth and sunshine of a Club Med vacation was going to be the perfect antidote to our recent troubles. The tropical heat would also bake away the pain of my first Valentine's Day alone with two kids since Arron's death. I had visions of lounging by the pool while Olivia swung high above the beach strapped into a trapeze and Carter paddled about with other toddlers under the supervision of a fun boy-counselor named Marco. I figured that Valentine's Day in a foreign country would be a nonevent, and a nonevent would protect me from the painful memories I was sure to encounter if I lingered here, pining away under New Jersey's winter-gray skies.

The reality was that I spent the first night of our getaway in a muggy Dominican Republic hotel room, administering Tylenol to my feverish daughter. The next day I left Carter in the "Baby Club" while I took Olivia to see the kindly doctor at the infirmary, where he promptly diagnosed strep throat and began administering amoxicillin. I felt terrible for Olivia, who looked so pale and sad. Two hours later, we picked up Carter from the Baby Club, where we found him sobbing inconsolably, neglected by the gossiping teenagers who were supposed to keep him entertained. From that moment on, he would not let me out of his sight. I negotiated the buffet-style cafeteria during every meal with a two-year-old clamped to my hip, making multiple trips. A bowl of pasta, a hot dog, a glass of milk. By the time I sat down my food was cold.

We spent our mornings by the pool and napped in our room

in the afternoon. Olivia would occasionally feel strong enough to enter the kids' club and swing on the trapeze or do crafts. During the flight from New York, we had met a group of three families from Manhattan who were traveling together. After hearing my story, they adopted the kids and me. The dads swung Carter into the pool. Olivia was invited to her new friend's room for a sleepover. I had adults to talk to. Despite their company, I felt lonely. Watching the dads play in the pool with their children was excruciating. Watching couples apply sunscreen to each other's backs was poignant after having Carter apply mine and later painfully removing my bathing suit to discover his tiny white handprints on my otherwise pink back.

I managed to forget about Valentine's Day until the morning we showed up for breakfast and saw red construction-paper hearts taped to the door. I squeezed my eyes shut tight, wishing Valentine's Day would disappear. Inside the restaurant, I touched the single red roses on each table. After breakfast we made a break for the pool. No hearts. No roses. Blue. Sun. Coconut. But the empty chaise beside me made a gaping hole, like a missing tooth. At naptime, in our turquoise room, bordered with seashell-and-starfish wallpaper, I watched TV while the children slept. There were successful dating stories on *Oprah*, couples in love on every channel. I lay on the bed, hot and sticky, listening to Carter's and Olivia's deep breathing, flipping through the channels aimlessly. I couldn't avoid the repeated images. Tears began falling from my chin, and I turned the TV off.

For Valentines' Day last year, I had hastily purchased a card depicting Romeo and Juliet for Arron and added my handwritten promise to love him until the end of time—and to provide a half-hour backrub, with "no complaining guaranteed." I had given each of the kids a small toy. I had prepared a nice dinner, which we had eaten from stools at the kitchen island, after the kids were in bed. We sipped our wine, smiling at each other over the rims of our glasses.

Remembering, I sobbed into my hotel pillow, trying not to awaken Carter and Olivia. How could I have been so stupid, so naive to think that this escape would be a solace? The days continued despite me, and this one was no exception. After the kids woke up, I took them back to the pool but found myself at the pool bar downing piña coladas at a two-for-one Happy Hour.

That night, there was to be a special Valentine's dinner at the cafeteria, and I had arranged to meet our New York friends. Reluctantly, I changed into the one dress I had brought. In front of the restaurant, two staff members dressed in red handed out single red roses. I gritted my teeth as I received mine, then did my usual balancing act with the tray and Carter and managed to get my veal scaloppini to the table without it hitting the floor first. I chatted with my new friends and marveled at how sweetly they were caring for me.

Like the rest of my life, my expectations of Valentine's Day were going to have to be redefined. I would never again experience the love that Arron and I shared together. But as I looked at my children and at my new friends, I realized that I was feeling less sad.

Later, after dinner, there was a singalong. Reluctantly, I waved my hands in the air and sang along to the Club Med theme song: "Hands up, baby, hands up. Gimme your heart, gimme, gimme your heart, give it, give it." Afterward, I clamped Carter back onto my hip and held Olivia's hand as we walked back to our room singing, "Hands up, baby, hands up, gimme your heart. . . ."

The following day Olivia successfully navigated the trapeze for the first time and came running over to me after her day at the kids' camp. "I swung on the trapeze all by myself!" she declared, plunking herself down on my chaise. Later she dragged Balloo, a male counselor from Quebec, to meet Carter and me.

"Olivia did great on the trapeze today," Balloo said, grinning. "And who is this?" he asked, tickling Carter, and was soon piggybacking him around the pool. Somehow the vacation was saved.

On the day we left, the kids ran up to Balloo and jumped on him as their farewell. I mouthed "Thank you" to him as he trotted around with Carter giggling on his back. He winked back at me.

It was a relief to be home, but now we had to brace for Olivia's surgery, only two weeks away. A week before the surgery, I called Encompys to clarify the status of our medical insurance, because it was still in Arron's name and I worried that I might run into problems at the hospital as a result. Kathleen told me that my medical insurance had been canceled on September 30, 2001. "I sent you a letter telling you how to sign up for Cobra," she said.

"I thought that was just a formality. I didn't think I needed to sign up for Cobra because Encompys was going to cover me for three years. Isn't that what you said?"

"No, Cobra was going to cover you for eighteen months. But we were never going to cover you for three years."

"So you're saying that I haven't had medical coverage for the past six months? I've been to the doctor in that time and I've never gotten a bill. . . ."

"I'll have to look into what happened there. But my understanding is that Encompys canceled your medical insurance on September 30, 2001. I'm really sorry, Abby."

I was shocked. Why was I only finding out about this now? Kathleen had told me verbally that I was going to be covered for three years, failing to mention it was through Cobra, coverage that kicked in for anyone who worked for a company for at least eighteen months and then became unemployed. But I would have to pay the high premiums myself. That was a large part of the equation to have left out of the conversation.

This was the second insult that Kathleen had bestowed upon me. Only a month earlier she had informed me that the free half-page obituary that had appeared in the front section of the *New York Times* in September would in fact cost me $6,000.

"But you told us it would be free."

"Abby, I told Selena when she asked me to place it that I *might* be able to get it free."

"Well, we would never have placed it had we known its cost. Why didn't you tell us it would cost $6,000?"

"I only just got the bill. But I've signed you up for the Robin Hood Fund. You will be getting $5,000 from them and that will almost cover it," she said. I thought she had done something special to cover the cost. Only later did I find out that all 9/11 family members were eligible for this amount from the Robin Hood Fund, a New York–based charity. Soon, the *New York Times* was calling me to collect their money. Kathleen had given them my number. It didn't occur to me to tell them that Arron's company had booked the ad and was therefore responsible.

I spoke with Jim, Arron's boss, and I was unable to hide my anger. Due to a fortunate glitch, the insurance company had not received the cancellation order, so Encompys had inadvertently been paying my insurance. Jim agreed to continue paying until April 1, which was the soonest I could get onto Audible's health insurance and at least ensured that Olivia's surgery would be covered. Jim later told me that when he confronted Kathleen about the obituary and the insurance issues, she had a temper tantrum and quit her job, on the spot.

I was rattled. My working suddenly took on a whole new importance.

On the day of Olivia's surgery, Diane, my neighbor, came with us to help. We got to the hospital early but waited in a prep area for three hours before it was Olivia's turn for surgery. She wore a sweet child's hospital gown covered in bunnies and a pair of fluffy pink slipper-socks that embarrassed her. She suddenly seemed so small sitting in an oversized blue vinyl chair. When Olivia's name was called, she bravely walked into the operating room and was lifted onto the table. I stayed as a mask was placed over her mouth and nose and she counted up to three until the anesthesia took hold. I glanced behind me as I left the room, her tiny figure lying there, arms out to the sides as if on a cross, and wiped away my tears.

Afterward, when Olivia was wheeled into a recovery room, she looked pale and skinny under a thin sheet. I held her hand until she was able to groggily prop herself up. We eventually got her to a room where she could sit and watch TV. She seemed surprisingly comfortable and even ate some ice cream.

A few hours after we got home, the anesthesia began to wear off. The doctor had recommended that she eat and drink as often as possible to heal her throat more quickly, but Olivia refused because it was painful. I became frustrated by her lack of cooperation and increasingly angry as the days turned into a week.

"You have to eat, sweetie. That's the only way your throat will heal. The doctor said that if you don't eat anything, it'll take much longer." She just shook her head.

Spring break ended, but Olivia was in no shape to return to school. The teacher sent her homework, but she refused to do it.

"I am losing it," I complained to the doctor, who had been calling regularly to check in. "This is taking so much longer than you said it would."

"You really need to get her to eat. It's the best thing for her." His voice was calm.

"But she refuses! She cries all the time and takes these long showers. They seem to be the only thing that helps."

"She won't even eat ice cream? Or gum?"

"No, nothing."

"Well, some kids do this and it just takes them a little longer to recover. Try to be patient."

"I'm afraid my patience ran out a week ago," I said, my voice wavering as I held back another bout of tears.

I had taken as many days off work as I could. Luckily Martha was there to help. She seemed to be infinitely more patient than I was. I didn't have the strength for the battles of will.

"Mama, can I have another shower?" Olivia whispered to me one evening from her nest on the couch.

"No, sweetie, you've already had four long showers today. It's a waste of water. How about you eat something instead. I'll make you a smoothie."

"No! I want a shower!" She immediately burst into tears.

"Well, the doctor says you need to eat. *That* is the only thing that is going to make you feel better!" My voice was getting louder.

Olivia shook her head no and pursed her lips at me. "It hurts!" she croaked.

"Well, you have to try. The more you try, the easier it will get! I am so sick of this! You need to eat to get better. All you do is mope around all day, watch TV, and take a million showers. I've had it! I am going to make you a smoothie and you are going to drink it!" I had hit my breaking point.

"No!" Olivia jumped up and ran to her room, crying. I was left feeling guilty, thinking about how difficult it must be, grieving and in pain the way she obviously was. I crept upstairs and knocked lightly on her door. I could hear her hiccuping.

"Can I come in?" The sobs continued, so I opened the door and sat on her bed, gathering her into my arms. I let her cry.

"I'm sorry. I'm just really frustrated that it's taking you so long to get better and you seem to be refusing to do the one thing that is going to help you, which is to eat."

"But it *hurts*!"

"I know, sweetie. But sometimes something has to hurt before it can get better." I meant her tonsils, but I could also have been talking about our grief.

13

EBB AND FLOW

One evening in early March, as I chopped onions for spaghetti sauce, I got the phone call from Jill that I had been waiting for. "It's a girl!" Her voice sounded shrill in my ears.

"A girl? No, no. I thought you were having a boy. You were going to name him Arron."

"Well, it's a girl. I guess I was wrong."

The happy news was tinged with sadness, not because it was a girl, but because the birth signified a new beginning in a world of endings and finality. I was surprised not to feel more moved. I couldn't remember if Arron knew of the pregnancy before his death, but I wanted to share this joy with him. There was a new member of his cherished family. I imagined the child containing a small part of him, or knowing him from another world.

I longed to be with Jill and Dan and their new baby, so that perhaps in proximity I could feel their joy. But I was far away and the event didn't seem real. Carter and Olivia received the news with glee. "What's her name? What color is her hair?"

My mother came on the phone, now a grandma for the third time. I heard a familiar blankness in her voice: joy tinged with sadness, and it was frightening to hear the dullness in her words. When the phone was handed back to my sister, I listened more intently. Surely a new mother's joy superseded all. But no, there it was again. Jill's voice lacked the excitement I had expected. I told myself that it was because of fatigue, relief, fear, the raw emotions of all new mothers. Was it because I wanted others' emotions to mimic my own? Was I glad for that sadness just a little? Or not? Surely they had to feel some sadness at this moment, for the magnitude of my own loss required it, demanded it. But was the depth of loss the same for other members of my family? I was not sure. But sadness felt right to me.

Then Jill said, "and her name is Caelin Hannah Nash." Somehow hearing her name made her more real to me, and something in me shifted.

"That's a beautiful name, Jill. I can't wait to see her," I said, genuinely happy.

Two days later, I was watching PBS, drinking a glass of wine, when the camera angle suddenly swung wildly to film the sky, just in time to capture the first plane hitting Tower 1 of the World Trade Center, Arron's building. It felt like I had been punched. I watched the sixty-second montage, filmed with a handheld camera, of firemen racing into the lobby of the building, the cameraman running from the collapsing tower and his jumpy images of white nothingness, and then the hazy pictures of the demolished towers. I could barely breathe. I immediately flashed back to that morning when I watched the towers collapse on TV, Carter on my hip, touching the screen. Thus began the flurry of television programs marking the six-month anniversary of 9/11.

This clip was the work of two French filmmakers who had been shooting a documentary about rookie firefighters that fateful morning. I watched it again a half hour later, mesmerized by the almost sickening swing of the camera from ground level to a shaky view of the sky as the plane flew overhead and careened into the building. These shots were the only moments caught on tape of the first plane hitting Tower 1. I closed my eyes, but the image was burned onto my retinas. Arron had told me it was a

THE ALCHEMY OF LOSS

bomb, so now I could see that he must have been on the opposite side of the building, facing Tower 2, when the plane hit. An uptown view would have guaranteed he would have seen the plane as I saw it now.

I couldn't understand why a six-month anniversary was necessary. Maybe TV ratings had been low or the feeding frenzy of 9/11 media had worn off to such an extent that the media needed something more to commemorate. Perhaps people were still thirsty for more understanding of what happened that day. I had not expected a barrage of television and newspaper articles and movies and commentary until the one-year anniversary. I had not had time to brace myself, to turn off the TV, the radio, to avoid the newspaper articles that were littered with "9/11's" and "September 11's".

Watching the preview, unable to turn it off, I felt shaky and delicate, as though I had just recovered from a fever. I was only beginning to emerge from the murky numbness of my grief. I began to breathe shallowly and wished I still had the recently finished vial of anti-anxiety pills.

"It's disgusting!" was Selena's take on the coverage. "I'm not turning on my TV until it's over!"

But I found myself drawn to the documentary. I wanted to know more, see more, have a clearer sense of what happened that day. I couldn't decide whether or not to watch it.

"Don't do it. It'll be agonizing," Selena said. "There's no way I'm going to." I wondered if that was really true. She was a news junkie, and I suspected she would want to watch for the same reasons I wanted to. To know. To make sense of what had happened. I wanted to know why the buildings had failed so catastrophically, I wanted to see the reality of what had happened, if it had been as bad as what I conjured in my imagination. Arron's last moments continued to haunt me. Why had the buildings fallen? Why wasn't Arron able to get out? What did he experience in that hour and a half? Did he consider jumping? Did he jump? Did he cry? Did it hurt? At what moment did he know he was going to die?

So I watched.

Again I saw the first plane lurch into Arron's tower. I watched as the fire chiefs set up a command center in the lobby of Tower 1, as firefighters raced up escalators. The pictures were hazy with smoke. Robert De Niro's voiceover explained that the periodic banging noises in the background were the impact of bodies crashing through the glass overhangs that protected the street-level entrances to the buildings. Suddenly there was a large rumble and the screen became white. The cameramen were running through the whiteness, unable to see anything other than the ghostly images of people they passed. Tower 2 collapsed and the cameraman could be heard over the sounds of sirens and screaming and moaning, wondering aloud if he had just died.

I watched in fascinated horror, appalled at the lack of foresight on the part of the firefighters who had set up a command station in the lobby of a burning building. I was disappointed that they had not thought to have someone watch the TV coverage, convinced that if they had been in communication with someone who had witnessed Tower 2 being hit by the plane, they would have understood how unstable the impact had made the building. They could have attributed a similar instability to Tower 1. They would have moved their command center. They would have done more to save people had they known there was even a remote possibility of the buildings falling. When I had watched the building being hit that September morning, I was certain, given how dramatically the plane had sliced through three of the four walls of Tower 2, that the top of the building was about to teeter off and fall into the street below. Later in the day my father, an architect, had explained how the building was engineered.

"Don't forget, the building was built to withstand a 737 hitting it," he had said. "It was made with all its supporting structure on the outside, so that if a plane did hit it, it would implode and not wipe out entire city blocks."

It made sense. But the firefighters seemed unaware of this

engineering failsafe. It became clear from the film that the fire-fighters were unable to properly communicate with one another. Everyone seemed to be talking into radios and then becoming frustrated by the lack of response. Firefighters ran around with no apparent coordination. The scenes were devastating. There had been no hope of Arron's rescue. There had been nothing but chaos and confusion. This film proved to me the hubris of the great New York City Fire Department. Of course it didn't matter. Arron was still dead, but I wanted to believe that he at least had had hope in his last moments. Watching the film, I felt sad that the firefighters had been let down by faulty equipment and by their hubris, thinking that nothing this terrible could ever happen in the United States. Everyone in the building had been let down. They were lulled into a sense of false security by the building's apparent infallibility. On some level every system to prevent such a catastrophic attack had failed: the airlines, the American government, the military, the building, George Bush. Watching the film, I grew angry at the firefighters for not saving Arron and all those innocent people. I was angry that engineers would plan a building that was designed to implode. I was angry that the door to the roof had been locked, so that there had been no hope of escape. I was angry that helicopters couldn't land even if people could have gotten onto the roof, because of the great billows of black toxic smoke. I was angry with the American military, which took too long to respond to the reports of hijacked airplanes, though I knew that wouldn't have saved Arron.

Oddly, I was still unable to get angry with the people who had actually committed the crime. Osama bin Laden. The Taliban. The Saudis. Who was to blame anyway? They seemed faceless and anonymous. They were either dead or very far away. They committed this crime for reasons I could not fathom, and yet deep down perhaps I did understand. The tallest buildings in the world marked the epicenter of American wealth, democracy, freedom, and global power: a perfect target.

That night I was unable to sleep. Selena had been right. I shouldn't have watched the documentary. I had learned more details about Arron's last minutes, and the horror he had suffered seemed more real. Now I couldn't get those images out of my head. I cried for him all over again, imagining his fear and regret. In the film, I saw the shiny lobby of the World Trade Center and the bank of elevators he would have used that morning. I saw hundreds of lucky people riding escalators down into the lobby and then walking outside, escorted by the firemen, and searched their faces for Arron's. I heard the bodies crashing through the glass and tried not to imagine the desperation that would make someone jump from such unbelievable heights. I saw Arron's nightmare up close and now it was mine.

I spent the following few weeks reliving the early days of my grief. I could feel the familiar numbness creep into my body, and I operated on autopilot, unable to express my emotions. I had not foreseen the damaging effects that the documentary would have on me. I was haunted by Arron's last moments at the top of the tower and began to have vivid dreams about him, where I could never see his face.

One afternoon, about a month after watching the film, I found myself staring out my office window. To the right I noticed with surprise that a tree bloomed with tiny, newly formed, jade-green buds. Under it, a small patch of bright green-yellow grass grew between cracks in the pavement. When had spring arrived? How had I not noticed? Then I was confused: *was* it spring, or still fall? The day was so similar to that September day—beautiful, sunny, warm. I could suddenly see colors, and they were blinding after my long uninterrupted days of gray. Somehow I had missed the passing of winter. The days had simply blended together, mimicking the grayness of my moods.

I woke up suddenly as if from a dream, disoriented, feeling as though I had lost months of my life. It was one of the strangest, saddest moments I could ever remember experiencing. I continued gazing out of the window, now with tears in my eyes, my loss like a cold wind blowing through my hollowed-out chest. Pain flooded a place in me where numbness had once been. I was breathing again for the first time, the burn excruciating as fresh, clean air flooded my body.

Perhaps I should have dashed outside to feel the spring-scented wind in my hair or smell the bright gold grass, but this awakening wasn't like that. I was simply filled with sadness. Summer was coming and it would be fraught with memories. Summer was when family memories were made: vacations, barbecues, swimming, gardening. Warmth. Sunshine. Light. Color.

I realized I could no longer hide behind my numbness, allowing it to shield me from the painful memories of Arron. I had to stop denying my emotions and give way to feeling pain. I was scared that waking up out of my numbness would cause my memories of Arron to be more painful and leave me raw, or that my connection with him would seem more distant. But wakefulness felt better than numbness, which was like a walking death. I hoped that this awakening would mean that I would soon find joy in the freshly painted hues that now surrounded me. Despite my fears, I was beginning to have hope that grief might not be all sadness but could perhaps encompass the full spectrum of emotions, both good and bad.

[14]

FREEING THE BIRD

Something in me had shifted and I felt as though a film had been lifted from my eyes and I could see more clearly. Lying awake at night worrying, I felt driven to calm what felt like the chaos in my life. The kids still needed my close attention and I continued to worry about Arron, that his ghost was unsettled: concerned about the kids and me, or seeking revenge for his death. I also needed to get my finances in order once and for all. The Victims' Fund was finally up and running and the forms, still in their manila envelope in a corner of my office, waited to be completed. At the suggestion of Liz, another 9/11 widow, I soon found myself in the dark oak-paneled office of an investment company, peering into the fluorescent blue water of a huge tank of tropical fish. I had let my one year with Jennifer, the financial advisor provided by the insurance company, elapse. Now, I finally felt strong enough to face the process of managing our financial assets and had sought help.

I turned at the call of my name to find a fit woman in a crisp green business suit barreling toward me. She flashed me a dazzling white smile and I held out my hand for her brisk handshake.

"Hi, I'm Debra! So pleased to meet you at last!"

Sitting in the black leather boardroom chairs, I felt secure that I had found a reputable company and yet out of place knowing the company handled the investments of only very well-heeled clients.

"I want to go over what you gave me and explain a few things." I had given Debra the cash flow report that Jennifer had prepared for me six months earlier. Not much had changed financially, other than the growing trust fund. Like Jennifer, Debra provided me with several scenarios for investing my money, all with varying returns. She made ratio recommendations for how I should invest in the various asset classes. My mind was swirling with percentages and returns on investment, details of small cap funds and stock indexes. She explained the company's fees, which were substantial.

"What I really want to know," I asked Debra at the end of our meeting, "is do I have enough?"

"Well, I would love to give you a nice, easy, straightforward answer, but it depends on how you invest that money. I think it would be wise for you to spread your principal across a variety of investments, so that you can earn the greatest amount of income from it. I think you could invest the children's trust fund, so that it also extends its earnings. But basically, I think you will be fine."

I left Debra's office feeling in control of our financial picture for the first time. I could finally exhale as some of my financial worry fell away. "You will be fine," rang over and over in my head. But my fear was replaced with another. What if I did invest Arron's insurance money with this woman, this company? Wouldn't that be putting all my eggs into one basket? I Googled the company name and Debra. I went to the Better Business Bureau website. I found glowing articles in magazines such as *Money* and *SmartMoney* and found that many of the firm's financial advisors appeared regularly on CNN and other channels' financial reports. I was satisfied by their apparent legitimacy. But handing over a huge chunk of money to an unknown company was still daunting. I was alone in my decision. I turned to what I was beginning to rely on more and more: my gut. Intuitively, I felt that Debra was a good person, who wanted more than anything to help me. I connected with her and understood even the more complex financial concepts that she explained to me in her clear, concise manner.

On Monday, I called Debra and told her I was ready to invest with her and her company. It felt good to make my first solo major financial decision. I hoped it would be a profitable one, something Arron would approve of.

At the prompting of my "pro bono" lawyer, Lenore, sister of Rob, my boss at Audible, I began filling out what were supposed to be "simple" forms for applying to the September 11th Victim Compensation Fund. There were twenty-four pages of forms, along with a forty-five-page *Helping Handbook*, and a densely worded, seventeen-page *Rules and Regulations* booklet. There was also a claim assistance website and a hotline.

I was one of the lucky ones. I had Lenore to help me. Pro bono lawyers, who were supposed to be available for every 9/11 family, were in fact scarce, and many families were required to pay their lawyers substantial fees.

Other 9/11 family members protested to the administrator, Kenneth Feinberg, about the unfairness of the fund. They were unhappy that insurance payouts, Social Security, workers' compensation, and pensions would all be subtracted from the final awards. They and their hired experts considered the "non-economic loss" payout of $250,000, the amount per victim awarded to families for pain and suffering, too low. If they had been allowed to sue, the families argued, this amount would have automatically been much higher. Complex tables allowed family members to calculate approximately how much they would receive, based on the victim's age, salary, and the number of descendants. According to the tables, I would receive a reasonably high payout, because Arron made almost the highest level that the tables accommodated for. If he had earned more than the cap on the tables, the payout would have been less than his salary, as happened with many of the million-dollar earners.

I sat at the kitchen table one evening after the kids were in bed and carefully filled out the many pages of the form in black ink, printing Arron's Social Security number into the box provided at the top of each page. I set about finding tax returns going back to 1998, making copies of Arron's death certificate, pay stubs, 401(k) statements, insurance payouts, Social Security awards, pensions. I created Excel worksheets showing "latent losses," fees I had to pay now that Arron was not around to do certain tasks: lawn mowing, financial investing, sports lessons, home renovation. I had to choose between two ways of filing my application. With Track A, the reward would be predetermined based on the application, and then, if the amount was considered by the recipient to be inadequate, a hearing could be requested afterward. Track B meant going directly to a hearing, and the award would be determined there. Lenore advised me to opt for Track B.

I left the signature section of the form until last: Part III, Acknowledgment of Waiver of Rights. My pen hovered over the page. I was not a person who would ever consider a lawsuit. I was a Canadian, after all. But my six years in the United States taught me that in America, lawsuits ensured accountability and sometimes changed policies or procedures. Flaws in airport security procedures had allowed fifteen terrorists to board planes with box cutters. The door to the roof of the World Trade Center was locked. The stairs were blocked by drywall and were impassable. The buildings collapsed despite being built to withstand a plane crashing into them. By signing the waiver, I might be preventing advances in building design that would protect against future catastrophic failures. I might be allowing the airlines to continue operating with slapdash security and motives centered on profit rather than their customers' safety. But if I refused to sign, my only other option would be to sue, an uncertain, time-consuming, and costly venture. My own and my children's financial security was at stake. I took a deep breath and signed. I felt as though I were signing in blood.

With money from the fund, I could quit my job and take care of Olivia and Carter full time. I wouldn't have to worry about my expenses: the kids' educations, health insurance, mortgages, food.

A big part of me, however, was frightened of receiving such a large sum of money. I feared that I would lack the integrity to spend it wisely, like lottery winners who spend their windfalls frivolously and wind up more destitute than they had been before. I feared the money would cause ill feelings among my family or with my kids when they grew older. My future responsibilities settled on me like a lead blanket.

One sunny May Saturday I saw two of my neighbors, Diane and Jennifer, walking by my house. They had come to ask me if I wanted to go to see a local psychic named Concetta perform. I was intrigued. I was in a mode of settling Arron's estate and our family, so he could rest and not worry about the kids or me. The Toronto psychic's words "she is very lost, cold" still burned in my mind. I still feared that he, too, was lost, like the bird in the fireplace. I had worked to get our finances in order and to apply to the Victims' Fund. I was making sure the kids were healthy and had someone to talk to about their grief, and I was planning what I hoped would be a happy summer for them. But I still didn't have a sense that I had calmed Arron's fears from beyond the grave, perhaps because I wasn't sure if he still saw me as "lost." Diane and Jennifer's invitation came at the perfect moment. Perhaps a psychic could help me to resolve these feelings of unrest, tell me that Arron was fine, that I was fine. I was willing to worship at the altar of the psychic if one could offer me peace of mind about the state of Arron's afterlife. But I worried that I was attaching too much importance to them, in a desperate attempt to hang on to my dead husband.

The Toronto psychic's unsolicited message, real or not, was a turning point for me, settling my tumultuous thoughts about where Arron might be. It gave me a faith in the afterlife, which in turn eased my fear of death. The message had been simple and yet it freed me from my own thoughts of Arron's last moments; it calmed me. It was only natural that I wanted to explore more, learn more about the afterlife in whatever way I could.

I wrote a check to Jennifer for the forty-dollar ticket and hoped that my desire for mutual communication wasn't overtaking my common sense.

A month later, the three of us carpooled to a New Jersey community center. As I walked through the door, my stomach fluttered. A woman at the door handed Diane, Jennifer, and me a preprinted raffle ticket, ripped from a giant wheel of them, explaining that they would be calling numbers printed on each ticket, five at a time, for five-minute readings from Concetta. I felt certain that my number would be called.

After a brief and heartfelt introduction from her childhood friend, Concetta appeared, practically skipping into the center of the room. She was tall, with perfectly coiffed blonde hair and a blue polyester pantsuit, brimming with giggly excitement like a kid.

"If you look around this room," she began, "you might think that there are only about sixty of us here, but I want you to know that your loved ones are here, too. They surround us. When I look around the room, I see thousands of people." Her New Jersey accent added to her charm.

The first five numbers were called and people jumped up, excited, like they had just been told to "come on down" on *The Price Is Right*. Each took a seat, beaming. Concetta wasted no time. She spouted names: "I'm getting a Martha, or Muriel." She almost always described how the person died. "Was it a stroke?" she would ask, as she clutched her head. "She is showing me something to do with her head. . . ." Often the information was extremely accurate. "She is showing me a baby—did she have a miscarriage?" "Yes!" the person would exclaim. "No one knows that!"

During breaks, while new numbers were called, Concetta, seemingly unable to stop herself, walked among the audience and continued to give mini readings. In one, she identified two men, similar but wearing different uniforms. "One is like a navy uniform and the other is more army." A man jumped up. "My father and uncle were twins!" he declared. "One was in the Army and the other in the Navy!" Finally, after almost three hours, Concetta announced that the next five numbers would be the last called for the day. I clutched my red ticket. When the final number was read, I was one number off. I looked up to see Diane spin around and hand me her ticket.

"This is yours," was all she said.

"Are you sure?" I stammered.

"Go."

I took the last seat and faced the audience. Concetta began at the other end of the row. I didn't hear any of the readings. My heart pounded in my chest. Finally it was my turn. Concetta was by now visibly exhausted. Her face was pale and she had lost her giggly demeanor. She dragged a hand through her hair. She pulled a stool over toward my chair and perched on it, the first time she had sat down in three hours. Concetta looked at me expectantly.

"My name is Abigail Carter and I would like to contact my husband."

"Who is 'A,'" she began.

"My husband's name was Arron."

"Okay. I see him. He is a very nice man. I see him surrounded by animals."

I smiled at this image. Every animal we ever saw, Arron was drawn to, claiming they looked like Harley.

"Who is Tom, Thomas, Tim?"

"That would be Tim. He was a friend of my husband's and he died shortly before my husband did," I said amazed.

"Okay. Good. Who is Nicole, Nicky?"

"I don't know."

"It's okay. It might come to you later. Now, honey. I don't want you to get offended by this, but he has a message he wants you to have. You are going to meet someone. And that's okay. You need to carry on with your life. He loves you and he really wants you to understand this."

Hearing this was nice in a way, but it also seemed a little

cliché. I was obviously young to be a widow and this was something I heard a lot. "I understand."

Concetta put her hand on her chest. "I feel there was a problem around his chest. He stopped breathing, couldn't get his breath. . . . ?

"I don't know."

Concetta continued to tap on her chest, her eyes closed, face pointed toward the ceiling. Suddenly she opened her eyes and looked at me. "Oh my God! Was this 9/11?"

The audience gasped.

"Yes," I whispered. Had she simply figured it out? I was young to be widowed and we lived in the 9/11 neighborhood. It made sense.

"Oh, honey. I am so sorry!" She began to cry. She took a small break and whispered to me how deeply the event had affected her. Then she turned to the audience and told them the same thing. She was about to continue with my reading when I blurted, "Oh! I thought of who Nicole is! She is the wife of the man that Arron was with on that day. I just thought of it now." I had spoken with Nicole only once and I knew very little about her.

"That is good," Concetta replied, unfazed by my outburst. "They went very quickly. I feel that they did not even realize what happened. I think everyone that day was chosen to have this fate. They knew they had this fate." How could she have known that I had been contemplating the issue of fate? "He is showing me a fish and some sort of table. A trout maybe?"

A year earlier, Arron built me what he called the "fish table" to congratulate me for a promotion at Audible.

"That's the fish table," I told her. "He built it for me last summer." Something about her was so genuine, heartfelt. I knew I was vulnerable, but nothing about her revelations seemed harmful. I was hungry for more and filled with questions. "How is he now?" I wanted to ask.

"Okay. He is around that table. He is nearby. He is giving you lots of signs that he is near. He is giving you signs that he is nearby and watching over you. He loves you very much."

Concetta told me what I had been longing to hear. Arron's spirit was intact, providing me with messages: he was nearby, still loved me, and assured me that I would find new love. I was relieved to learn that I was no longer "lost" or "cold," that he saw me as approachable again. Real or hoax, I didn't care. I walked out of the community center, still slightly shaky after my reading, and turned my head toward the sky to bask in the warm late-spring sunlight. I felt rejuvenated, ready for my next challenge.

15

ZOOMING

"Zooming" was what I started calling my escapes from grief. Escapes into the physical world, avoidance of the inner one. I accepted every invitation for dinners, parties, weekends away, barbecues, afternoons at the pool. I overplanned birthdays, anniversaries, and holidays, to the point of my own exhaustion. A hectic lifestyle shielded me from what was missing.

My summer always begins with Olivia's birthday, on June 2. *2002* Her seventh birthday would be the first without Arron. She wanted to celebrate at a local art school, where we had also held her fifth birthday party. I could still see Arron and Bruce leaning against the wall of the school, drinking beers in the dappled sunshine that streamed through the windows. I hoped we wouldn't be replacing a perfectly good memory with a sad one.

I called the owner of the school and made the arrangements. I ordered the ice-cream cake. I wrote the list of kids to invite and the items I would need for the party in the same green spiral notebook that held the telephone messages my family and friends had jotted down in the early days after September 11. I printed out invitations and mailed them. Every single person accepted. I suppose no one wanted to decline the party invitation of a 9/11 orphan, and as a result nineteen kids were showing up.

The day of the party my mother came to help, and I was glad. She greeted guests, worked with the kids (and was better than the art school staff), served the cake, handed out goody bags, and cleaned up. She joked with the kids while I walked around in a daze with a smile frozen to my face. Every kid découpaged a handmade cardboard box, cementing a clay frog or owl to the top (in keeping with the Harry Potter theme). I looked at Olivia, a pale seven-year-old who could barely smile when she blew out her candles, and Carter, a clingy two-year-old boy who cried and whined often, exhausting his already exhausted mother. The room seemed dark, despite the sunny day. I missed the proud smirk Arron used to give me at every birthday party, that look of "Can you believe this?"

The party ended with me writing a big check to the art school and feeling ripped off. But when I got back in the car, I saw Olivia in the rearview mirror, looking at me with her slopey eyes and grinning crookedly. It had been worth it. I had not seen even that half-smile in a long time.

School plays, end-of-year presents for the teachers, summer camps, summer tutoring, report cards, more birthday parties, backyard barbecues, street parties.

Zoom.

On the afternoon of July 4, after attending Montclair's annual Independence Day parade, I cranked up the air conditioning in the car and we sped along I-5 toward Scituate, Massachusetts, to visit our old friends Beth Ann and Donald and their two kids, Tess and Dean. Arron and I had spent idyllic days as first-time parents here, and I braced for an emotional trip down memory lane. Once we got there, I was surprised by how at ease I felt. I loved being back in Scituate despite Arron's absence. It felt safe. After whoops of greeting and the kids had dashed off to play, Beth Ann, her dark hair now cropped but her vivacious laugh unchanged, handed me a Fresca and began to tell me all the news of my old town. That afternoon, we took the kids to the beach, where the boys frolicked in the sand and caught hermit crabs, clutching them in their cupped palms, racing toward us as we drank more Frescas on the beach. The girls climbed the big rocks and settled onto their haunches as they compared seashells. We walked into town for ice cream and later drank glasses of red wine while we watched the kids play in the sprinkler in her backyard. Donald grilled steaks. We talked nonstop about Arron, about our common friends, about the kids. For a while I was the woman I had been when I lived here—a new, young mother, not a care in the world. I was glad I came. And I was surprised not to be riddled with sad memories of Arron. Scituate remained my happy place, perhaps because it was full of memories of being a mom for the first time, or because Arron and I had spent a simple existence there. I was also determined not to let sadness take hold, to stay busy, go to the beach, drink wine, talk nonstop.

Before our long drive back to New Jersey we briefly visited our old next-door neighbor, Sheila. The kids ran happily around her yard, Olivia not remembering her old house, which we could see from Sheila's driveway, since we had left just after her second birthday. The new owners had cleared more land and I was shocked to see how big the property really was. I laughed, thinking how Arron would have balked at the amount of lawn they now had to mow. As we stood there, the new owner came out and, recognizing me, invited us in. It was strange to be inside the house, especially without Arron. The walls were painted in tasteful shades of blue and green and our bright blue kitchen cabinets were now white, giving the place a clean, fresh feel, but otherwise the house was unchanged.

Happy memories washed over me—Olivia in her high chair in the kitchen covered in spaghetti, or taking running swings from her Jolly Jumper hanging from a bolt in the ceiling in the living room. I missed being in this house and in this town and the carefree life we lived here. As we left, I took one last glance at our rock, still sitting at the edge of the garden where we had placed it, having spent hours digging it out of the ground. It was one of many rocks that made up the low wall surrounding the property. For the first time, I wondered what other histories each of the rocks in the wall contained, what toils, what hardships had been required to place each rock in its spot. They had all survived, while those who had placed them might not have.

Soon, we were speeding along a highway headed toward home. I was sad to leave. I felt at home here among my caring friends. Scituate was a place where Arron had been alive and happy. Now we were heading back to Montclair, the place where he had died. In bumper-to-bumper traffic near the Merritt Parkway in Connecticut, the kids got cranky. It was late, they were tired and hungry, and we were getting nowhere. I took my frustrations out on them: "Be quiet!" "No whining!" "Stop fighting!"

The kids were worn out for the next week. Olivia woke up every morning looking gray and tired and refused to go to day camp. An old lady of seven. Day camp exhausted her. She averaged three days a week, and I didn't have the heart to force her to go the full five. The camp's founder had given Olivia a free summer of camp. I was indebted to them and felt guilty that her attendance was so erratic. I wished I could take the summer off from work and just hang out doing nothing with the kids. We all needed that. But I also needed to keep busy.

Zoom.

The next day, I sucked in my breath as Arron's truck pulled into the driveway. The sun struck it in a familiar way. I expected Arron to get out, but instead it was Bruce, with his wide grin. I had given the truck to Bruce and Jacquie, and in exchange Bruce had offered to come and fix our roof. Giving the truck to them made sense. I didn't need it, and Bruce was driving a van that looked ready to spontaneously combust at any moment. Bruce and Jacquie were reestablishing themselves in Toronto after a long stint in Manhattan, and I was certain that they could use the extra vehicle, especially now that they had a baby on the way. I was pleased that Arron's truck was going to a good home. It was irrational, but selling it to a stranger would have been unbearable.

Arron had been proud of his truck. He loved piling the kids into the back jumper seats and driving to Home Depot. To him the truck represented a life that eluded him: a rough-and-tumble man's world full of off-roading excursions, hauling loads; a world of tangible rewards. He loved coming up with home construction projects, just so that at the end of the day he could see and touch his creations. In his life as a businessman, his products were virtual and his hands lacked the calluses that manual labor creates. To me, the truck represented these aspects of Arron.

When Bruce arrived, the kids were immediately all over the truck and in it, laughing and sitting in the tiny sideways-facing, folding seats in the back. For them it brought back many happy memories, but I couldn't go near it.

Soon, the yard was mayhem as Bruce got to work. He assembled a motley crew of workers with the help of one of my neighbors. Having Bruce around was like having Arron around. They had a similar, irreverent sense of humor; they both had nicknamed their hammers and both would spontaneously break into "hammer" songs. The familiarity was strange. Carter began following him around like a puppy dog.

For the next three weeks, I cooked steaks on the grill and made salads, which we would share on the patio with a glass of wine, discussing our latest reads, or movies, as we always had. We were both aware of the strangeness of these dinners, where to the outside world we might appear as husband and wife and where one chair always seemed to be empty. It was Bruce I told one night about Encompys, Arron's company, closing its doors in bankruptcy. "It feels like another death," I told him.

"Yeah, that's a real shame," Bruce commiserated.

The July heat was blistering, often reaching 103 degrees. Bruce and his crew worked forty feet up on hot, black tarmac. Bruce's fair complexion forced him to wear jeans and long-sleeved flannel shirts, and by the time he had finished the roof, his clothes hung off him, he had lost so much weight.

One evening as we sat on the couch watching TV, Bruce blurted, "I saw Arron on the roof today." He said it as though bumping into Arron on the roof was perfectly normal.

"Lucky you. I wish I could see him." I imagined Arron up there, legs draped on either side of the peak. I could see the grin on his face, and I felt happy for Bruce and jealous at the same time.

"I don't know if it was the heat and I was hallucinating or what, but he was sitting up there smirking at me. It was as though he was checking up on me, making sure I was doing a good job." Bruce was very private with his thoughts, but in that moment I could see how much he missed Arron.

"That sounds like him," I said, laughing. "He always had to make sure the job was being done right!"

When he had finished our roof, Bruce headed off to another job in California for a few weeks, leaving the truck in our driveway while he was gone. One day, I had to move it and found myself sitting in the high driver's seat for the first time since Arron's death. I held the steering wheel in my hands, imagining his hands there. Arron was this truck. Happy, strong, tough, practical, cool, fun, rough. I backed it up the driveway and parked it on the street. I sat there for a while and bid it a quiet farewell. I folded in the side-view mirror the way he had taught me, so that it wouldn't get hit by the traffic that raced along our street.

Zoom.

On August 7, we celebrated Carter's third birthday party. Kids ran around our yard playing in the kiddie pool and I cooked hot dogs. Carter, obsessed with Thomas the Tank Engine, inspired me to find a cake decorated with a little toy train. It was a hit and became the favorite toy of all the presents he received, even topping the tricycle I had given him. The four or five kids who came played while my neighbors and friends drank wine with me, trying to fill the gaping hole that Arron's absence left in the day. I stood grilling hot dogs at the barbecue, where Arron would normally have stationed himself with a beer. I carried the cake and watched as Carter blew out his candles, remembering other years where Arron, gleeful, "assisted" with the blowing. I could feel him as I cleaned up, giving me that look again of "Can you believe he's already three? Where has the time gone?" or if Carter was being particularly whiny, "When will he be four?"

Zoom.

Earlier in the summer, I had received a phone call from CBC Television asking me to do an interview with them for the one-year anniversary of September 11. Initially, I had refused. I was afraid they would scrutinize me to find out how I was doing, if I had finished grieving, had moved on, had begun dating, or had married. I worried that perhaps I would be perceived as not coping well or else coping too well. I feared judgment that I was receiving special attention only because of the way my husband had died. I had visions of the camera narrowing in on my tearful face. On the other hand, I reasoned that an interview could become part of an archive for the kids, a time capsule. Here is Mommy at one year. But I worried about the toll such an interview might have on me. I could only imagine what chalky emotions would be stirred from the bottom of the pot and the ripple effect on my family and friends that their expression might have.

The piece was to be broadcast all over Canada. If I was honest, I was just a tiny bit pleased with this new notoriety. It felt good to feel special, to be fussed over, to have people take an interest in what I was saying. The lure was captivating, and I understood for the first time the many 9/11 widows and family members who enjoyed basking in this limelight. I couldn't help wondering how they would feel once the lights were turned off and everyone got bored of 9/11. How would I feel?

Still, this was not how I wanted to gain distinction. If I were to have recognition I wanted it to be because of my accomplishments, not because of something that happened to me, something I had no control over.

Yet I agreed to the interview.

The film crew arrived a week after Carter's party, in the still-blistering heat. The interviewer, Sylvène, put me at ease while the camera crew set up. She had gone to Jarvis Collegiate, Arron's high school, and although she hadn't known him personally, she had known many of his friends. I felt comforted.

When the setup was complete, I coaxed the kids into the cool sanctuary of the basement to play. Sylvène sat opposite me, out of camera shot, and began with the words "First time you met?" And so I talked about Arron. Happily. It was not about me. I spoke about the building falling and knowing the unlikelihood of his survival. I didn't cry. I was determined not to. I wanted the interview to be fun, humorous even. I wanted people to know Arron. I didn't want to be seen as the weeping widow. A few times, the kids appeared and I had to shush them. Their peeking faces made it difficult to concentrate and I barely contained my giggles.

Later, we all went outside, so the crew could film us doing "normal" things. The kids clambered onto their bikes and I helped Carter manage his new tricycle, holding the handlebars for him. I agreed to let the kids be filmed from behind, so the final piece ended with a shot of me helping Carter ride down the street, away from the camera.

Zoom.

I had purposely booked a vacation during the last week of August to visit Jill, Dan, and Caelin on the west coast, where we had rented a cabin at Tyax Lodge on Tyaughton Lake in Gold Bridge,

British Columbia, near Whistler. I wanted to be out of reach when the media began calling in earnest. Newspapers and radio and more television stations would be looking for stories to fill their pages and hours of intense coverage during the one-year anniversary. I would not do any more interviews.

Our vacation rental sat on the shore of an incredible turquoise lake surrounded by lush forest. Despite being part of a lodge, our cabin seemed remote, hidden in the woods. When we arrived, the kids ran free, finally released from their car seats.

The first sight of my niece, a sweet, strawberry blonde, blue-eyed kewpie doll of a baby, had the kids and I arguing over who would hold her first. She showed her pleasure at seeing her cousins with lovely baby belly laughs. Both kids doted on her. Carter proudly sat in the big chair carefully holding his baby cousin, patting her cheek with big-boy solicitude.

The week continued as uneventfully as I had hoped. There was no TV and the quiet was wonderful. Dan and the kids fished from the dock while Jill and I sat in the sun and took turns holding Caelin. Despite bouts of sadness, I finished the week feeling calmer than I had felt in many months. I actually felt peaceful. My sleep was rarely disturbed by the pangs of anxiety that been regularly waking me. For the first time, I could sit still and not leap up every few minutes. For four whole days I did not think once about 9/11.

But as we bumped along trucking roads back toward civilization, my jumpiness returned. By the time we had reached Whistler, I had a flat tire, which Dan replaced for me. The next day, we said our farewells to Jill, Dan, and Caelin and continued our drive. Careening along the suburban highways of Seattle, after five hours of driving with the kids fighting in the backseat, I tried to read the directions crumpled in my hand. As I clutched the steering wheel, looking for the highway exit that would get us to the home of an old high-school friend, I caught sight of the swirling lights of a police car in my rearview mirror.

"Shit," I said.

"Are we going to jail?" Olivia's voice was panicked. Carter began to cry. The officer stood at the passenger window for a few moments before I could remember how to open it. Cars whizzed by on my side of the car, where there wasn't enough room for the officer to stand.

"Are you aware," he said, "that you passed right by me?"

"No. I had no idea," I said, trying to keep the quiver out of my voice.

"You were going seventy miles an hour, in a fifty-five-mile-an-hour zone."

"I was?" The kids began to fight again in the backseat. Carter was still crying. "Hush!" I said, a little too loudly.

"Are you distracted in any way?" the officer said. It was all I could do to suppress an explosion of laughter.

"Yes, perhaps I am, Officer," I managed to squeak with what I hoped was a straight face.

He must have recognized the crazed look of a desperate single mother, because he leaned into the car and said to the kids, "You need to be quiet for the rest of the way. Your mother needs to concentrate."

There was shocked silence from the backseat.

"Thank you," I managed. The police officer helped me figure out where I was and then let me go without writing a ticket.

"Take it easy. And slow down!" he said as he walked away.

"I will, I promise!" But I knew it was a promise I would break. *Zoom, zoom, zoom.*

16

MOVING ON

In the months leading up to the first anniversary of 9/11, the office of Michael Bloomberg, mayor of New York City, polled family members to gather ideas for how to mark the occasion. I envisioned each of us holding a single red rose while encircling the pit area that had once contained the World Trade Center, and at a single moment, we would drop our roses into the pit. I wanted to recapture Arron the way I had when I visited Ground Zero for the first time. I e-mailed my idea in.

Perhaps at the one-year anniversary I would finally be able to let Arron go. I imagined the roses turning into doves and flying off, free. I wanted the sappy movie ending. I wanted closure. It seemed that no matter how many memorials I attended, no matter how much I cried, no matter what I did, I couldn't shake my grief. My fear of forgetting Arron kept me bound to it. Perhaps the memorial would allow me to show him how much I honored him, allowing me to move on. It would give me a place I could come and be with him. Ground Zero would become a kind of sanctuary of spiritual convergence, like a cemetery where I could go and lay my single rose.

Finally Mayor Bloomberg announced his plans for the ceremony: the family members would receive a flower and walk down into the pit to lay it. Names would be read by family members, a group of five at a time. We were all invited to volunteer to read. I was flattered. Maybe they had actually accepted my flower idea. More likely, it was a common idea among family members, but at that moment, I felt singled out. I had not planned on going to Ground Zero, given my previous experiences there, but when these plans were announced, I took it as a sign. Perhaps my dream memorial could be realized.

I debated bringing the kids to the ceremony. Someday it would be important for them to see Ground Zero, but they were still young and I worried that it might be too scary for them now. I was also concerned about the crowds. The invitation allowed each family to bring ten guests, which amounted to a potential crush of 30,000 people. I decided to let Olivia choose whether she would attend, knowing she was likely to say no. She told me she just wanted to go to school that day. Janet had offered to take her to Montclair's 9/11 ceremony early in the morning, before taking her to school, and Olivia readily agreed. Carter would go to nursery school. Neither of the kids seemed to understand the meaning of the anniversary, but Carter sensed something was happening and started clinging to me more. Olivia didn't want me talking about it.

Selena made it clear that she would join me in whatever I decided to do on the anniversary. When I told her of my plan to go to Ground Zero, she was not thrilled about the idea but was nevertheless willing to go. I was glad to have company on the pilgrimage. I didn't choose who attended memorials with me. I went with whoever showed up. It never occurred to me to ask my family to join me at the ceremony, because it didn't occur to me that I might need them there. I was independent and I wasn't used to asking for things. My mother was spending the day at our cottage in Quebec with her cousin Barbara. My sister attended a memorial service by herself, in Pemberton. They seemed to stay clear of my relationship with Selena—out of respect or resentment, I could only imagine. My father and stepmother had opted to avoid the anniversary altogether by heading to Europe for three weeks.

I tried to understand, knowing their desire to "move on" and their avoidance of everything 9/11, but it was hard not to feel as though they were trying to escape me.

The Canadian consulate, working with the Ontario Victims of Crime unit in Toronto, had arranged for the other Toronto-based families to travel to New York and stay at the Empress Hotel near Central Park. Selena and I decided to go into New York on the afternoon of September 10 and spend the night, so we could attend a pre-anniversary reception and avoid an early-morning commute to Ground Zero. I asked Martha to spend the night with the kids.

Selena and I left for the city, and as we said good-bye to the kids, I was overcome with sadness. I knew they must have been feeling the strange mood in the house for the past few weeks. I tried to say good-bye as lightly as I could. "Be good for Martha," "Give Mommy a kiss goodnight now," "I love you." I wasn't sure if I was feeling guilty for leaving them on such an important day, when perhaps they would need me most, or if I felt sad because I knew it might be me who needed them. As I drove away, watching them wave to us from the yard, I had to swallow back tears.

We arrived at the hotel, a lovely twenties-era building overlooking Central Park, and had just enough time to get ready for a cocktail reception at the home of Pamela Wallin, a former Canadian TV journalist, who had recently been named the Canadian Consul General in New York City.

We gathered in the hotel lobby with other families whom we had met at previous memorials and events planned by the Canadian consulate and greeted each other with grim warmth. We would not naturally have come together for any other purpose. As a group, we possessed a false closeness that comes of macabre discussions about recovered remains, last phone calls, and charities.

"They found Peter," one of the widows told me as we walked from the hotel to the party, referring to her husband.

"Really?" My response was hesitant. I knew there was more coming.

"Yes. Almost his entire body. Only his leg was missing. They identified him from the brand of pants he was wearing. It was something I included in the missing person report."

"I'm glad for you." I couldn't decide if I was horrified or jealous.

We arrived at Pamela Wallin's apartment, a cheery, brightly lit space at the top of a building on the Upper East Side. The apartment was tastefully decorated with paintings by well-known Canadian artists and was well suited to entertaining, clearly a large part of her new role. Various officials, including Michael Kergin, the Canadian Ambassador to the United States of America, and the consulate staff who helped us were also there, as were the representatives from the Ontario Attorney General's Office for Victims of Crime, John and Tracy. Selena and I were becoming good friends with these OVC reps and admired their wonderful ability to make us laugh. Despite long, sad days of working with the families of crime victims, John's ice-blue eyes always twinkled and Tracy was constantly laughing and upbeat. We clung to anyone who could provide that magic.

I had lectured myself not to drink too much at this affair, but it felt good to numb my emotions, bracing for a difficult few days ahead. I made small talk with other family members, some of whom I was meeting for the first time, but I was more than content to let Selena dominate the conversations and later egged her into flirting with an older gentleman. After two hours, both Selena and I were becoming more animated. I could feel my cheeks beginning to flush.

We found John and Tracy, whom we had planned to have dinner with, and feeling as though we were clinging to them for support, we bid our farewells to Ms. Wallin (now Pamela) and left the party with our new friends linked securely to our elbows. We wandered the streets around Central Park looking for some proper dinner, settling on a sports bar, and were soon ordering chicken wings and more drinks. Several other family members joined us. The evening became louder as we forced our fun. We laughed too hard at each other's jokes. We needed a release, to forget our tragedy. Or perhaps it was a celebration of sorts: casting off grief, and moving into something new, like a graduation.

We woke the next morning a little worse for wear and quickly attempted to dress. We had brought clothes for a warmer day, but the news on TV told us that despite the sun it would be in the low sixties Fahrenheit. Not sure what one wears to a one-year anniversary at the site of a demolished building, I imagined a black cocktail dress and a big floppy hat, like widows wore in old movies. I could wear dark movie-star sunglasses and be Jacqueline Kennedy. But I knew we would be traipsing around in dust and grit in the morning and then meeting a prime minister in the afternoon, so I settled on black pants, practical shoes, and the one sweater I had brought. The outfit was a far cry from the fashion-plate widow and something Arron would have called "unsexy."

On the bus, everyone was mute, lost in their own thoughts, as the bus worked its way through the early-morning New York City streets. At seven, the city was just rising, but there was a tension in the air. People on the street seemed frenetic, moving too quickly, honking too loudly, even for New York. Sirens and flashing lights were everywhere. The mood was terrifying in its anticipation. I had never loved New York the way I loved other cities—Paris, London, Boston. Those cities were green and beautiful with splendid old buildings and flowers brightening dingy corners. New York held no magic for me. I saw nothing but garbage, ugly grated storefronts, potholes. Occasionally I would pass a classic brownstone stoop, or a meticulously planted three-foot square of garden, but these small oases were not enough. For Arron, New York had been pure power. He loved the hustle, the aggression, the ambition it took to make it there. New York always gave me an uneasy feeling that I was never able to articulate.

Maybe it was that the entire city seemed too tall. It was cocky in its attitude. That morning, I cursed New York, as if a city could be blamed for my husband's death.

As we drew closer to Ground Zero, we stopped. Slowly, one by one, the buses passed a police checkpoint. Barriers held back crowds of people who had come to watch the ceremony. I began to regret my breakfast. I felt queasy. I wasn't prepared to be on display. I felt stupid for not having foreseen that. Our bus parked near the family members' entrance, and we all got out and melted into the crush of people. At the entry, our identification was checked, P-numbers verified, all within view of a crowd of onlookers. I felt like they were all studying my face, trying to see my grief and take it for themselves.

Following a bobbing Canadian flag held by John, we made our way deeper and deeper into the throng of grieving families. We got within fifty feet of the podium where family members would recite the victims' names. Directly in front of it a large set of bleachers groaned with the weight of reporters and photographers, TV crews and cameras. Wires snaked the stands and the ground, squirming toward the noisy tractor-trailers providing them with power. I felt panic. I did not want my picture taken, and I hoped I was well hidden and anonymous in the gathering.

As we neared the edge overlooking Ground Zero, the wind whipped dust upward from the pit in a circular pattern, and then the swirls engulfed the crowd. I could taste the grit in my mouth: Arron's dust mixed with the toxic poison of cement and plaster and asbestos and death. Blinking back the sunshine, I could feel the grit in my eyes and I wished that I could cry it away.

I stood shoulder to shoulder with the throngs, Selena beside me, each of us clasping our familiar Red Cross bags. Not many people were wearing their face masks this time, despite the dusty wind. Around me huge groups of people wore T-shirts emblazoned with photos of their loved ones and sayings such as "We will never forget," one face repeated across chests small and large.

I hadn't thought to make a T-shirt of Arron's face and wondered how so many people had had the same idea. Was it an American custom to make T-shirts out of the photo of a dead loved one? I felt inadequate without one, as though in not advertising my husband in this way, I had again failed him.

Behind the bleachers a mother posed her small blonde daughter, clad in a T-shirt bearing her grinning father's image and wearing a Stars-and-Stripes bandana while a camera snapped photos. I missed Carter and Olivia, but I was glad they weren't part of this. People were hugging and crying and many wore that hideous mask of numbness that I knew so well. The throng was overwhelming and there were a few moments when it would swell and propel us in another direction. Between the swirling dust and wind and the undulating masses, I felt uneasy and it was hard to breathe.

At 8:46 AM, the moment the first plane hit Tower 1, a fire bell rang and a moment of silence followed. The wind seemed to gain momentum, swirling dramatically among us, like a movie cliché. Soon a few dignitaries stood up and began reading names alphabetically, Rudy Giuliani and Michael Bloomberg among them. Then the family members who had volunteered to read took turns, one by one stepping up to read five names from the long list of the dead. I had chosen not to read. I wanted to mourn privately. It was a sombre affair watching the names being read. When people listening in the crowd heard their loved one's name they moved toward the ramp, collected a flower, and made their way down into the gaping pit. We waited patiently through all the As and Bs. The wind continued to buffet us. The crowd undulated.

By now, I was covered in grit. It was in my eyes, my mouth, my hair, my ears. My feet were sore and I was dying to sit down. The readings took forever. We stood through all of the C names, our hair whipping, the grit like sandpaper on our skin, waiting to hear the name DACK. An hour passed, perhaps more. My heart began to pound as the Cs neared their end and the Ds began.

Another fifteen minutes. And finally, a pale, slim young man wearing a sombre black suit stood up. I knew it would be him who read Arron's name. He read each name carefully and then he said it: CALEB ARRON . . . BLACK. I looked at the man to see if his blunder registered on his face, but he continued with more D names, unaware. Then, he turned and walked off the podium. Selena and I looked at each other with our mouths hanging open.

"He was in the Ds!" I said, aghast.

"What an idiot!" was Selena's response.

Was DACK not a simple name? Messing up Caleb I could have understood, but Dack? When you are reading D names? I just sighed. Another perversion of a memorial.

We pushed our way through the crowd and collected the carnations being handed out by people holding baskets. Soon we stood in a long traffic jam of people, bumper-to-bumper on the ramp into the pit. We had lots of time to watch others lay their carnations in a knee-high ring that was set up on the floor of the pit. The flower stems were jumbled together like a giant game of pick-up sticks. People stood around the ring and cried or prayed. Some posed their families and took photographs. I felt like a sheep being herded to its slaughter. But I played my role, the martyred widow, hating it. I let out a little baa-ing noise, as Arron would have done. I needed to laugh.

It seemed like hours passed before we finally made our way down that ramp. As I walked, I began cursing Arron for being here that day, making it so I had to be here now. When I got to the pit, I wanted to whip my flower into the ring and run. Instead, I had to push my way through more children posing in red, white, and blue bandanas; more uncles and aunts and friends wearing T-shirts; more uniformed firefighters and police officers. Finally, I made my way to the edge of the circle and dropped my carnation onto the pile. It looked tiny in the mass grave of flowers. I tried to calm myself down by studying the huge steel girders that were sticking out of the cement wall encasing us. They had once held the floors of the parking garage. We were in a giant tomb. The more I thought about it, the more ghastly it became. *Ashes to ashes, dust to dust* repeated over and over in my head. I wanted to huddle in a corner and rock like a disturbed child.

I had to leave. I made eye contact with Selena, who was lost in her own thoughts, and we slowly made our way back out. My legs were heavy and climbing the ramp was painful. But then we were up and out. We exited the site through a tall chain-link gate, which clanged shut behind us. And that was it. It was over.

Selena and I walked down the road, our ID badges still hanging from our necks, past police and firefighters, and onlookers who watched us with what I supposed was pity in their eyes. We came upon a group of Royal Canadian Mounted Police, who were endearingly comical in their big jodhpurs and Bullwinkle hats, and I wanted to hug them. They seemed completely out of place there but to me they represented something normal, something that made sense. I felt homesick for a Canadian sensibility, a Canadian way of memorializing the dead, though I had no idea what that was. Surely Canadians would mourn more quietly, more beautifully.

We got to the bus, exhausted, and I was lost in my sadness. I felt empty. Flat. Deflated. The Ground Zero Memorial had failed me, failed Arron. I wished I could call the kids. I was desperate to see them and longed to have them both in my arms. I wondered how the town memorial was for Olivia, how her day was going at school. She would be eating her lunch now. Did she miss me, too? Was this day significant for her? Perhaps now she could finally understand what this day represented. Was this day significant for Carter?

We waited for more people to return to the bus and were soon easing through traffic and lines of buses on our way back to the Canadian consulate. When we arrived, I went to wash up. I had smudges of dust all over my face. For an instant, I didn't want to wash it off. Was there some small remnant of Arron in this grit? One tiny particle of him clinging to my ear lobe? My eyelash?

I looked at myself in the mirror, but the person looking back at me was unrecognizable. This woman was so sad! So old! Who was she? I applied lipstick and then tried to smile. Off to meet a prime minister.

After a quick lunch, everyone moved to stand around the perimeter of the room as Jean Chrétien made his rounds. When he reached Selena and me, he moved toward me and held my hand. "Nice to see you again." I was flattered that he remembered meeting me a year ago. Still clasping my hand, he said to both of us, "You two are very tall women!"

"And proud of it!" Selena said.

I just smiled at him and he moved on.

When he finished his rounds, he spoke to the crowd. "September 11th has been a terrible experience for all of us, but it's time for all of us to get on with our lives. It is time to move on."

Move on? Move on to what? I hadn't realized that the passing of one year meant everything was suddenly all better. I resented the expectation that the families would now move on. It implied that Mr. Chrétien could wipe his hands clean of the nasty affair. No more awkward receiving lines. No national memorial in Canada. Done. Over. Case closed. Beside me, Selena seethed, "We're outta here!" I didn't argue.

Some of the families were heading back down to Ground Zero to meet with George W. Bush. I couldn't imagine anything worse. I was dying to get home to see the kids, so after a few farewells, we made our way out. At the bottom of the escalator, we saw one of the more outspoken family members holding a one-woman news conference. She was surrounded by reporters in a blaze of lights. As we ascended, we could hear her laughter, and I wondered what on earth she could be laughing about with those reporters. All I wanted to do was cry.

We got back to New Jersey just in time to greet Olivia's bus. The child who bounded off the bus was not the one I had said good-bye to the day before. She leaped into my arms gleefully and exclaimed, "Mommy, I saw Daddy's name on the stone today and we talked about Daddy in my class!" She had a huge smile on her face. In a flurry of words, she described the town's memorial, where a fire bell was rung and a fireman had lifted the cardboard hiding the plaque so she could see her Daddy's name. "I didn't know his first name was Caleb!" she said to me. I was confused. Was it possible that she really didn't know? Or had she just forgotten? Had I really never told her? Anything was possible. Then she told me how her teacher had told her whole class that her daddy was one of the people in the building that day. I am not sure if Olivia felt pride, or relief, but for the first time in a year, her father's name had been spoken at her school. It was real for Olivia for the very first time. I tried to hide my tears. It had been a year since I had seen this happy little girl and I didn't want to spoil it.

That night, the town of Montclair held a "cultural" 9/11 memorial where dancers and singers and poets performed tributes to the town's 9/11 families. Although we were exhausted, I felt we should go, but I soon questioned my decision. The kids were not interested in sitting still, and as no one in town, other than the other widows, knew who I was, we were asked to move to seats off to the side because of their behavior. It was humiliating. I was already angry at how the Montclair mayor's office had handled the town's public memorial. Despite soliciting my ideas for its design, the mayor's office managed to create a mockery of a monument: a small rock holding a cheap plastic plaque embossed with the Twin Towers and the victims' names, with tiny embossed leaves falling among the names. A motley display of flowers was planted around the rock, installed by the Junior League, who agreed to its upkeep. I had stood with the woman hired to design the memorial and made suggestions such as "keep the plaque simple, just the names" and "perhaps something in brass." It turned out she was employed, not by the mayor's office, but by the plaque company, and this was an opportunity for her company to display its garish creations.

My attempts to donate a park bench in our neighborhood park in honor of Arron had met with several unreturned phone calls. I gave up. Other widows described elaborate memorials, street name changes, and gardens that their towns had commissioned. It felt wrong to expect anything from Montclair, and yet I felt let down.

It was slowly dawning on me that no public memorial service or ceremony would ever satisfy me. What was missing in each of them, what I had failed to realize before now, was that none of them was about Arron. Or me. Or the kids. Or our families. Public services were for the masses—a one-size-fits-all solution. If Arron's body had been found, the finality of his death would have been acknowledged during his funeral. We wouldn't have been subjected to any more memorials. A burial plot or special place for his ashes would have given us a place for a headstone, or an urn and a place to commune with him. The one-year anniversary of his death might have been a simple, private affair: a bouquet of flowers on a grave, a gathering around a tree. Instead, the memorials seemed to fulfill the public's need to confirm the deaths of each victim, especially those whose bodies had not been found. They seemed to ensure the media's ratings. I began to see that without a private monument for Arron, we had no physical place to be with him. The only thing that would ever make me happy and properly honor Arron would be a monument that I would need to create myself.

That night, I was consumed by raw, bitter disappointment. I had a long, exhausting bout of tears. It felt good to release the last two days' emotions. I mourned that a whole year had passed without Arron. He was still as real to me as the day he left, and as I thought of all the things he had missed in a year, I was engulfed in my own sadness and it seemed I would never stop sobbing. But I welcomed the tears. I wanted to sob so that he could know how much I loved him and missed him. I wanted him to see my pain

and sorrow and know that I mourned for him properly. My puffy
eyes were my own personal monument, proof that I still loved him.

There was yet another memorial for the kids and me to attend.
This one would take place in Ottawa on September 14 and had
been arranged by a private cemetery out of respect for the
Canadians who had been lost on September 11. Hopefully this
would be the Canadian memorial I had longed for, with a quieter
sensibility. We had been asked to bring objects that were meaningful to our loved ones so we could place them in a box that was to
be buried beneath the monument. The kids and I filled a small ziplock baggie with items for the box. There was a British beer mat,
from an assortment Arron had collected, hoping to frame and
hang them around our house. I had (barely) managed to convince
him that they would clash with our decor. We added a drywall
screw, an homage to his love of homes and building, a picture
that Olivia had drawn, and a small toy that Carter had selected.
I contemplated adding Arron's old dentures, which had remained
sealed in a small Tupperware container for the past ten years, but
they seemed too grisly. I laughed at the comic touch they would
have added, but I wasn't actually prepared to give them up. They
were a part of him for a long time, the result of his losing several
teeth in a nasty bicycling accident when he was nineteen. His most
recent pair of dentures had been lost with him.

The night before the memorial, the kids and I had dinner in a
lovely restored train station with my mother and grandfather,
who had driven to Ottawa to be with us. My relationship with my
mother had begun to swing back into more familiar territory. She
was more secure now in her role as my mother and as someone
who was helping me through my grief. She had been working with
Larry on the divorce settlements and this had helped her see that
her grief over Arron had reopened old wounds from her divorce.
She seemed more confident now, and I felt safe to depend on her

again, knowing she had the strength to support me if I needed it. My grandfather was also a quiet pillar of strength. At almost ninety, he carried on in life with the spirit of a much younger man. His motto was simply to "keep moving." Since my grandmother's death only three years earlier, he continued to spend his winters in Florida, and his summers in Montreal playing golf, maintaining a very active social life in both places. He had adored Arron, and in many respects they were very similar. Both shared the somewhat unnerving trait of being unable to sit still. They used to discuss stocks or mutual funds at length. My grandfather was a man of few words, but he seemed to be showing me through example how to remain graceful and alive despite losing your life's companion. He was a true example of how life should be lived and how I needed to keep moving.

At the cemetery, a tent had been set up a short distance from the monument, which turned out to be a rock, perhaps four feet tall, and on it a brass plaque with a list of the twenty-four Canadian victims, a depiction of the buildings, and the Canadian government logo. Below the plaque, on the ground, was an empty box made from deeply stained cherrywood and lined in green felt. We sat under the tent, along with about eighty people, mostly families. It was Carter's naptime and he was tired and not doing well on this trip, being out of his usual routine. We sat near some very sympathetic older people but soon I was up chasing Carter, or trying to keep him quiet during the speeches. His backpack stuffed with toys held little interest and lay neglected under his chair.

After a few short speeches, the families began lining up in front of the monument to place their items into the box. I looked in my purse and around my seat for the ziplock bag. I flew into a panic as I realized that I must have left it in the taxi. My mom went and spoke with Maureen and Clara, our liaisons from the Canadian consulate. Without any fuss, they quickly and quietly made a call to the taxi company and were soon at my side, assuring me that the taxi was on its way back with the bag. They suggested that we go and have our moment and that the bag would probably be there by the time we reached our turn. I managed to calm down but felt very flustered and sheepish at the same time.

The kids and I walked up to the stone. Olivia asked me to show her Arron's name, so I leaned over the open box and together we touched his name on the plaque. Carter stood under us but couldn't quite reach so just watched from beneath. We didn't speak. My mother and grandfather hovered behind us. After a few minutes, I took the kids' hands and walked away. A photographer approached us, a journalist from one of the newspapers, and he had snapped a picture of the kids and me as we touched the plaque. He asked for our names, and the picture appeared the next day in many newspapers across Canada. In it, I look tired but determined. I was angry with myself for having lost the mementos. And yet, they seemed to lose their importance in the end. The most meaningful moment had been the simple act of touching Arron's name, as though we could finally touch him, together. I had come to Ottawa for that moment. Perhaps that was what had been missing for me at Ground Zero: time with the kids; a way to touch Arron.

A while later, Maureen and Clara from the consulate came running over, holding up the ziplock bag triumphantly. By now the box was closed, but Maureen walked over to it with us and re-opened it. I tried to look somber as I placed the bag carefully into the box, but the mementos had lost their meaning. These were just things. The kids were impatient at being made to endure another moment of forced remembrance. Even I was impatient and quickly touched Arron's name once more in farewell. The moment had passed and was now already locked away and buried deep within us.

Home once again, the memorials gradually began to work some sort of strange magic on me. Unexpectedly, I was feeling light—the weight of anticipation was gone. I felt renewed, fresh. I wasn't alone in this feeling. I sensed in the media a relief that the anniversary had passed, that we had all survived. I got this same feeling from my friends, other widows, and my family. It *was* time for me to move on, just like Mr. Chrétien had implored us to do. As angry as I had been at his words, I now thanked him for giving me the permission I needed to "move on" or, as my grandfather said, to "keep moving." My friends' visits and phone calls were becoming less frequent, and tiny suggestions about dating or relocating began to creep into our conversations. It seemed as if my moving on might allow everyone else the same freedom. The people who had helped me had done their duty and now it was time for all of us to get back to our lives. I wanted this for myself as much as for those who had ministered to me.

But sometimes I couldn't tell if people wanted me to move on so they wouldn't have to worry about me or if they wanted me to stay the "grieving widow" so they could continue to comfort me. One of my neighbors became angry when I told her I missed her frequent visits, because she thought I had found her to be overly obtrusive. I swung like a pendulum, both wanting to move on and needing to be cared for.

I seized on to the idea of a new beginning. It was time to define "moving on." The bouts of tears were becoming less frequent, though I still relished them. They were my insurance that I had not forgotten Arron. I knew that moving on didn't necessarily mean forgetting him, but the thought was still frightening. My drive for an appropriate, meaningful memorial stemmed from this fear of forgetting. Arron's closet became a makeshift cenotaph. During happy periods, I opened the closet, his clothes still stacked neatly inside, exactly as they had been the day he died. I would clutch one of his overly starched shirts, or imagine him in his favorite shirt (which everyone else hated), and then sob into his navy-blue bathrobe, which still smelled of him. Soon, the act became almost masochistic. A crying dry-spell would send me back to the closet for a rain dance of tears. A whiff of his bathrobe was a reliable shaman. The tears would cleanse my body, washing me with relief that I still mourned my husband honorably, appropriately, with tears and sobs. I knew I could always cry if I opened his closet. I kept it intact, not willing to move anything or give anything away.

I started to feel a small spark of excitement thinking about all the opportunities I now had ahead of me. I could move to a glamorous city, discover a new passion instead of work at my old job, paint my bedroom pink, and all the decisions would be mine and mine alone. I could create a new life for the kids and myself, full of possibility. But with excitement came fear and loneliness. What if I made a wrong decision? Which direction should I choose? What if I wound up even more miserable? With each decision I became conscious once again of my aloneness. At first I had comforted myself by bringing Arron into my decision-making process. Would Arron have done this? What would Arron think? But the more I did that, the more I rejected his "opinions." Soon I was saying things like "Arron would have hated this!" or "I know what you're thinking, but this is *my* decision!" I felt like a small bird on the edge of a cliff, looking out onto a vast landscape. I knew my wings were getting stronger, but I remained on the cliff, unsure of their ability to carry me. I wondered, if my wings *were* strong enough, in which direction would I fly? In the end I decided that direction didn't matter; I just had to keep moving.

PART THREE

THE REDDENING

"... and the time came when the risk it took to remain
in a tightly closed bud became infinitely more painful
than the risk it took to blossom."

Anaïs Nin

17

YEARNING FOR LOVE

"Moving on" proved to be more difficult than I had anticipated. My sister and my niece Caelin flew in from Vancouver and my mother drove down from Toronto to celebrate my birthday. I was happy to see them but exhausted. I wanted September to end. I wanted a quiet house and my routines to resume. I wanted to have my cup of tea each morning and read my paper at the kitchen table. Instead, my mother set the dining-room table for breakfast the night before, her habit whenever there was a crowd in the house: tiny glasses for orange juice, cloth napkins. In the mornings, I brought my bowl of oatmeal out to the table to find a bowl had already been set at my place.

Jill, in one year, had grown up in my eyes. Her almost daily phone calls had been buoying me in a way I had not expected. She knew me better than any other person, other than Arron, and I knew her equally well. She laughed at my black humor. She cried with me. She mourned Arron as much as I did. More than any other friend or family member, I had come to rely on Jill and was amazed at her wisdom, something I had never seen in her, despite knowing her intimately her entire life.

"I know you don't really want to celebrate your birthday this year," she said suddenly, as she stood in front of Caelin's swing, bending to grab Caelin's feet as it came toward her, making her giggle. Somehow my mother had managed to plan a party, convincing me to invite my close friends and neighbors over for dinner. At first, the distraction seemed appealing, but now that the day had arrived, I was dreading it. My birthday was another reminder of the passage of time: another missed sushi dinner, another missed red rose. I wanted my birthday to be forgotten, as if in forgetting the milestones I could forget Arron's absence.

"Is it that obvious? I hoped no one would notice. But I guess I'm not very good at hiding my feelings."

Jill laughed. "No, you're not at all!"

"Don't get me wrong, I'm really happy you're here, but I just don't want a big production for my birthday and suddenly it seems to have turned into that."

"I know. I think Mom just wants to do something special for you. We all do."

"I know you do. But it's not necessary. It's not going to make anything better."

"We all know that, Ab. We could call it all off . . ." she suggested.

"No, no. I'll get through it. It's just not going to be as easy as I thought." I was grateful not to be feeling the strange hazy numbness that I had been feeling at last year's birthday. At least this year I knew I could smile and laugh without feeling like I was about to crack. But I still felt as though a black cloud was following me wherever I went. I began to worry that the seemingly perpetual frown on my face might become a permanent fixture, like crossed eyes in the childhood warning.

Later, my mother and I prepared an Indian feast: curried chicken, lentils, potatoes, spinach, basmati rice. The bright yellow food looked festive and hopeful in my white wedding china.

I went upstairs for a quick nap and fell into a heavy sleep. A tentative knock at my door woke me.

"Abby, it's six. People will be here any minute." My mother's voice annoyed me. I didn't want to get out of bed. I wanted to lie there for the rest of the night. I wanted my birthday to go away and never return. Instead of being four years younger than Arron, I was now only two. Soon I would be older than he was when he died. I wanted the process to stop, so that I would not grow old while Arron remained thirty-nine forever.

It wasn't until I heard a knock on the front door that I actually rose. I pinched my cheeks, knowing that if I didn't, my mother would. "You look so pale," she would say, as she pinched me painfully the way she had when I was a child.

Downstairs, I feigned joy. I smiled and even laughed. I ate the colorful dishes, though I tasted nothing. I opened presents guiltily. Every kindness seemed an act of pity. I knew my friends didn't pity me, not really, and yet I knew on some level they did. They empathized with my situation, imagining what it would be like to lose their spouses, to raise their children alone. I recognized that they wanted to be there for me, to ease me through another painful event. I loved them for it but I was tired of being grateful. I was tired of thanking everyone. I didn't need more gifts. I didn't need more sympathy. I wanted to step out of the spotlight and resume my place in an everyday life, one not marked by my specialness.

Cleaning the kitchen after everyone left felt rejuvenating. I craved mundane tasks these days. They reminded me of my old life, my normal life. Later that night in bed, I cried for the loss of the old me, the one who died with Arron. I was still uncertain about this new, grumpier person who had taken her place, unable to feel deep emotions, unable to taste food, and yet learning and growing and at times even hopeful about what her future might hold.

Next stop on September's emotional rollercoaster was our wedding anniversary, a week after my birthday. My family had gone home and the kids and I celebrated with a trip to the playground, ice cream, running Saturday errands. Carter missed his nap and fell asleep on the couch as I made dinner. Olivia and I sat on the too-high window seat that Arron had built, eating the simple dinner I had cooked, silent. Another year alone, I was thinking, both despondent at this thought and proud. I had accomplished so much without Arron. I never would have imagined it was possible to raise a two-year-old and a six-year-old through the monstrous year that we had had. I looked at Olivia, her posture as ramrod straight as her father's had been, and marveled at her. She was so intelligent, silly, beautiful. It was almost possible to imagine her as the magnanimous woman she was certain to become. Carter was still young, but I tried to imagine him in the coming years, losing his clinginess and regaining the self-confidence he had lost this year, becoming the faithful, gifted, commanding individual that he was destined to be. I wished Arron could see them, could walk in that door for just five minutes and hold them.

Suddenly there was music: Macy Gray, our family favorite. The lyrics seemed to carry significance, as though Arron was talking to us from beyond the grave. As a family, we used to sing along together to her song "I Try." Even at five years old, Olivia could sing the complicated quick changes of the song's melody. Now Macy Gray was singing the words *I thought I'd see you again.*

Olivia and I sat quietly for a while, listening, surprised that the music had suddenly turned on without our doing anything. She looked at me and pointed to the ceiling. I nodded. We both were content to know that our own special ghost was paying us a visit. We listened as we continued to eat our dinner, and I tried to figure out an explanation based on logic, but I couldn't imagine how the CD player could have turned itself on. I smiled, thinking about Arron and our anniversary, and a tear escaped down my cheek. You finally remembered the right day of our anniversary! This year, now that you're dead, you actually got it right.

My world crumbles when you are not near. . . .

The song had taken on new importance.

The rest of the week, as soon as I walked into the house from work, the CD player would again turn on and begin playing Macy Gray. Martha just shook her head. "An angel," she would marvel and return to cooking dinner. I let the CD play during the bustle of dinnertime, allowing Arron to be a part of the fray.

My longing for Arron began in the pit of my stomach, stinging and yawning like a canker sore. Loneliness found its most secure foothold at night, as I lay down to sleep. I longed for his weight to hold me down, keeping me from floating away into an abyss; I longed for the crush of his kiss, the crook of his arm that was my nest. I longed for the physicality of his body reminding me of mine. I longed to make love.

The truth was, I thought about sex often. It surprised me. I thought about sex while I was married, but it wasn't quite as obvious then. And occasionally, Arron was there to indulge me, if he wasn't too tired. He could also offer kisses and cuddles, which sometimes fulfilled my desires. Now, my urges were more frequent, HBO-fueled. I began to see a pattern in my lustful cycles, tied to my menstrual ones. Had marriage sheltered me from my own sexuality so completely that I had never noticed these patterns before?

I began to wonder what real-life fantasies might look like. What did real Manhattan or New Jersey men have to offer a lonely thirty-something widow?

"Online dating is kind of fun," a colleague told me one day as she scrolled down a web page looking at thumbnail headshots. "You write a profile and post a picture and guys e-mail you if they're interested."

"Wow," I managed, trying not to sound taken aback that my demure colleague engaged in such activities.

"You should try it," she cheered. "You'll have a million guys writing you."

After yoga class one night in November, I asked Jen and Corny, my neighbors and friends, what they thought. "Too soon, you think?"

"No, no. It's great! You should definitely do it."

In one of our daily phone calls, Jill, too, seemed pleased that I was considering dating. "It's a great idea, Ab. It will be really good for you to get out every now and then and meet some new people."

But I wasn't sure. It had only been fourteen months. I was curious and anxious to speed through the natural process of mourning, but I didn't feel as though I had fully accepted Arron's death. I still expected him to walk in the door from an extended business trip at any moment. His closet was still full of his clothes. His dusty flip-flops were still under the back porch where I had left them, unable to put them into a garbage bag.

I browsed Match.com one day to see if it was possible to be attracted to other men. I found a widowed Manhattan architect who loved to garden. My imagination took over. He would understand my loss. We would go to sweet, hole-in-the-wall restaurants in the city and sip Merlot. He would take me back to his tasteful loft and. . . . My fantasy stopped there. What would happen then? Would I go home and hold Arron's imaginary hand? I pictured myself in a *Sex and the City* episode, carefree, kidless, and sexually liberated.

After a few weeks of prowling the man-site anonymously, and bolstered by my friends' and sister's encouragement, I resolved to write a profile of myself. Everything I wrote sounded ridiculous. *Tall, attractive (?), sexy (?), 9/11 widow, mother of two, hasn't dated in eighteen years, seeks handsome rich prince who loves kids and is not afraid of a ghostly dead husband in the closet. . . .*

My choices of photos were limited because I was always the photographer in the family. There was the coy one, with an infant Olivia standing beside my grandmother, now deceased, both of whom I would have to crop delicately out of the picture. And there was the serious one, posing primly for a corporate newsletter in a turtleneck.

Where, I wondered, were all my sexy shots? I sneaked glances at the other women's profiles, to see what I was up against. Fifty- and sixty-year-old women looked sexier than I could ever imagine being. I settled on the coy-girl-next-door-with-cropped-out-baby-and-grandma shot.

I posted my profile and photo to the website and then waited for some kind of response. Almost immediately, I got a few "winks," one from an elderly-looking gentleman claiming to be forty-four; another from a man showing his nude torso wearing fireman's hip boots and suspenders; and one from an orange-tanned jock with no neck. I was pleased to be getting winks, but disappointed by who I seemed to be attracting. I had envisioned a wink from one of the tall, dark specimens that I had already added to my "favorite" list.

Deciding to take matters into my own hands, I browsed the site as though I were in a giant man-superstore: Nice eyes, but too pudgy; funny profile, but too short; great in every way, but a smoker; tall and handsome, but doesn't want kids; wonderfully intellectual, but weird bulbous nose; sincere, but can't spell. Maybe it was too soon to be looking.

My eyes were beginning to glaze over when the widowed architect again caught my eye. I spent two weeks working up the nerve to write him an e-mail. What to say? *Hello, fellow widow person. Isn't this a strange club to belong to? I am absolutely terrified of dating and still love my dead husband, but would you consider going out with me?*

Finally, I wrote him: *Hi* [trying to sound upbeat]*! Loved your profile* [flattering the ego]. *I like to garden too* [showing common interests]. *I look forward to hearing from you* [positive, yet noncommittal]. *Regards, Abby.*

I waited for a response that never came. It was humiliating.

I retreated from the site to lick my wounds. My worst fears of being undatable were being realized. I was never going to meet someone. Perhaps deep down that is what I wanted: to remain single and widowed and forever devoted to Arron. I felt as though I might be subconsciously sabotaging my own chances by being so picky and posting a demure photo. Now I was the one who was too tall, too widowed, had too many kids, was too unsexy, too *something*. Having a dead husband seemed to be a deal breaker. Perhaps online dating wasn't going to work for me.

I considered my other options. Perhaps I should resort to the traditional bar scene: hire a babysitter, get all dressed up, and drink a gin and tonic while sitting alone on a stool. I hated the bars and clubs even when I was twenty and single and I couldn't imagine it had changed much. Even if I knew where a hip bar might be, it would likely be full of twenty-somethings.

Maybe I should join a church. (Does one "join" churches, or was it more of an initiation process?) Did single men even go to church? Now I was grasping at straws. I would never join a church.

I had heard that the grocery store was a good way to meet men, but I only ever met other moms and the grocery store pharmacist (who, come to think of it, had been getting awfully friendly lately).

I loathed the idea of letting fate take its natural course and waiting patiently for things to happen to me. If Arron's death had taught me anything, it was that there wasn't time to sit around waiting for life to happen. But I wondered why I was so desperate to have a man in my life. I was lonely, that was obvious, and I missed having an adult around to talk with and tell about my day. I envisioned someone who might provide the kids with some male influences: how to fish, roughhouse, offer some new points of view. I fantasized about how it might feel to be in love again and how my being happier would affect the kids, lightening up the stale, tomblike house. New blood in the house might also even us out, reset the balance of our lopsided family, giving us each more confidence to move forward.

Olivia still asked me regularly when she would have a "new daddy," still convinced that a man was all we needed to make us happy. Perhaps she was right. My biggest motivator to start dating, though, was my determination not to waste a moment of my life. Whatever dating might result in, from making a new friend to having a meaningful relationship (even by the dubious man-site methods), I hoped it would enrich my life. I resolved to get myself out into the world by whatever means necessary, no matter how painful it might prove to be.

After my defeat with the architect, I continued to browse the site, finally coming upon the profile of a good-looking bald man who seemed witty and could spell. From his description, I could tell he was bright, funny, and lived close by. Besides, he was one of the few who actually wrote me back. He had recently moved to Montclair from Florida and was willing to meet me for coffee.

I lay awake the night before our date trying to figure out what to wear. I made a mental note to replace my white cotton Hanes underwear. "God! No wonder Arron and I had sex so rarely. I wore Hanes undies! I still wore my nursing nightie!" This thought met with a pang of remorse. I had fallen into the mommy trap of kids and jobs, forgetting my husband, and he had done the same. I had sometimes blamed him for our infrequent sex life, which had led to my feeling insecure about my body. I had thought Arron wasn't attracted to me. Now I could see that this thinking had led me to hide my body and deny my sexual desires behind large pairs of Hanes. I wished I could rewind time and recast myself in my marriage as the sexy wife, the kind with hot lingerie and an alluring wardrobe. Now I had no clothes suitable for a date besides a pair of unflattering jeans or perhaps a skirt that I hadn't worn since I was in my twenties. I dressed like a mom, like someone who didn't care what other men thought of her. Only now did I realize that that must have included Arron. Why hadn't I seen it before? I finally opted for black slacks and boots, casual yet smart. I hoped there was something marginally flattering about the outfit and that it was appropriate for an 11:00 AM date at a local French café.

My palms were sweaty as I maneuvered the car into a space near the coffee shop the next day. Breathing deeply for a few minutes, I stared at my hands on the steering wheel, trying not to panic. Oh God! The wedding ring! I had forgotten to remove it.

I looked at my hands, admiring the chunky gold band on my left ring finger. It seemed to cling adoringly there. I slid it up my finger, revealing the shiny white skin beneath it. Hesitating, I pulled the band all the way off and held it in my hand. I had forgotten how heavy it was. I slipped it onto my right ring finger, struggling to push it over my knuckle, and held my hands out to survey the effect of this transition. Both hands felt strange and backwards, like they weren't mine at all. They seemed sad and alone—like those of a single woman.

I wiped a tear from my eye. "I'm sorry, Fab." I had betrayed Arron's love with my impulsive move, unceremoniously, sitting in a car, with just a cold, gray December sky to accompany me. I recalled a similar ring ceremony.

Arron's wedding ring had belonged to his father and his father's initials were embossed into its rose-colored gold. Though beautiful, it had proved to be problematic as a wedding ring over the years, given that Arron wore it on his left pinky finger, as his father had. "I keep getting hit on by gay men!" he declared one day. I laughed.

"Well, Mr. Homophobe, why don't we get you a regular ring, one that you wear on your ring finger." I had always wanted him to have a regular ring but had deferred to his wishes when we were married, knowing the sentimentality he had held for his father's ring since his father's death when Arron was seventeen. He immediately agreed.

On a sunny early spring Saturday, a year before his death, the kids and I had waited in this same car while Arron dashed out to the jewelers. He came back clutching a small blue velvet box. He opened it and held up the bright, shiny ring, which we had chosen together, ready to slip it onto his hand. "Shouldn't there be a little ceremony, or something?" I said.

"Okay. Here." He handed me the ring. It was a lovely gold band, strong and simple.

I slid it slowly onto his ring finger, smiling at him, and then kissed him gently when it was in place. He held up his hand and we were both pleased with the effect. I loved Arron's hands—strong, creative, sensitive, loving. The ring was beautiful and I felt proud being bound to him by it. That simple ceremony felt like an instant renewal of our love, unspoken but mutually understood.

Now, staring at my own hands, gray in the dim light of the mid-winter morning, I mourned him once more. "It's just coffee," I told myself. I fingered the strange object now on my right hand and hoped that my first-ever blind date would not notice the glaring whiteness of my loss, wouldn't see my hand shake as I held my teacup. I hoped my voice wouldn't crack when I answered the inevitable question, "So, how did he die?" I touched my ring once again for reassurance as I opened the coffee shop door.

I sat down with a tea. As soon as he walked in, I knew this date would not turn to romance. "Nick" got coffee and sat opposite me. I began to worry that one of my friends would come into the shop and wonder what I was doing having coffee with a bald man. They would know. I felt myself blush, feeling as though I was cheating on Arron. Nick told me he wanted to be a comedian, so I found myself laughing nervously at his strange jokes. There was something desperate in his humor. It was not the silly, lighthearted humor Arron had used.

"I'm in the process of writing some new material. I want to write funny things about difficult events. Like the Nazis. I think there could be some really funny stuff there."

I tried to picture something funny about Nazis but only came up with a Monty Pythonesque sketch. Was this guy serious?

We continued to talk, avoiding the obvious questions. An hour later, Nick could no longer avoid them. I could feel the walls of the maze I had backed myself into close in around me with each question.

"So, you're divorced?"

"No."

"Oh. Separated?"

"Um, no. I'm widowed."

"Oh! I'm sorry. That must have been really rough. How long ago?"

"It was about a year and a half ago." I could feel it coming, dreaded the impending question.

"So, do you mind if I ask . . . how?"

And there it was. Was I ready for the shocked look? The pity? The end of the conversation?

"He died on September 11. In the Twin Towers."

His jaw dropped and his brow furrowed. "I'm so sorry. I sort of guessed when you told me the timing. That day affected me a great deal. It's what made me move back here from Florida. I wanted to come to New York and become a teacher. I felt stuck in my software job in Florida."

"Teaching would be good," I said, hoping to change the conversation.

"Wow. That's huge. How are your kids?"

I could feel myself crawling deep inside myself, like a turtle, trying to avoid Nick's questions, trying to avoid my emotions. I wasn't angry, or annoyed with him. He was human and therefore curious. Had I heard from Arron? Which tower was he in? Did he work in the building?

"Is it okay for me to be asking you these questions?"

"Yes, it's fine," I answered him. And I realized it was. My mind had become numb, and my robot self had taken over. I could answer any question, albeit emotionlessly.

Then, as is often the case after I have told someone of my tragedy, he told me his. His older brother died when Nick was ten. "My family never talked about it. It was taboo."

"That must have been very difficult for you. . . ." And I began to understand Nick's underlying sadness. He was the younger brother who could not live up to his dead older brother. His lack of self-confidence seemed to show through his skin like rust. I felt bad for him. We became friends united in sorrow.

Over the following few weeks, Nick and I went out for dinner, a lunch, and even took Carter and Olivia to the Museum of Natural History. "As friends," I was quick to assure him, the kids, and myself. Still Olivia asked the question: "Is Nick going to be our new daddy?" It was a fun day at the museum, but I realized that I would have to be careful about introducing the kids to my dates. I also needed to be careful about what I told Selena. I mentioned one day on the phone that I had been thinking about joining Match.com. Instinctively, I didn't tell her that I had actually been on a date. I knew it was not going to go anywhere with Nick and I wasn't ready for her reaction. Up to that point I had told her everything that had been going on in my life, but for the first time I could feel myself holding back from her. She told me how difficult my dating was going to be for her.

"I guess it's normal for you to want to begin dating again," she said. "But I have to tell you it's going to break my heart when you start seeing someone."

"Why on earth would that be?" I asked, wondering if she somehow knew about my date.

"Well, for one, because it's going to be difficult for me to see you with someone who is not Arron, but also because I'm afraid that when you're with someone new, I won't be part of your lives any more." She used a strong voice, trying to sound rational, but I could hear her desperation and fear.

"Oh, Selena, that's ridiculous. You're the kids' grandma and you will always be in our lives. Even if I remarry, that will never change."

"I hope so," she said. But she didn't seem convinced. I wondered if our relationship really would change if a new man came into my life.

One afternoon, several weeks later, over a lunch of chicken tikka masala, Nick handed me a letter. He had poured out his heart. "I respect everything about you. . . . I think I might have fallen in love with you. . . ."

"Oh Nick," I stammered as I read it in front of him. "I'm sorry. I just don't feel the same way." I felt his disappointment in my bones, like it was my own.

I wondered sadly if I had given Nick anything in return other than heartache. We tried to remain friends. I got him a job in the customer service department at Audible. But then one day he abruptly quit without warning and was gone.

Janet had heard all about my forays into the dating world.

"I know Nick was not the one for you," she reasoned, "but he taught you that you are attractive to men and worthy of being loved."

She was right. Seeing myself in another man's eyes had opened my own. Going out with Nick had prompted me to buy pretty clothes, to wear more makeup, to begin to feel like I might actually be attractive, something I had forgotten about during eleven years of marriage. I had allowed myself to wallow in the doldrums of motherhood, putting kids first, husband and myself last. I was remorseful that I had not been at my best for Arron, had not provided the tiny pleasures that he might have appreciated.

18

TANTRUMS

Jill begged me to join her at my dad's in Port Hope for another Christmas. "I really want to see you and the kids and this is one of the only chances we'll have. We all need to be with family right now," she reasoned. I knew Jill had been feeling isolated in her townhouse in Pemberton. Dan worked long hours and she was alone in a very secluded place with only Caelin to keep her company. She was the one who needed family. I wasn't so sure I wanted to endure another Christmas fiasco but decided that with her and Dan's company, it would be fun.

Selena flew to New Jersey again to help me with the drive, but once we reached Port Hope, we dropped her off. "I'll call you tomorrow," I said, feeling like a traitor. She was still bitter toward my father and Sheilagh and was again hurt that we weren't staying with her. The next night, my parents, Jill, Dan, and all the kids and I spent an idyllic Christmas Eve decorating the tree, with Christmas carols playing in the background. We ate tourtière and drank wine. Later, sitting around the kitchen table, I thought of Arron and my dad the year that Arron got his Fender Stratocaster, jamming one night after dinner. Arron was playing his guitar and my dad was on his banjo and they were both hunched over a Rolling Stones songbook, plucking out the notes to "Brown Sugar." My dad sang too loudly and off key and Arron kept laughing throughout the song, trying to keep it on track. I loved the memories of Arron that were here, as agonizing as they sometimes were.

The next morning the kids woke up to a frenzy of gift-opening reminiscent of the previous year. Overflowing gifts, kids flinging packages at recipients, impossibly packaged toys. Later in the day, I bundled the kids into the car and nearly skidded off the road in a snowstorm on our way to Selena's house.

"Dammit," I said out loud. I was seething that we had to be out in these dangerous conditions.

"Mommeee!" Olivia said from the backseat, annoyed that I had sworn.

"Sorry. I'm just really mad that we have to drive to Grandma's right now. I wish she could just come to Grampa's."

"Why can't she?" Olivia asked.

"I don't know. I guess because Grampa and Sheilagh are mad at her."

"Why? Did she do something bad?"

"I'm not sure exactly." I couldn't explain it to a seven-year-old.

I hated that the kids and I were caught in the middle of their feud. Selena had told me about seeing my father and Sheilagh at several town-related functions during the past year, and how they had snubbed her, refusing to respond to her hellos. I was embarrassed by my parents' juvenile behavior. I wished they would just talk to her and tell her why they were angry with her. I knew it had to do with how Selena had seemingly taken over my life. I was still allied with her, but I was also slowly rebuilding my relationship with my mother, who had obviously been most affected by Selena's strength of will. It had taken me longer to realize that my dad and Sheilagh might have felt excluded as well. The shift in our various relationships was subtle and none of us could figure out how to manage our hurt feelings, so they festered, unspoken.

At Christmas dinner back at my dad's, a dozen of us sat around the long mahogany table wearing cheerful paper hats, anticipating turkey. My dad stood at the head of the table, carving.

When everyone had received their food, Jill stood up, raising her glass of white wine in the air. "I want to make a toast to everyone, including those that aren't here. I want to remember Arron—"

Xmas

"Hey! Who wants turkey!" my father suddenly announced, cutting Jill's speech off.

"I'll have some!" Sheilagh's voice seemed unexpectedly loud.

I looked at Jill, who sat down, deflated. There was an awkward silence as we all looked at each other, my dad and Sheilagh apparently oblivious, still passing around plates full of turkey. Jill glanced at me, shocked. "Can you believe that?" her look said. We were used to their hearing loss. We were used to making accommodations, speaking more loudly, facing them as we spoke. Had they really not heard Jill? Not seen her standing? Yet, I couldn't imagine why they would have intentionally squashed her toast to Arron. All week, it seemed that conversations with my dad and Sheilagh had been peppered with the words "move on," and talk of Arron carefully skirted. That night, I ate my turkey but tasted nothing. Messy emotions were not tolerated in this house. Instead they were carefully bottled and put down like good wine—reserved for a date far in the future, when age had mellowed their flavor.

Later, Jill ranted in the living room while my father and Sheilagh smoked cigarettes in the kitchen. "I can't believe it! Why did they do that? I was just trying to make a simple, lighthearted toast to Arron! What was the big deal?"

My anger was slower to reveal itself. During the rest of the week, I was emotionless, unable to shed a tear. I felt my jaw clench tighter and my neck began to seize.

In the car ride back to New Jersey, Selena complained bitterly about my father and Sheilagh as I drove, white-knuckled. "I thought your dad might invite me over just once since you were here. . . ." "I wish you guys would stay with me. . . ." "You stayed with your dad last year. . . ."

"I know. I'm sorry." I could feel the snakelike muscle in my neck constricting, until turning toward Selena in the passenger seat became excruciating. After eight hours in the car, Carter was becoming tired and grumpy. "When are we gonna get there?" he whined. The last remnants of dusk were turning to night as I merged onto the highway that would take us into New Jersey. I failed to see a closing lane sign and slammed on the brakes seconds before careening into a semi-tractor-trailer. We were all silent for the final half hour of the drive.

Home again, I craved time alone to think and to process my feelings, my grief, my anger. I felt like the parent, dealing with all the frightened, angry, grieving children in my life. My emotions torpedoed around inside me, producing rage. Opaque, uncontrolled, blind rage. I was angry at my dad and Sheilagh's behavior: their cold silences toward Selena, their avoiding talking about Arron or anything painful, their interrupting Jill's toast. I was also angry at Selena: her guilt trips, her disparaging remarks about my parents, her anger.

I tried to disguise my rage as grief. But grief couldn't hide all of it. Some of it was old, something I had carried around with me like a blanket for decades. Childhood frustrations and an inability to show my emotions, especially anger, stemmed from my fear of hurting someone's feelings. I was caught between my divorced parents, constantly appeasing their individual wishes, denying my own feelings in the process. My emotions were either not to be discussed (when I was with my father) or overly hurtful (to my mother). I had taken on a divorced child's guilt, trying to please both parents, not understanding that their anger was toward each other and not me.

I spent several angry days at work writing a letter to my dad and Sheilagh, trying to express my angst. I poured my rage into the letter, essentially blaming them for my grief over Arron's loss. It was their fault that their house caused me to remember Arron while they seemed to want to forget him. The letter was an irrational rant. I had no one else to be angry at. They were safe because I knew they would still love me, despite my emotional outbursts. I should never have sent the letter, but I did.

My anger spread through my family like a virus.

One night, after a particularly trying day with Carter, I longed for just an hour without his hot hands clasped around my neck, his whining, his refusal to let me out of his sight. He wouldn't go to sleep. Each time I put him down in his bed, he would wail and get up, following me. I put him back, he got up. I went downstairs to watch TV and I could hear him shuffling around upstairs in my office. I went up to find him lying on the floor, just outside the door to my room. I put him back to bed, but he continued to wail. Olivia, sleepy-eyed, came to my door.

"I'm sorry Carter is waking you up, sweetie. Go back to bed." She obeyed.

For over two hours, the pattern continued. Finally, I went to bed, closing the door against my three-year-old oppressor. He lay down outside my bedroom door, crying. I put him back in his bed and forbade him to come near my door, so he lay down on the floor outside his own bedroom.

I stood, rigid with rage, at the end of the hall. It was now 2:30 AM and Carter was sobbing. "Please, Mama, I want to come with you!" he begged. "I want to sleep in your bed!"

I was beyond coherence, beyond sanity. I was desperate to get away from him, afraid of what I might do to him if he came close to me. For the first time, I felt frightened of myself.

"Carter, go to bed! This is ridiculous! We are both exhausted!" I bellowed.

"But I scaaaarrreeed!" he wailed.

"You can't come near me!" I screamed, desperate to run away from him. "I need to be alone! Can't you understand that? Can't you see that I NEED to be alone! I am going to hurt you if you come near me! Stay away from me!" I screamed, alarming us both.

He convulsed with wails, and as I stood watching him I heard my own voice. Horrified, I crumpled to the floor, extending my arms so that he could finally come to me and get the comfort that he needed. "I'm sorry, I'm sorry, I am so sorry. . . ." I choked out between convulsive breaths.

His body made a tight little ball in my arms and slowly his hiccuping sobs melded into the heavy breaths of sleep. I eased him into my bed and tucked him under the covers. I crawled in beside him and soon I was mimicking his howls, my despair complete. I choked with tears, gritted my teeth, pulled my hair. I wanted to run away, to escape my children, to throw myself into bed and never wake up. I wanted Arron to hold me tight and tell me everything was going to be all right. He would get Carter to sleep.

The tears continued to burn, until slowly they dissipated, and I fell asleep, an empty shell.

I woke up to the sweet smell of Carter, nuzzled in the crook of my arm, reminding me of Arron's cuddles. I felt newly cleansed. I touched his soft cheek and smiled, feeling as though I had battled a demon and won back my freedom.

In the morning brightness, I reflected on my black night. I was panicked by my anger, scared that I might have actually hurt my son. I thought I had been coping, but with absolutely no break from my clinging child, I was exhausted and unable to maintain rational thought. I had lost perspective and hadn't realized that Carter and I had entered a vicious cycle of rage: to give him comfort and attention, I needed time alone to regroup and heal, time that I was never allowed to have because Carter constantly needed comfort and attention. There was no reprieve. This cycle had been ongoing and had resulted in other meltdowns on my part, but this had been the worst. Our emotional Christmas seemed to have exacerbated my feeling of being trapped by rousing my anger and physically exhausting me. It had been a long two weeks, and without Martha giving me periodic breaks from Carter's demands, I had cracked.

I knew that all parents experienced frustration. I knew other families had to endure such tantrums from their children. I knew that in some respects, Carter's behavior was normal. But the question always lingered—was this usual childhood behavior or was this Carter's way of expressing his grief? Was this anger my way of expressing my grief?

Such rages were not discussed among my parent friends. Admitting rage was like admitting to a criminal weakness. I was used to being strong. I was used to having people perceive me that way. But now I was proving to myself that there were cracks in my armor.

Carter and I continued to fight our battle of wills, which seemed to get worse over the following weeks. Like any three-year-old, he was testing his limits and mine. One afternoon, after he had hit Olivia, leaving her in tears, I gave him a time out on the stairs, but he simply stood up and walked away. I set the timer on the microwave to ensure he sat for three minutes of punishment, but he flung his body in frustration and hit his head on a step. I attempted to carry his writhing body up the stairs for a time out in his bedroom and slammed his door so hard that it flung back against the wall, leaving a hole in the plaster. I came downstairs shaking.

I stood rigid in the kitchen, jaw clenched, willing myself not to turn around and shout at Carter, who had defied me once again and come downstairs. I was convinced that if his father were alive, things would be different. I wouldn't ever be this mad. Carter would be more docile. Arron would have ruled with an iron fist or jostled him out of his angry moods with giggles. Carter would have been secure about his place in the family. He would have clearly understood his limits, his responsibility to treat everyone with respect.

But Arron was not here and at that moment I hated him for leaving us. I hated him for not allowing us to be like other families, whole, complete. I hated him for leaving his children with the constant fear that their only living parent might not return to pick them up. I hated him for causing his kids to feel uncertain and insecure by being different from their peers. I hated him for leaving us all with our insidious anger, which burned even a year and a half after his death. I hated being angry with him, blaming him for his own death.

Several days later, after another night's battle getting Carter to bed, my heart told me that this was not a war that would be won or lost. My anger was volcanic, erupting, magma-grief that had nowhere to go but up and out, destroying all in its path. The next day I had an emergency meeting with Janet.

"Anger is a typical response to difficult, emotional events." I drank in her rationale.

"But I scared myself," I pleaded.

"I understand. You're in a difficult situation. You're human. You're not a bad mother because you had a temper tantrum at your son." I folded and refolded my seventh Kleenex, using it to catch the tears as they spilled off my chin. The others, all soaked, were piled neatly on my lap.

"How do I make it better between Carter and me?"

"You're going to have to retrain him."

"How?"

"First, you will have to set consistent limits for him. When you say 'no,' don't say yes after he begs and begs. Don't raise your voice. Say 'no,' in a quiet voice. As soon as you raise your voice, you've lost the battle."

"Okay. I think I can do that." I could feel myself being bolstered by the practical advice. The tears stopped.

"If you need to give him a time out, do it consistently and calmly. If you set him on the stairs, and he gets up, simply walk him back without saying a word. Keep doing it until he stays. Same with bedtime. Just keep putting him back in his bed until he stays. Don't engage in conversation with him. Just explain calmly that it is time for him to go to bed now."

"That makes sense."

"Consistency and follow-through. Be consistent with your punishments and follow through with what you say. If you tell him that he will have a time out if he keeps hitting Olivia, and then he doesn't get one even after hitting her, he learns that you don't really mean what you say."

Janet's instructions were clear. I left feeling renewed, like I finally had the tools to take on my three-year-old. That night, after I put Carter to bed, he cried and came into my room. Without a word, I took his hand and led him back to his bed. He cried harder and came back out. This time I was waiting in the hall for him.

"It's time for bed," I said gently as I tucked him back in. I don't know how many times he came out of his room that night, or the next, but he soon got the picture and resorted to yelling "Mooommmmmeeeee!" from his bed. I ignored him. It wasn't perfect every night, and he still had difficulty getting to sleep, but it did get easier. We both calmed down and the angry nights became less frequent. I got better at saying no when he begged me for things, and sticking with it, even if it meant a tantrum in the grocery store.

Using the same tools, I also handled my own anger and frustration better. I learned to give myself time outs when I felt the steam rising in my ears, retreating to my bedroom to bite my pillow.

"My bear is coming out!" I warned the kids if I felt myself being pushed too far. The kids knew what this meant and to my amazement stopped whatever behavior had prompted it. I growled aloud my frustrations and felt better.

But old habits die hard. I tried to accept my imperfect, growling mothering.

I hoped my children would forgive me for my continuing rages. I tried to forgive the kids for theirs. The question remained whether I could forgive myself.

Comfort Zone Camp began offering an overnight camp at a YMCA campsite in New Jersey and that spring Olivia was old enough to attend. She had loved the two other one-day sessions that we had attended since that first one in Montclair. Carter, however, hated the nursery and I was growing weary of the adult support sessions. We sat in circles under the fluorescent lighting of suburban schoolrooms, passing boxes of tissues. Although the sessions were mediated, there was always one person who seemed to need more attention than the rest of us. Each time anyone expressed a difficulty, such as one widow's inability to sleep alone in her house, the attention-seeker would turn the discussion to herself. "I know what you mean! I have the same problem!"

Although I could do without the weepy "closing ceremony" songs, it was still intoxicating to watch hundreds of balloons float into the sky, and cathartic to imagine Arron getting messages from his children: "I miss you daddy."

But I eventually began to feel that my tears were being yanked from me against my will at the support sessions with sad stories and women who still seemed stuck in their early grief. I heard stories of women who still couldn't get out of bed, who were frightened to leave the house, or whose children were struggling through school. I was pleased to realize that I had moved past these stages. Despite my lapses with Carter, I could see that I was moving forward, finding a new path. One of the rules in the sessions was not to offer advice, and so I had to bite my tongue at times. "Get out of bed!" I wanted to scream. "Go outside and see the sun rise!" But I knew that each person would move ahead at her own pace.

Olivia came alive after each session, finishing the day with a smile on her face, having finally unburdened herself of her pent-up grief. She had a place where she could talk about her dad and how she was feeling. She had found a place where she saw that it was all right to cry. She began to learn that she could cry and be sad and still be a happy person. Despite her initial cheerfulness, I had to brace myself after each session for a difficult week of bickering and whining, homework tantrums, and contentious bedtimes while Olivia raged, something I was learning was a guaranteed result of expressing the emotions of our loss, not just for Olivia, but for all of us.

I was thrilled when she turned seven and could begin attending the overnight sessions. It meant that Carter and I no longer needed to participate. Each child was paired with a volunteer buddy, often someone who had also suffered the loss of a close family member. They spent the entire weekend together, eating, sleeping, and buoying each other through "Healing Circles," where they talked about their loved ones and their loss, cried openly, and explored their emotions. For Olivia, this was her safe place where she could talk to other kids who understood and were experiencing the same emotions that she was having.

One bright April Sunday, Carter and I arrived to pick up Olivia from her weekend. We found her being pushed on the swing by her buddy, Kim, who had been Olivia's big buddy at the previous day-long session. Kim welcomed us with a flash of her white smile and a flick of her strawberry-blonde hair. She was as tall as I was and about my own age, with an infectious vivaciousness that belied her history. She had been through more than I could fathom anyone experiencing in a lifetime. By the time she was nine, both her parents had died from illness and her older brother was raising her and her younger brother. In 1998, her younger brother and her nephew were killed in a car accident. The family seemed to be cursed. Despite her losses, she was still a happy person, always giggling, something I found inspiring. I watched Kim, seeing a future Olivia. Kim and I instantly liked each other and I could tell that this was going to become an important friendship for Olivia and perhaps for Kim and me as well.

Olivia was squealing with delight from the heights of the swing and she pretended not to see me, not ready to give up Kim's exclusive attention. Carter ran over to an empty swing and began swinging face down, his hands and feet touching the ground.

Kim walked over to me. "Hi!" she said, giving me a big hug. "Hi Carter!" She waved at Carter, who was now rubbing his hands in the dirt under the swing. "We had an amazing weekend. Olivia really opened up. She talked a lot about her dad. At one healing circle, where we sit with our healing group and tell our stories, we both cried a ton."

"Really? She never cries with me." I was relieved that Olivia had opened up to her, though I had to admit that I was a little bit jealous. I wished Olivia could open up to me in the same way.

"She thinks you'll be upset if she does." I knew this, but it was hard hearing it from Kim. Olivia finally jumped from the swing and ran up to me and gave me a great big hug. Something in her had changed. She seemed lighter and strangely confident.

"I missed you," I said.

"Me, too, Mama."

I smiled as I watched her walk off toward the dining hall with Kim, pleased that Olivia had found such a good friend. Kim got it. Olivia had spent the weekend being heard and understood.

Each child-buddy team that wanted stood up and performed during the closing ceremony. Some simply played their loved one's favorite song on a CD player, others recited poems, and some sang songs. Each was more heartbreaking than the next and I swallowed back tears several times. Boxes of tissues were passed among the audience of parents, volunteers, and kids. Olivia was shy about performing, so opted out, but she and Kim got up as part of their healing group. Each child held up a hand-drawn letter, their loved one's initial. One by one they recited something they remembered about them. Olivia looked at me nervously and turned to Kim, who put her hands on Olivia's shoulders and bent down to whisper something in her ear. When it was Olivia's turn, she turned again to Kim, who smiled, and Olivia stepped forward.

"'A' is for Arron who loves olives. That's how he named me. My name means an olive bush." Olivia stepped back and Kim hugged her. This time I couldn't prevent a tear from escaping.

When they were all done, I clapped vigorously. Olivia sat down and gave me a sheepish look. I gave her a thumbs-up sign.

After another heart-wrenching sing-along and the balloon whoosh, it was time to head home. Kim helped us carry Olivia's things to the car.

"Will you be my buddy, too?" I asked her, smiling.

Kim giggled. "Sure. We will definitely stay in touch."

"Maybe you can come over for dinner sometime."

"I would love that!" Kim said, as she gave me a big hug.

"I can't thank you enough. Olivia seems to have had a really great weekend. She seems lighter somehow, happier, I guess."

"Well, it's been amazing for me, too. She's a really amazing kid, Abby."

"I know," I said, smiling at her. I busied myself getting Carter into the car while Olivia and Kim said their good-byes. By now they were both crying and I was trying not to watch them, holding back my own tears. We got in the car and waved good-bye to Kim, all of us crying as we drove away.

"When will I be able to see Kim again?" Olivia asked.

"I don't know, sweetie. We'll call her soon."

"Can we call her when we get home?"

I looked in my rearview mirror and saw the tears falling down her cheeks. "Oh, Mousie. I know you're going to miss her." I tried to swallow my own tears. Olivia sobbed the entire two hours it took to get home. I had never seen Olivia cry this way before. She howled. And it didn't let up. It was her first real emotional release since her father's death. When we got home, although it was frightening and painful to watch her, I just held her, knowing how good it was for her to let it out. My tears mingled with hers. At first she seemed concerned. "Why are *you* crying?" she asked.

"Because I know how sad you are, and how much you're going to miss Kim." This made us both weep harder. Finally, later that night, we called Kim. My voice wavered as I told Kim of our afternoon. "Olivia has bawled for four hours straight. I've never seen her do anything like that before. You two really connected, didn't you?"

"Yes." I could hear Kim's voice wavering as she swallowed back tears, and I was on the verge once again.

"I cried all the way home, too," she admitted. "I had no idea how emotional this experience was going to be."

"No, me neither. But I think it's been a huge turning point for Olivia." Olivia took the phone and I left her alone to sob into it with Kim.

In the weeks that followed, Olivia seemed more confident. She began working harder in school and began to have a few successes in some of her math and reading tests. She decided she wanted to join a soccer team with her friends. She giggled and joked around more.

Kim became like an aunt to the kids and a sister to me. We spent the occasional evening drinking red wine while the kids pulled her by the hand into their rooms to show her their latest treasures. I sat with her and listened while she cried during a breakup with her boyfriend and then tried to be there during her older brother's cancer treatments, and again when he ultimately succumbed to cancer, leaving his own twelve-year-old daughter fatherless. Kim's tragedies seemed never-ending. I marveled at her strength. Despite feeling downtrodden by life, she was secure in the knowledge that whatever losses life threw at her, she could weather them and become even stronger. She passed her strength on to us all.

19

SHEDDING SKIN

One morning at work, tea in hand, I opened my e-mail and was confronted with a note from my boss, Rob, that began "Abby, I am really disappointed in your performance. . . ." I had forgotten to get his approval on a specification, which subsequently caused a delay when a problem was found in some programming. His words stung. Rob was an inconsistent boss, one who yo-yoed between micro- and macromanagement of his staff, but I had always respected him. He was smart and I had learned a lot from him. In the past I had tried hard to please him, but lately I seemed to do nothing but annoy him.

A year after returning to Audible, he had asked me to resume my old position as Web Project Manager. It meant upping my three-day week to four days but also more pay. I had finished the small project that I had initially been hired to do and had begun working on small parts of the website. I felt ready to take on more responsibility at work and was eager to reclaim the old, reliable person I once was. I wanted to get back to a job I had once loved and feel the flushes of success I had once felt. I worried that a four-day week would be too much for both the kids and me, but I was enjoying my adult days at work and the break it gave me from my kids' unrelenting demands.

I accepted the position and moved back into the other side of the office, the living side. I immediately began writing a functional specification for a new search engine for the site. It was a daunting task and my concentration wandered frequently. As I wrote, I would remember e-mails that I had forgotten to send, or I would get a phone call or an instant message and forget what I had been doing. Interest rates dropped and soon I was refinancing my mortgage, the search engine forgotten by the stack of mortgage applications that accumulated on my desk. I no longer seemed able to prioritize my tasks. I had lost my powers of concentration. I would walk over to speak with a programmer but get asked a question by the designer and would forget my initial quest. My list of tasks seemed shorter than it had in the past and it worried me, knowing that it meant I was forgetting things. I stared at my list trying to remember what I was supposed to be doing.

Soon a complete site redesign was added to my plate. I sought and interviewed freelance designers, finally settling on a woman whom I ultimately hired for a full-time position. I worked to determine the reconfiguration of hundreds of pages. Developers and programmers were frequently in my office asking questions about things that I had neglected to include in my instructions, which would have been complete and concise in the old days. I worried about my ability to do my job, and only three months into it, with the redesign on my plate, my fears were being realized.

Rob had taken to deriding me publicly during meetings. "Abby, you should know that information. . . . You're the Project Manager. . . ."

When I received the e-mail, I reread it twice before crumpling into hot, embarrassing tears. I called Janet, who agreed to see me an hour later, and I slunk out of the office without a word to anyone, feeling broken. I was ashamed that so little could turn me into an emotional mess. Rob's e-mail confirmed my own disappointment in myself. I wanted to love my job again, to feel unconquerable as

I once had. I wanted to feel that sense of pride again.

Instead I retreated to Janet's basement therapy room in tears in the middle of a workday.

"How badly do you need to work . . . ?" Janet let the question hang.

"I can't quit. . . ." As I said the words, I was aware how hollow they sounded. "What would I do about health insurance?"

"I know you can find a way if you really want to, Abby." In my despair there was hope. I played hooky for the rest of the day and took myself to see the movie *Chicago*. I sulked, feeling wronged. I wanted Rob to feel punished by my absence.

I pondered the idea of quitting for several weeks before knocking on the office door of Don, Audible's feisty, bearded founder.

"I'm tendering my resignation," I said quietly, hunched in a chair in front of his desk. I watched his surprise turn to acceptance.

"May I ask why?"

"To be honest, I just don't feel capable of doing a good job. I used to love this job and be good at it, but now I can't concentrate. I'm scattered and I'm disappointing everyone, including myself."

"I understand, Abby. I know you have to do what you have to do, but we'll all be sad to see you go. What will you do?"

"I don't know exactly, but I'm thinking of writing a book about my experiences." Don had begun his career in journalism and had written a couple of books before starting Audible. I knew he would appreciate my choice of careers.

"That's wonderful, Abby. Good luck."

For the following month, I continued to work, to launch the redesigned site. I was excited about the relaunch and was happy with the new designs. The redesign was something that I had wanted since I had begun working for Audible three years earlier and I was determined to see it to fruition and leave Audible on a high note. But I was nervous about leaving my job, both financially and mentally. I would soon have to pay full price for health coverage, and I would lose my salary. My finances were going to have to adjust. I also worried that I would be bored being home full-time, but I placated myself with my fantasies about writing. I had no idea if I even *could* write, or if it would quickly become boring, but it felt like my story was desperate to be put onto a page, and I had been waking up periodically with entire paragraphs drafted in my head.

I knew the time was right to say good-bye to Audible, and I felt good about leaving the site newly designed. A week after a successful launch, I sipped green-apple martinis at a combined site launch and farewell party. Another long-time employee, a developer I had worked with for three years, was also leaving the company. It felt like the proper end of an era. As I stood in the door of my empty office, I said a final farewell to the person I once was, then carted my boxful of office supplies to the car for the last time.

That evening, the night of Canada Day, I had my second blind date. It had been six months since Nick disappeared. "Brian" and I had met online two weeks before and I had spent my final days at work writing jovial e-mails to him, full of silly, flirting wit. He was a boyish-looking thirty-two-year-old with two small boys and was recently separated from his wife. I was attracted to his large academic vocabulary, his sense of humor, and his puppyish brown eyes.

I was late for our date at a restaurant and then giggled too much, thanks to the two farewell martinis. We laughed and talked and drank wine and ate marvelous French cuisine. We clearly had what so many Match.com profiles called "chemistry." I felt an unfamiliar longing to touch his hand, to feel the electricity pass between us. Later, by my car, we stood like awkward teenagers, not knowing if we should kiss each other goodnight, each knowing that if we did we might not be ready for the consequences.

Summer holidays kept us from seeing each other again for two weeks, and in that time, something in me had come alive, and I ached for this man to touch me. Like a sixteen-year-old, I dreamed of our first kiss, which finally came after an intimate dinner of vegetarian Indian food. It was full of electricity and promise. The inevitable question of sex was just around the corner.

But a second annual girls' weekend to Montreal interceded, and I found myself giggling over wine, telling Jocelyn and Jacquie about Brian, and getting their opinions on a pink skirt and jacket combo at Les Ailes de la Mode for an upcoming trip to London. Selena and I had been invited to visit the Prince of Wales's gardens at his home, Highgrove House in Gloucestershire. I was feeling indulgent. I was in the first flush of lust with Brian. I was having a weekend without my kids, drinking wine on a Saturday afternoon with two wonderful friends. I was about to head to London at the invitation of Prince Charles. Selena and I had been invited along with the Bali bombing victims' families—one of the privileges of tragedy. It was an opportunity, we decided, that could not be missed, though it seemed crazy given that we had also planned to spend the second anniversary of 9/11 in London. It meant two trips to London in six weeks.

A week after returning home, Brian and I had a polite third date, before rushing back to his apartment, where he brought his fingers to my cheek tenderly and then ran his hands through my hair. My body trembled and my muscles felt rubbery, a long-forgotten feeling. His lips against mine tasted sweet, tangy. But I held back. It was only our third date. I had rules, from an unknown place, from unknown authorities. It was not quite two years since Arron's death; I chastised myself—too soon.

I peeled myself away from his tight embrace and kissed my farewell, a longing, thankful kiss. I went home and hugged myself as I dreamed of more. Arron was far away.

I surrendered to Brian completely only a few nights later after a prelude of slow dancing to Stevie Wonder in my living room while Carter and Olivia slept upstairs. We swayed together and kissed again softly until finally, impatient, I grabbed his hand and pulled him upstairs. I held his warm body against my own and breathed him in, quenching a thirst, relieving a hunger. The tears

I had expected came, but not for the reasons I had imagined. These tears were joyful, relieved, fulfilled. The loss inside me was, for the moment, lightly patched and temporarily healed.

I had thought the first time I had sex after Arron's death I would weep and feel remorse, guilt, and sadness—that is, *if* I were ever to make love again. Instead, I was rocked sideways by my own desire, fervor, and heat, the persistent ache of my loneliness forgotten, or perhaps soothed. My new partner, equally willing, had endured two years of unrequited love from his soon-to-be-ex-wife.

In the ensuing weeks, we wrote more flirty e-mails full of desire. He wrote me a poem. *Is this a phoenix love we have, rising from the ashes of other lives and other loves to clutch life as it passes?* We mooned at each other over more vegetarian Indian meals and I found myself in a lustful relationship, based not on reality, but on a sleepy, hazy, live-in-the-moment dreamscape.

I met his six- and three-year-old boys for the first time at the park and watched as they wheeled around on their bikes, my own kids getting ice cream with Martha instead of me. I felt like a traitor. We didn't hold hands in public, hiding our connection from his kids and people who might know us, but he sat close to me on the park bench. I became annoyed when his six-year-old kept yanking him away from me. "C'mon, Daddy. Push me on the swing." Brian turned back to look at me apologetically.

A week later our kids met for a playdate at our house. "These are our 'new friends,'" I told Carter and Olivia. They were happy to have playmates for the afternoon. Another day we piled our kids into our respective cars and convoyed to the beach, a Brady Bunch family. When Brian's kids were with his wife, he would ride over to my house on his recumbent bike and teach me to make dinners of mung beans to suit his vegetarian diet. He taught Carter and Olivia how to scoop the fruit from a kiwi and to open a pomegranate and warned of the perils of McDonald's, a warning that has endured. Occasionally his kids came over, devouring my hot dogs and Oreos. No Newman-Os or veggie dogs at *my* house. He was a natural teacher and I began to watch in fear as my kids hung from his shoulders and sat happily in his lap. I was still just dating Brian and I was uncertain of where it might lead, but I could tell the kids were getting used to having him around.

"Are you going to be our new daddy?" Olivia asked him one night. I took a deep breath, feeing certain then that I should have waited to introduce them to Brian.

"Nah, your mom and I are just good friends," Brian said with a twinkle in his eye as he winked at me. I was pleased to see them happily engaging with a man, a solid father figure. They craved male company, something that was sorely lacking in our lives, but I worried suddenly that they might get hurt if we were to break up. Another lost man. Better to know a wonderful man, I consoled myself, than to be sheltered from him for fear of his loss.

Sleepovers proved another puzzle. At first, it seemed natural for my children to find a man in my bed in the mornings, because they used to find Arron there. But I began to realize that finding their dad in his bed was different to finding Brian there. Carter would stand beside the bed to demand, "I want chocolate milk!" instead of crawling into bed with me. Could lust make me blind to the emotional needs of my children? No doubt I had scarred them for life, ensuring therapy sessions into their twenties. But slinking around after hours seemed sinister, dishonest. Brian's children were safe from confusion, as we never slept at his house.

In late July, I left Carter and Olivia in the care of my mother and reluctantly parted from Brian at the Newark airport. The following day, Selena and I pulled into the driveway at Highgrove House for a garden tour. For forty-five minutes, we walked around the estate and encountered some of the most exquisite gardens I have ever had the pleasure of visiting. I was particularly taken with an area known as "the stumpery," a series of overturned tree stumps planted with a woodland garden. In the "kitchen garden," a brick-walled enclosure the size of a lawn-bowling field that supplied the entire estate plus the local food bank, Selena leaned over a low fence and picked a pea pod from one of the plants.

"A souvenir," she giggled as she put it in her jacket pocket.

After the tour Selena and I sipped Pims in the Orangery, a large hall built by the Prince to house the many tours and events he conducted on the estate. We waited in a casual group of British 9/11 and Bali bombing victims' families for our turn to meet the Prince. I hated the doleful look on his face as he spoke with other families, one I was sure he had practiced on his visits with the poor AIDS orphans in Africa or the lepers in Asia.

When it was our turn, Selena thrust at the Prince the pea pod she had pilfered from his garden. "I stole this. I hope you don't mind."

"Ah, yes. From this garden, is it?" He seemed mildly amused. He was smaller than I had imagined but more dignified than in pictures. It was clear he was very intellectual and I was surprised to find myself admiring him. Selena peppered him with questions about the garden and his boys. Pictures of the day show me looking resigned (or maybe annoyed), standing slightly behind Selena as she and the Prince engaged in lively conversation. I waited politely to ask him about his garden, something he was clearly passionate about. A break in conversation never came.

"I loved the stumpery!" I managed to stammer as he walked away to talk with another family. He turned and waved at me. Our time allotment was over, consumed by the pea.

2003

I returned to New Jersey feeling energized by the trip, and for a while during August my relationship with Brian seemed to flourish. My car followed his as we drove down the highway on the way to another all-kids excursion, and I could see his head bobbing to music or occasionally turning around to talk with his sons. We would eat picnics in the park and steal kisses when the kids ran off to play.

He took us on a tour of Yale, his alma mater, showing us his room just off the main quad, and we watched the kids running together through the expansive park opposite. We huddled together in Brian's favorite vegetarian restaurant, while I coaxed Carter to eat a veggie burger and Olivia scrunched her nose at the smell of the artichoke quiche.

Brian was patient and caring toward all of us. I still had many melancholy moods, which he seemed willing to indulge. I talked at length about Arron, no doubt ad nauseam, but Brian didn't complain. He hugged me tighter and looked into my eyes, thirsty and reverent. I sometimes tried to imagine what our life might be like together— one large car, four children—but the image never quite came.

We both had messy lives. We both knew that we were holding each other back from dealing with them. Because of his desire to be near me in New Jersey, he was refusing to settle the terms of his divorce and the custody of his children with his wife, who wanted to move to Connecticut. They spent long weekly meetings with a mediator trying to work things out. I wasn't yet ready to commit so seriously to a man who would sacrifice what was best for him and his kids to be with me, so I began to pull away.

I was able to find some needed breathing space from him by traveling to London once again, with Selena, Olivia, and Carter for the second anniversary of September 11. The ceremony took place in Grosvenor Square, where folding chairs had been set in rows before a large wooden arbor surrounded by a quintessentially English cottage garden. Inside the arbor was a wall of bronze with the names of the 9/11 victims impressed large enough to read from where we sat. During the ceremony, the kids dressed in their finery with Selena sitting between them, we enjoyed a poem read by Judi Dench and listened to a few speeches given by Princess Anne and a variety of consular officials. I took a deep breath, soaking in the serenity of the scene before me. But then I glanced at Selena as she tried to hug the kids simultaneously in an odd grasp, one whose apparent intention was to mark her claim on them, one that seemed meant to depict her grief as more devastating than anyone else's. Olivia, sitting next to me, gave me a pleading look. Selena's strange, needy hug annoyed me. Her grief at this anniversary seemed as fresh and raw as it had been a year ago. In fact, she seemed as grief stricken over Arron now as she had been in 2001. As I worked to let grief go, she seemed to cling more tightly to it, like a drowning person clings to a rescuer. In the past year, our bonds had been loosening, and I knew I was drawing away from her, calling less often, only now telling her with trepidation about my dating Brian. While on the trip, I had had to defend an article that Brian had sent me through e-mail, which discussed how many of the 9/11 widows were dating and even marrying.

"I can't believe he would send this to you now, while you are here in London!" she said. I realized too late my mistake in showing it to her.

"Brian is just missing me, I guess."

"It's totally insensitive. I really don't like this guy for you, Abigail."

I couldn't tell if she was threatened by my dating, by Brian himself, or by the article.

I had been suggesting to Selena that she find a grief therapist but it was something she felt she could not afford. At my suggestion, she had begun working with the Red Cross, which was able to find her a free therapist, but the woman lived an hour and a half away by car. Despite the long weekly commutes, Selena persevered and she seemed to be getting stronger, our conversations more forward-facing. But on this trip Selena appeared to be sliding back into her grief and I wished there was something I could do. I hoped it was just a temporary effect of yet another anniversary.

After the garden ceremony, each family was given a single white rose to place onto an oval engraved in the cement floor of the entryway to the garden, which had been inscribed with a poem in a spiralling string of words. The roses piled up on top of the inscription, obscuring it. "Love" and "Time" were the only words I could make out.

Selena's brother Laurie and his family had traveled from Wakefield in northern England for the service, as had Arron's paternal uncle Ted and his wife, Shirley. I wandered the garden with Kirsty, my cousin who lived in Windsor, and her thirteen-year-old daughter Cleo. Some of our group stood by Arron's name on the hand-forged bronze wall. "Beautiful," I heard Arron's Uncle Ted say. I sat on a bench with Olivia and Carter, tickling them out of their boredom. "I wanna go!" Carter begged. We were all sick of memorials.

Afterward, we stood sipping wine near a circle of people speaking in hushed tones with Princess Anne. Carter and Olivia chased pigeons, a skill that Arron had taught them on the long white sandy beaches of the Jersey shore. The group suddenly shifted with a squawk and I turned just in time to see Carter barreling through them on his pigeon quest, practically knocking the Princess to the ground. I turned away, letting Kirsty be his mother. "Carter! You must watch out for all the people!" Princess Anne's lips pursed tightly.

For dinner that night, Kirsty and Cleo, and David, Selena's nephew, Olivia, Carter, and I went to an elegant restaurant with white tablecloths and crystal wine glasses. I had met David only once before, when he was ten. Seeing him for the first time as an adult, I had to stop myself from staring at him. He was the twin of Arron in his early twenties. I felt transported back to my early courtship with Arron and was horrified at my urge to grab David's hand. Carter refused to move from David's lap.

After my four-day tour of London, something between Brian and me began to shift. Perhaps it was a seed of doubt that Selena had planted over the article Brian had sent, or the effect that September always seemed to have on me, but small things about Brian started to annoy me. His vegetarian smell, grassy like hay, and his big brown eyes, just a few months ago so alluring, now seemed cow-like. The stares he received riding his recumbent bike around

239

town wearing his floppy sun hat, protecting his delicate complexion, began to embarrass me. I found myself buying him clothes to augment his university professor's worn and unflattering wardrobe and to expose his muscular physique. But slim-fitting sweaters could not mask our differences. I ate steaks on the nights that I didn't see him. I gleefully fed his kids hot dogs whenever they arrived at our house. "When in Rome," he took to saying, to rationalize their defection.

I had tried not to fall into the trap of comparisons that I thought was the pitfall of dating after widowhood. I celebrated every difference of character with glee. I loved this man's velvet lips and luscious kisses, so unlike Arron's. I admired his patient fathering, his kind, gentle mannerisms. I loved that he was encouraging me to begin writing. But soon I became annoyed with him for not being Arron. I missed Arron's giggles, his silly sense of humor, his cockiness.

I had managed to convince myself that I had easily accepted this new person into my life, and in doing so I had created an ersatz husband. But it was Arron I wanted. It was a cliché, but no one quite lived up to Arron. I knew I had the capacity to love someone else, but I was frightened that my subconscious would always find a way to sabotage any new relationship. I was terrified that I would spend my life alone.

In the weeks after the second anniversary of Arron's death, my crying jags worsened. Arron began to slide his ghostly form more securely between Brian and me.

I began to smell Brian's desperation in his more frequent night visits, in the words in his e-mails, in his poems.

> Morning brings light, memory, shame.
> That we betray another's name,
> Hunger sated, thirst slaked,
> Cannot divine if hearts have faked.

"I really think you need to get out of this house," Brian said to me one night. "I think it's holding you back."

"You may be right." I busied myself trying to adjust the thermostat. I was cold, now that October had arrived. "I know I'll have to move at some point, I can see that." This house, which had once been comforting because of all the reminders of Arron, now felt claustrophobic. Having Brian in the house intensified the feeling. I knew Brian was right, but I also knew he wanted to persuade me to move to wherever it was his wife wanted him to go. "I do want to move on, but I don't think I'm quite ready yet." I knew he could read between the lines. I would not be moving to Connecticut with him.

Several weeks later, after the kids were in bed, Brian and I snuggled on the couch, watching a movie. I traced his hands languidly with my finger and then I played with his ear, stroking it, distractedly as I always had, contented and happy. But then he turned toward me and I froze with the realization that it was not Arron's fingers that I caressed, not his ear that I held. I had anticipated the familiar ski slope of Arron's nose, the jovial, loving gleam in his eyes, but instead I encountered a stranger's features—fearful and unsure, imploring me to disclose my thoughts. I recoiled.

"Are you okay?" he asked.

How could I tell Brian that I had mistaken him for my dead husband? How could I explain that after five months of intimacy a kinetic memory had overtaken me, allowing me to behave toward him the way I had with my husband of nearly eleven years? I had longed for companionship and intimacy, but now that I had it, it felt false. I could no longer pretend to Brian that I didn't miss Arron. The reality was that it was Arron's ear I longed to caress. How could I tell Brian that in that instant I had realized my mistake: I was not yet ready to love another.

I felt something akin to heartache, a dull ache of regret and immense sadness for Brian, who wanted nothing more than my love.

"Are you okay?" he asked again.

"Yes. Just a sad memory," I said as I pulled my hand away from his ear.

But for me, something had suddenly changed. Brian had become Brian.

20

SLEEPLESS IN SEATTLE

I n the calm after the storm of the second anniversary and the whirlwind visits to London, I was finally able to sit in Arron's black swivel office chair facing my brand new Mac and begin to write. Brian, a writer, had inspired me to give in to a yearlong urge. I wrote "September 11, 2001," at the top of the page and made it bold. I needed to unlock my stories, stories that I wanted my children to know. I hoped that in writing down the last two years I could let them go, secure in the knowledge that they would never be lost, and thus that Arron would be preserved forever. I wrote what I could remember. I wrote whatever flew to my fingertips, amazed by the speed at which the pages filled. Sometimes large salty tears would fall onto the computer's shiny silver surface and I would smear them away, annoyed that they were slowing me down but glad for their scouring effect.

As I began my writing, I discovered a class for 9/11 widows being offered by Tuesday's Children, an organization founded by a man whose brother died on September 11. His goal was to help children, including his own nieces and nephews, who were directly affected by the tragedy. He began by offering families free Mets tickets and expanded to offer tickets to other events. The kids and I attended a Father's Day event at the Jersey Shore where a row of sad mothers stood in the sand watching our orphaned children build sandcastles. "Crappy day, eh?" was about as far as our small talk would take us. Tuesday's Children provided a lunch of grilled hamburgers and hot dogs, the male volunteers at the barbecues reminding us of what we had lost. I took the kids to a Mets game where I did my best to explain the rules. There was a Christmas event at a fire station in Manhattan where the kids decorated cookies and sat on Santa's lap inside a fire truck.

I learned about the class from a brochure mailed to me by Tuesday's Children. They were offering a course called "Creative Insights," intended to encourage 9/11 widows to find a way to move forward with their lives by tapping into their creativity. The next course was to be held in ten sessions in New Jersey, meeting every other week from ten to two-thirty, starting in October 2003. I immediately signed up.

The first classes were held in the nondescript boardroom of a New Jersey company located in an office park just off the Garden State Parkway. Thirteen 9/11 widows stood at one end of the room, pouring coffee, picking at muffins, and murmuring shy hellos. Julia and Athena stood up and introduced themselves as our guides. "In finding your hidden talents, your creativity, you will learn to open up new aspects of yourselves and find new ways to live your life!" Julia's exuberance was intoxicating. Her background as a corporate leadership trainer fit her energetic style. She bounced around the front of the room, raising her arms in the air to demonstrate her conviction.

"Life is about living your dreams, and we are going to teach you how!" Athena's dancerlike hands seemed to scatter magic dust around the room. Her fluttery blonde hair and upturned, mischievous eyes gave her an ethereal and slightly fairylike quality, easily convincing us all that anything was possible. I drank in every word.

Our homework for the following two weeks was to "live our lives with no expectations," which would let us be open to possibilities and give us confidence in our abilities to adapt to new situations. I realized that I was guilty of harboring expectations everywhere I went. I had expected we would toast Arron when I went home for Christmas. I had expected Selena would recover from her grief at the same pace as me. I had expected that my relationship with Brian would turn out happily ever after. I had expected that I could be a good mother all on my own. But my expectations were unrealistic. They did not take into account the fallibility and imperfections of others, or of myself. As I drove home after the class, I realized that I was hard on other people because of these expectations. My mother, my dad, Sheilagh, Selena. I realized that my anger at them stemmed from my unspoken expectations of how they should behave, how they should grieve, how they should care for me. Each of us was muddling our way through our grief. I needed to stop assuming that their grief would match my own in its length or its expression. I needed to be kinder and gentler with the people in my life and accept that I could not prescribe their behavior. We were all equally fallible.

I stepped from the car, feeling freer and calmer than I had in a long time. I thought of how I could apply the "no expectations" rule to other situations: social events, future Christmases, how I cared for my own children. Of course, it would be impossible to eradicate all expectations, but I was beginning to see the freedom that this could bring to my life.

Our next "live with" was to observe our "V.O.J.," our voice of judgment. This voice was our inner critic, who blamed and shamed and discouraged us from experimenting. My own V.O.J. had been telling me for a year that I couldn't write, that I didn't know what to write or how to write it, thereby preventing me from writing at all. It wasn't until Janet suggested I just *write* that I actually began the process, and finally I simply started from the beginning, not caring what came, having no expectations and no judgments about what I wrote.

Christmas 2003 at Jill and Dan's house was decidedly jolly. We went to the French caterer in Squamish and bought our traditional tourtière and a buttery Bouche de Noel. Jill's Christmas present to Olivia was to have her ears pierced and we all sat and watched as Olivia stoically endured the gun and came away looking grown-up in her sparkly pink studs. Jill taught Olivia a crazy Ethel Merman version of "Rudolph the Red-Nosed Reindeer," kicking her leg up backwards during a pause after the word Rudolph, which had us all in hysterics. Caelin and Carter bounced naked on a mattress on the floor.

After Christmas, the kids and I drove to Seattle to see Deirdre, Jack, and their daughter Rosemary. We walked in the door to squeals and hugs, all of us delighted to be in each other's company again. Arron and I had met Deirdre and Jack in Brussels, where Jack and Arron were the only married students attending Boston University's international MBA program. Arron and I had giggled at this tall couple as they crouched onto the bus for a tour of Brussels put on for the students. They both had enormous eyes and dazzling white-toothed smiles, and each carried a tiny chihuahua. They sat down beside us on the bus and enchanted us with their easy humor; by the time the tour was over, we were friends.

On December 30, Deirdre and I snuck out of the house, leaving the sleeping kids in Jack's care, and met up with Deirdre's friends, Michael, Kat, and Kat's boyfriend. Deirdre had told me a little about Michael. "I met him in an improv class in the summer. Very funny! I just adore him! He was divorced from his wife about two years ago. I think you'll like him because he's quite spiritual. He's a student of Pastoral Sciences at Seattle University and wants to become a minister."

"Hmmm. He sounds interesting. But a minister?" The very idea of meeting someone who might someday be a minister put fear in my heart.

"I know, it's weird. We're all trying to get him to quit."

"Why?" I asked.

"It's not him. He's just not the minister type."

Over drinks at a local bar, I sat with Michael, laughing at his improv-trained style of humor. The belly laughs were intoxicating. Brian did not make me laugh this way. I admired Michael's curly salt-and-pepper hair, almost to his shoulders, his ice-blue eyes. For some reason, it was easy to tell him my story.

"Wow. You've come a long way. And so now you're dating someone?"

"Yes, but it's been pretty rocky lately. I'm not sure I'm quite ready for a relationship."

"Do you think you'll ever love again?" Michael asked, hitting immediately on the issue that I seemed to be having with Brian.

"Yes. I'm sure I will. I know I have the capacity," I said, taking another sip of my gin and tonic as I glanced into his eyes nervously. I didn't know how the conversation had gotten so intimate.

When the bar closed at one, we walked outside to find chunky flakes falling lazily from the sky. People streamed out of bars along Pike Street and scraped up the snow into dirty balls, throwing them at one another, intoxicated by the rare Seattle snowfall. We ducked behind cars, then stealthily leaned out to wallop one another with carefully aimed lobs. We found an empty parking lot filled with virgin powder and lay down to make snow angels, and Michael and I glanced sideways at each other as we rolled lopsided lumps for the head and body of a miniature snowman. Then we made our way to Neighbors, a local gay nightclub still open, and we all spent the final hour before its close twirling each other around the dance floor. Michael grabbed my hand and pulled me onto a platform where we danced together, holding hands. Afterward, as we walked toward the car, Michael and I fell behind the group, talking. Suddenly, he pulled me into a doorway and we kissed briefly, and I could feel the rush of excitement throughout my body.

Deirdre soon came looking for us. "Ahem! Are you guys coming?"

I was happy and embarrassed and guilty. This meant the end for Brian, who waited for me in New Jersey, sounding jittery in his e-mails. At Deirdre's house, Michael and I found ourselves alone on the couch. We kissed some more, before I pulled away.

"I have a boyfriend. . . ."

"Do you want to stop?"

"Not really. But I should. I also need to get to bed. My kids will have me up early tomorrow. It's almost four." He sat up, and I couldn't tell from the expression on his face if he was disappointed or relieved. What was I doing?

The next day, in the bright sunlight, he gave me a hug next to the rental car. I wondered if I would have kissed him if the kids hadn't been there. We waved our good-byes and I wished we were staying for Jack and Deirdre's New Year's party that night, but I had promised Jill that we would be back in time to spend New Year's with her and Dan and their friends.

Home in Montclair, I posted the photos from my trip onto the Internet for friends and family to see. Brian saw them. too. "So who's the dork in the necklace?"

"Necklace?" I was taken aback by how quickly he had zeroed in on a picture of Michael and me. Michael was wearing the necklace that Deirdre had given him that night, from a recent trip to Ethiopia. What had Brian seen in that picture? My happiness? Could he tell that I was laughing, something I didn't do enough with him? Of course he sensed instinctively that something between us had changed.

Michael and I began e-mailing as soon as I returned to New Jersey. I felt a little guilty about Brian, but at first convinced myself that Michael and I were just friends and that distance would prevent anything more. But our e-mails became flirtier and I began looking forward to them. One evening, Brian came over to bake cookies with the kids and I snuck upstairs to read another e-mail from Michael. It was becoming clear that I would have to make a decision about Brian soon.

In early January, Brian and I celebrated his birthday with dinner at a fancy sushi restaurant, drinking miso soup and eating sushi rolls topped with unusual sauces. Brian was in a black mood, perhaps sensing that my mind was elsewhere.

"Where do you think people go when they die?" he asked me suddenly. "Do you think there's a heaven?" I was startled by his line of questioning.

"Well, I'm not sure if it's a heaven in the Hallmark sense of the word, but I have to believe that Arron is somewhere."

"Why? Because he gives you 'signs'?" Brian held my gaze, challenging me.

"I know you don't believe that my 'signs' are messages from him, but they help me. I need to believe that he didn't just disappear into nothingness. I need to believe that he exists on some other plane, and that we still have some kind of connection. Who cares if it's real or not?" I was confused. Why was Brian being so querulous with me?

"I think when you die, that's it. There's nothing more." Brian suddenly looked like a sulky four-year-old. I was certain he could tell that I was ready to break up with him, which was causing this confrontational attitude. But I hated that he was using his existential beliefs and Arron as revenge.

"That's such a sad way to think. So fatalistic. How can you have a happy life if you believe the ending will be so grim?"

"Who ever said I live a happy life?" We continued to eat in silence. Our relationship seemed doomed to meet a similar end.

A week later, at our Indian restaurant, I told Brian I wanted to break up.

"It's because of that guy in Seattle, isn't it?" Brian pouted. He looked down, trying to hide the tears that had formed in the corners of his eyes.

"No, Brian. It's not because of him. I barely know him. You and I have messy lives right now. You need to work things out with your wife. You need to make decisions based on what's best for you and your kids, not what's best for you and me."

"Yes, I suppose you're right about that. I was just hoping that you'd be part of the equation."

"I know, Brian. I'm sorry." I had persevered for the last two months, hoping that I would fall in love with Brian, but instead I realized that the kind of relationship that Brian wanted with me was not the same as what I wanted. I wanted something fun and carefree. I wanted sex. I wanted to fall in love and be deliriously happy. I realized that I didn't want to become a Brady Bunch family with Brian. I wished I did. I knew he loved me. I feared now that I wouldn't ever love another man, that Arron would always get in the way, and it seemed that Brian had been another of my victims. Was Michael next?

Michael and I began speaking regularly on the phone and, to my surprise, at the beginning of February he came for a visit. My heart beat faster as he descended the escalator at the airport, wearing his brown suede jacket, a black bag flung over his shoulder.

"Hi!" he said when he saw me, pulling me into a bear hug. We kissed, quickly, nervously. As I drove along the Garden State, I quietly took his hand. He looked at me and smiled, squeezing it. He stayed in the guest room. During his four-day visit, he made us all laugh and the kids forgot to miss Brian.

On the Sunday of Michael's visit, Olivia's school had a skating party. At the rink, a kid crashed into Carter and me, sending us flying. The impact dislocated my knee and it swelled up instantly. I sat on the ice, unable to get up, teenaged skating guards hovering. Michael had left the ice with Olivia to buy hot chocolate. Eventually, I limped off, Carter still crying beside me, holding my hand tightly, terrified.

I spent the night in agony, hobbling around or sitting with my knee wrapped in a bag of frozen peas. Michael made me cups of tea and picked up takeout for dinner. The next day while the kids were at school, Michael sat with me at the emergency room, making me cry with laughter at his improvised doctor routine.

"Ma'am, I am going to need to listen to your chest. . . ." Drawing the curtain around the bed he tickled me as he poked and prodded, and then kissed me as I suppressed more giggles. It seemed like some kind of test for us, to see if Michael could take care of me, or to see if I could be vulnerable with him. I felt helpless and silly, hobbling around the house on crutches, as he patiently helped make dinner and learned to make Carter's Ovaltine, just the way he liked it. Maybe I *could* fall in love, I thought.

Selena arrived in March to take care of the kids and I flew back to Seattle for a weekend with Michael. Selena seemed to have resigned herself to my dating and implored me to have fun.

Alone at last, Michael and I spent hours in bed, getting up only to make tea and eggs. We looked deep into each other's eyes as we talked about spirituality. He told me about some of the ideas he was learning in divinity school, and I was drawn into conversations about God, Tao, the meaning of life, afterlife. He drank in my Sylvia Browne–induced image of the afterlife, praising my ideas, my cobbled-together beliefs, insisting that I was wise. He encouraged me to follow my instincts and seemed to trust them, sometimes more than I did. "You just know things," he would insist. I was willing to believe him. We did not speak of the future, content to live in the present, savoring the moments as they came.

We spent a day taking the ferry to Bainbridge Island, me still hobbling around in a knee brace. We stood for a strange, awkward photo at a quaint winery, Michael clasping my arm like I was his elderly wife. Another day, we drove up to Vancouver to spend the night at a hotel with Jill and Caelin. That night, Jill got a sitter and the three of us went out on the town, giggling as we handed a street comedian a dollar so that he would tell us a joke, which none of us could remember by the end of the evening. We had dinner in a wonderful restaurant, drinking too much wine. Jill was a litmus test for Michael. Watching her laugh at his silly humor, I was eager for her acceptance of him. That night, in our room I asked, "So?"

"Yeah, he's really nice. And funny. And you're obviously smitten by him and I think that's great. It's great to see you happy, Ab."

"Really?" I was insecure, still not certain Michael was the right person for me. I was convinced Jill was just saying what I wanted to hear.

"Yes. He's really nice."

The next day, we drove back to Seattle, my feet on the dashboard, resting my bad knee as Michael played a CD by Maktub, a Seattle band whose songs were becoming our theme songs. I was content being the passenger, to not have to do the driving, for once. I had forgotten what it was like to be taken care of.

At the airport, we both stood beside my bags, sad-eyed.

"I can't wait to see you in Mexico," I said. My mom and I had arranged a trip to Puerto Vallarta using her timeshare. Michael had found a room at the same resort and we were planning to meet her.

"Yeah, it's going to be great." We hugged one last time.

Within the month, we were all sitting around a shallow, aquamarine kiddie pool, taking turns throwing brightly colored plastic fish into the water so Carter and Olivia could dive for them. Carter whirled around on Michael's back and then sailed into the water, giggling, his arms and legs akimbo. Michael body-surfed in the waves with Olivia. He sat next to me on the lounge chairs sipping a piña colada and holding my hand. I looked to my mother to be another litmus test for Michael, and he was performing beautifully. My mother could see that I was happy and that was what mattered to her. She seemed willing to accept him, though I would have been blind to any other reaction. After the kids went to bed in the room we shared with my mother, Michael and I snuck off for drinks and talked. Later, we made love on his bed with the curtains blowing in the soft ocean breeze. At one point I went to the bathroom and saw bottles of medications tucked into his open toiletries bag. He had told me he had once been diagnosed with obsessive-compulsive disorder, but I had never seen much evidence of it other than the fact that he washed his hands a little more often than most men I knew. I hadn't realized there were meds involved. I didn't know how to broach the subject with him when I snuggled back into bed beside him.

And then the week ended. Big tears rolled down my face as we parted at the Puerto Vallarta airport. I sensed that the paradise we had found in Mexico would never be replicated. Our week together had been perfect, but I worried that it had been too perfect. We had pretended to be a family in an unreal fantasy world. I couldn't be sure if I really loved him, or if I had convinced myself that I loved him in my desperation to reexperience the love that I had lost, to prove to myself that I could love someone besides Arron.

I began reading a book called *Mindful Loving: 10 Practices for Creating Deeper Connections* by Henry Grayson, Ph.D. I seemed to be seeking clues into how I loved. Too quickly? Was my love one of the "counterfeit" forms of love that Grayson described in his book? Number one on his list was "infatuation or the falling-in-love syndrome," a form of counterfeit love "based on fantasy rather than a real knowledge of the self or the other person." I feared too that I was trying to "replace the loss," the myth that had haunted me from the very first book I read about grief. I now worried that this had been the problem for Brian and me and that I was about to make the same mistake with Michael. I exchanged ideas from the book with Michael, hoping that his understanding of counterfeit love might prevent us from basing our relationship on it.

My trips to Seattle had started me thinking about the possibility of moving away from Montclair. Since my breakup with Brian and the start of my new romance with Michael, Montclair had begun to feel as though it no longer fit me. The house and all its memories had been weighing on me for months and my fears about living in the post-9/11 New York area were taking their toll. The continuous "Orange Alerts," indicating the level of terrorist activity going on in the world and its risk to New York, made me nervous. During trips into Manhattan, I walked the subway platforms with trepidation and recognized my same stretched look of angst in the faces of strangers. Everyone was viewed with suspicion. Eyes darted around, looking for the owners of unattended bags. Plans were formulated in the event of a disaster in every place traveled during the course of a day: the subway, the bus, the street, the buildings. Who to call? Who to take care of the kids? Where to go?

Each time I had an event to attend in the city, Carter would wail and cling to my leg, not wanting to let me go. Olivia would call me on my cell phone constantly. "Mommy, where are you?" she would plead. Their fears were the same as mine. What if I didn't come home one day, just like Daddy?

I began thinking about where I might move. I started looking online at MLS listings in Toronto, the obvious destination. I knew the city and still had a few friends there. My parents lived there and could provide extra childcare. I looked at houses in all the areas of Toronto that I could imagine living. But none of them captured my imagination. My reasons for moving there began to seem flimsy. Babysitting and a few old friends were not enough of a lure. Instead, I found myself looking at Seattle MLS listings, getting excited.

"Omigod. I *love* that one. Oh! And that one!" I exclaimed out loud as I clicked on the virtual tours of big boxy Craftsman houses painted in California pastel colors with lush green gardens and mossy steps. Views of Lake Washington, the Cascade mountains, or, in the other direction, Puget Sound and the Olympic mountains. The pictures of houses in Toronto were taken in the winter, reminding me of the dreary, slate-gray skies and below-zero temperatures. Seattle lured me with its charms, its promise of a fresh start, where Toronto seemed dull and cold, full of memories of a life I had once led with Arron.

One day, not long after returning home from Mexico with Michael, I was speaking with my friend Cornelia. "I need to get away from this area, from the constant reminders of Arron and 9/11. I go to places like Seattle where everyone seems oblivious to 9/11 and it feels great. They were so far away that I don't think they really got what it was like. I love that innocence."

"So are you thinking of moving there?"

"I don't know. Toronto would make more sense. It's where my family is."

"But your sister would be close, right? What about Vancouver?"

"I really don't know anyone in Vancouver and I just don't get excited about it the way I do with Seattle. Every time I go to Seattle, I really like it. It makes me feel happy." I wished I could explain it better. There was something about the brooding skies, the infinite green textures of the landscape, the curiously cloud-diffused light. It reminded me of living in London, where I would walk along the streets with my hand brushing the rosemary hedges that lined the perfect gardens of the beautiful whitewashed houses. I marveled at the jewel-like flowers that sprung incongruously in December and January. I thought of Deirdre and her entourage of interesting characters, her and Jack's love of life. I loved Seattle's neighborhood coffee shops where people gathered and the bulletin boards were covered in notices for massage therapists and writing groups. I loved watching people hunched over their computers and imagined myself one of them.

"Is it because of Michael?"

"Yes. That probably has something to do with it, I admit." I smiled at the thought of what Michael and I might have in Seattle: a normal relationship, where I could see him regularly. I had no notions of marriage or even moving in together, but I relished the thought of seeing him more often.

"Maybe you should rent a house for a month in the summer and see if you like living there," Cornelia suggested.

On the phone a few nights later, I told Michael about Corny's suggestion. "The kids and I could come and see if we might like living there."

"Oh. That's a good idea." He sounded hesitant.

"What? Does that idea scare you?"

"A little, I guess."

"Don't worry. It's not all about you. I really do like Seattle and I'm thinking of checking it out. But I'm also thinking about moving back to Toronto." I could feel myself backpedaling. "An extended trip to Seattle would also give us a chance to see where things might go with us as well."

"It sounds like a good plan." This was not the exuberant response I had been hoping for.

Soon, I began to get sad, worried-sounding e-mails from Michael. He seemed plagued by some unnamed fear that he was never able to adequately explain to me. He seemed certain that another tragedy along the lines of 9/11 was going to happen again. I now knew he took anti-anxiety medication and wondered if perhaps he had stopped. Something was changing. Phone calls that had once been a half hour or more were now reduced to a few minutes. "I've just arrived at the theater. I'll call you later," he would say, sounding overly exuberant, as though he was forcing a false good mood. But later for Michael would be 4:00 AM for me, and the promised call wouldn't come for a day or two.

"Another drive-by?" I would say, as I had come to call his brief phone calls. I tried to keep the whimper out of my voice. In e-mails I found myself apologizing for whining at him and trying to sound nonchalant, attempting to give him time to figure out what he wanted from our relationship. This cooling off also gave me time to think about what I wanted and I began to see that Michael wasn't ready for me, wasn't ready for Carter and Olivia, wasn't ready for the instant family we presented. I realized the tables had turned, and I felt what Brian must have gone through with me.

Unexpectedly, Michael came for Olivia's ninth birthday at the beginning of June. Olivia had invited eight friends over for a sleepover, and Michael had them all laughing as he taught them improv techniques. We sat in the basement judging the girls' hilarious descents down the basement steps, "best glamour queen," "best puppy," "best baby." The girls were content to do this for over an hour. By the end of the evening, they were all hanging off him. I heard one of the girls whisper to Olivia, "Michael is so cool!" Olivia replied, "Yeah, he might be my new dad." Although I had imagined us as a family in Mexico, when I tried to imagine Michael and I as a married couple now, the picture wouldn't come. Although he was here at Olivia's birthday and seemed to be trying hard to make our relationship work, I could tell his heart wasn't in it. I knew how much he loved the kids and me, but I began to realize that it wasn't enough.

The following Monday, after we put Olivia on the bus, Michael stood at the kitchen door, watching Carter and me leave for his pre-K, Carter wailing at me as we struggled out the door. "I don't wanna go to school! I hate school! No, Mama, don't make me go!" I was inured to the routine, as it happened most mornings. Carter wanted nothing more from life than to stay home with me, watching TV. I was brisk with him. "Come on, Carter. Say byebye to Michael." Michael was standing in the doorway, shocked and distressed. "I know it seems bad, but this is our normal routine. He does this every morning, especially Mondays."

"I want to stay with you and Michael!" Carter, although only four, already knew how to manipulate Michael.

"Abby, maybe. . . ." Michael was starting to panic.

"No, Michael. Don't make this harder than it already is." Carter and I walked off, leaving Michael at the door looking like he was about to burst into tears, Carter wailing, "I wanna stay with you guys!" all the way to the car.

When I got back, Michael met me at the door. "Was he all right when you got to school?"

"No, I had to do the usual and spend five minutes prying him from my thigh. But the teacher is used to it, so she helps me."

"God, I don't know how you do that. I know it's not, but it seems so cruel."

I couldn't help being hurt by the implication. "I'm sure it only seems cruel to you because you're not used to it." I was surprised by how strongly Michael was reacting. "Come on, little boy, life isn't *that* tough!" I wanted to yell.

That day, Michael accompanied me to New York, where I had to meet with Lenore to go over the final details before we had our hearing, only two weeks away, for the Victims' Fund. I had hoped that we would have had our hearing quickly, perhaps within a few months of filing the forms, over a year before. But I had heard nothing from Lenore. Occasionally I would call, only to be told that she was working on a big case and would take a look at everything, soon. But the big cases kept coming. Occasionally, Lenore would request things to add to the file: letters from Arron's colleagues that would show how valued he was as a leader, copies of eulogies, pictures with the kids, a video of the CBC interview I did. They were all added to Lenore's big white binder, a testament to Arron and to what my family had lost with his death. The binder's purpose was to show that he was worth more than the U.S. Department of Justice tables indicated. His family deserved a higher reward. What amount of money could possibly replace a life?

As much as Lenore stalled, I stalled in equal measure. I was reluctant to endure a hearing, to assign a price to Arron's life. I didn't know how to reconcile my guilt for reducing his life to a dollar sign. I made secret lists of the charities I would donate to and fantasized about founding a widow's network, for women and young families who were not so lucky as to have their loved ones' worth measured against an actuarial table conjured by the U.S. Department of Justice.

And still I had waited, e-mailing Lenore every few months. "I'm sorry it's taking me so long," she apologized. "To be honest, I'm finding your case emotionally difficult. I seem to avoid it. I am truly sorry."

"It's fine. To be honest, I try to avoid it also," I admitted.

Lenore wanted to wait until she could hear from some of her colleagues who had already submitted to a hearing with their clients. She needed to know how tough or lenient the reviewers were; if more information was required; whether to pay for an economist to review Arron's case. I sent copies of more documents and a check for three hundred dollars to an economist in Pennsylvania. More weeks passed. When the economist's report came back, Lenore was still unhappy and felt he should have made a recommendation for a higher amount. She returned the report to the economist and more time passed. Finally an adjusted report was returned, and Lenore was satisfied. Another large case came up. Summer ebbed into fall. Finally she filed the forms and now, almost six months later, my hearing date was imminent.

While I met with Lenore, Michael wandered around downtown. Afterward, we had lunch outside in the sun at a little bistro. It was a perfect Manhattan scene. We laughed and enjoyed a glass of wine, and I felt the warmth from Michael that I had been missing. "I would love to live in New York for a while," he fantasized. "I would love to trade living arrangements. Someone could live on my boat in Seattle while I lived in their apartment in New York."

"That's a cool idea," I said, trying to ignore the irony of our disparate plans.

On the subway home, I still carried the briefcase holding all of the documents I always brought to Lenore's office. "You know," Michael said, "if you ever want me to take a look at some of your financials, I know quite a lot about investing, from when I worked in insurance." Our closeness that day had me grasping at more ways to draw him nearer to me, so I allowed him to look at the economist's report, which recommended an amount for my settlement. Michael was very quiet as he read, and I began cursing myself for breaking my own rule of never discussing money with friends. Michael lived a frugal life. His improv career was quickly depleting his savings account and I wasn't sure when his well would run dry or what he might do when it did. As he learned my financial realities I searched his face nervously for signs that he was surprised or intimidated, or dismayed, but his expression remained impassive, business-like. Suddenly I worried that Michael could see that it was not only our relocation plans that were separating us.

Later that night, Michael seemed to take a new protective interest in Carter. At bedtime, he asked to help me get the kids to bed, something that he had always left to me to do alone. We helped Carter get his pajamas on and sat on his bed together while I read a book. The phone rang, so I left Michael to finish the book with Carter. I was still on the phone with Jocelyn when Michael and Carter came downstairs. "He wants you to put him to bed," Michael whispered to me, over my phone call.

I held two fingers up, needing another few minutes to finish the call. After hanging up, I took Carter upstairs while Michael retreated to the living room. When I came down again, Michael looked angry.

"Can I talk with you?" His tone was ominous.

"Sure. What's up?" I said cautiously.

"Well, I really think that you should've told your friend that you would call her back. I think you should've made putting Carter to bed your first priority."

I was stung. "Well, Michael. I've been trying to reach Jocelyn for over a week now. I knew it would just be a quick call while we figured out our trip next week. You were with Carter and I thought that you would put him to bed after the book," I said, trying to sound calm.

"He didn't want me to put him to bed. He wanted you."

"Well, it didn't kill him to wait a few minutes. This is my reality, Michael. I am only one person and sometimes my kids have to wait while I take phone calls during bedtime." I was angry. How dare he insinuate that I had abandoned my child for a phone call! How dare he comment at all on my parenting!

"I can understand your need to be selfish . . ." he trailed off, realizing too late his mistake.

"Michael, this is your issue, not mine, not Carter's." My stomach filled with a heavy feeling. My jaw clenched.

"How about we finish this conversation in the morning, when perhaps we're both a little more rational. I think we must both be tired," I suggested. We ascended the stairs each lost in our own thoughts. I could feel the knot of anger just under my sternum, and I fought to let it go. It's his baggage, I told myself. I was tempted to tell him to sleep in the guest room when he followed me into my room.

"Do you want a back rub?" I could tell by his tone that he was trying to quell his own anger. I lay face down on the bed as he straddled me. He began rubbing, but the massage, usually gentle and satisfyingly hard at the same time, was now painful. "Ouch. Easy," I cried. His hands encircled my neck, crimping my jugular vein uncomfortably. We didn't make love that night, a first in all our visits together. The gulf between us remained undiscussed.

The next day, Michael's last morning with us, I got the kids off to school. When I returned, Michael pulled me down into bed with him. "I'm sorry about last night. I don't know what got into me."

"Yeah, it was a weird night," I agreed. He kissed me and it was clear that we were going to make love, but something had changed. The lightness of our relationship seemed to have disappeared. My thoughts were elsewhere, my lust squelched. His lovemaking was overly physical, a little too rough. Afterward I sat up feeling strange and immediately fell sideways onto the bed.

"Oh God. I'm so dizzy. Did you see that? I just totally fell over!" I tried sitting up but was again overcome by a wave of dizziness. I struggled to remain upright. I stood up and felt myself stagger to the right. I stumbled down the hall, my hands pressed against the walls.

"Michael, something's wrong with me. I can't stand up!" Something had shifted between Michael and me and now my body was reacting. Days later, a doctor diagnosed vertigo, but Michael and I would never get so definitive a diagnosis for our ailment.

[21]

TESTAMENTS TO LOVE AND LOSS

In July, Martha and I combed the kids' hair and drove into Manhattan to the New York County Courthouse.

Lenore had suggested that I bring Carter and Olivia to the hearing. "It will potentially mean more money for them in the long run," she said, reading my shocked reaction over the phone.

We met Lenore in front of the courthouse carrying her bulging briefcase, packed with Arron's white binder. Our small entourage was directed down into the catacombs of the courthouse basement to a waiting room where the kids were given Cokes and cookies. Soon we were escorted into elevators, and led past cubicles of the drab, fluorescent-lit fourteenth floor into a tiny boardroom whose walls barely contained the large table and chairs. We arranged ourselves around it, leaving room for the reviewer who would sit at the head of the table, near the door.

The reviewer entered the room, took her seat, and introduced herself and a court recorder who had taken a seat next to her.

"Since you have children here, I will start with them, and then they can leave if they want and go back to the waiting room until we are done," she began. She looked at the documents in front of her, presumably our claim forms.

"So, you must be Olivia?" she said, looking at Olivia, who shyly bounced her head up and down.

"And you must be Carter?" Carter did as his sister did, bouncing his head as he sat in my lap.

"Do you understand why we are here?" she directed her question at Olivia.

"To talk about Daddy?" Olivia said.

"Yes. What do you remember most about him?"

"He farted a lot," Olivia said, giggling. The reviewer smiled.

"Do you remember things you did with him?"

"I liked working out with him. On the stepper. And he made good pancakes. Minnie Mouse."

"Those are all good things. Anything else you can think of?" Olivia shook her head.

"Carter, do you remember anything about your daddy?" Carter shook his head as he looked down at the table.

"That's okay, Carter. I think that's about all I need from the kids. Does your nanny want to take them back down to the waiting room?" Martha had already leapt up and was gathering the kids' coats. She gave me a look as she left that wished me luck and seemed full of caring.

The meeting continued. I had prepared a bullet list of items I was going to talk about: Arron's background and upbringing, his father's death when Arron was seventeen, his schooling, his MBA. I talked about his phone call on the morning of September 11. I talked about his personality traits: "irreverent, quirky sense of humor. Brilliant, infectious giggle." I told the panel of his business aspirations. "Entrepreneurial, ambitious, wanted to run his own business." I told them of the music lessons he would never teach the kids and the other latent losses. I discussed my need for a therapist, the kids' fears of separation, and Arron's mom and her potential financial needs. Our life together was reduced to bullet points. Lenore let me do all the talking. The reviewer asked very few questions. I wasn't sure what I was supposed to be proving with my descriptions. Was I giving proof that Arron had really existed?

These facts about our life seemed to change nothing. Did the fact that I needed to see a therapist or that Olivia still feared the dark or that Carter still asked where Arron's body was equate to more dollars? But I did what I was told to do. I trusted Lenore's expertise. She had vast experience with civilian lawsuits and knew how to persuade a jury to give a defendant more than was required. When I was done speaking, I felt like a deflated balloon, empty and limp.

A few weeks later, on the first of August, Carter, Olivia, and I arrived in Seattle, rewarded with a perfect summer day with clear blue skies and a golden sun. I negotiated the rental car up a very steep driveway and fiddled with the code on the lockbox. The house I had found to rent for the month was on the market for sale and had been "staged" with just enough furniture to live with, nothing more. There were no curtains on any of the windows and we opened the door to a rush of hot air. The kids raced around the house. I had hoped that Michael might come and meet us, but he had other plans. I had spoken on the phone with him at the end of June, after his disastrous visit.

"You say you want a relationship with me, but your actions tell me otherwise. I am tired of the drive-by phone calls, Michael. I need more in a relationship. I don't want to have unrealistic expectations when I come in August. I think we should just be friends, at least until then." He had agreed, though I hoped it had been reluctantly. Our phone calls and e-mails after that centered around finding this house and his recommendations on areas where we should look. His absence this day squashed my hope that we might rekindle our romance during my month in Seattle.

"This is my room!" I heard Olivia declare as I lugged suitcases into the house. The kids' footsteps raced further up the stairs.

"Mommeee! They have tons of DVDs!" I couldn't tell which child was yelling down at me. The house was pristine, a show home, complete with vases of fake flowers that I hid away in a closet.

I could see Lake Washington from both my bedroom and from one side of a big third-floor rec room. From the other side, I could see the city skyline, including the Space Needle.

I was pleased with myself. I was spending a little more for the month than I had intended, but now I was happy that I was. In a couple of days, we would be able to sit in this room and watch the Blue Angels fly their F-16s around the city, here for the weeklong Sea Fair, and celebrate Carter's fifth birthday.

That first night, the kids and I snuggled in my bed to watch TV, content. The next morning I awoke at 5:30 to a fiery red sunrise peeking over the Cascade Mountains in the distance, across the lake. I watched, awestruck, as the ball of orange drifted along the tops of the mountains, lighting the sky in hues of pink, purple, yellow, and orange. I could get used to waking up to *this* every morning.

A few days later, Jill and Dan arrived like a whirlwind. Caelin, now three, Tulie, Jill's dog, and the kids all clambered up the stairs to mark their territories. Later, I took everyone to Pike Place Market and to the kids' favorite store, "the mummy store," known for its displays of actual mummified bodies and shrunken heads.

The F-16 jets zoomed around the house like giant mosquitoes for several days of practice. They were so close it was almost possible to see the expressions on the pilots as they whizzed by, the deafening noise of the engines taking several seconds to catch up to them. Michael had been determined to be at Carter's birthday and over the past two days we had managed to forge a respectful friendship. Deirdre, Jack, and Rosemary joined our Sunday party and we snacked on cupcakes as we watched the final Blue Angels show.

I don't know when I stopped feeling sad during the kids' birthdays. Perhaps having a birthday in a strange house was the trick. No memories. No images of Arron at the barbecue roasting hot dogs. It was nice to make new memories, ones without Arron's ghost tricking me into a melancholy mood.

Seattle was perfect for that entire month of August, with clear, royal-blue skies every day. We spent our days alternating between the beaches along Lake Washington Boulevard and the playground in Madrona or Madison Park. The kids listened intently for the now familiar jingle of "When the Saints Come Marching In," signaling the arrival of the ice-cream truck. Olivia and Rosemary did a couple of weeks of "acting" camp on Mercer Island while Carter protested loudly about being dropped off for sports camp. I cried into my tea at Tully's one morning with Deirdre after one of our harrowing partings.

"Am I being cruel, forcing him to go to camp in a strange city? I just need a few hours without kids," I moaned.

"No, Abby. You're not cruel. In fact, I don't know how you do it. I really don't." Tears were welling up in Deirdre's eyes.

"Let's go get our toes done," she suggested. "We should have just enough time before we have to go get the kids!"

The reality was that I had no nanny in Seattle. No school. Nothing to give me recharging time away from the kids. A friend of Deirdre's came and babysat a couple of nights but other than that I was alone 24/7 with two kids. If we did move, how would I cope without my support system? Martha was like a mother to me, and a grandma to the kids. It almost brought tears to my eyes just thinking about leaving her. Her tough, no-feeling-sorry-for-yourself attitude had buoyed me through many difficult days. Her first husband had died leaving her with four young boys to raise alone in Montclair, after they had emigrated to the United States from Argentina.

"I have four boys, no husband, no money. Eese very tough! I know!" She was sympathetic, but only to a point, and I appreciated it. It could be worse. I could be raising *four* children, with no money, and little English. I admired her strength. Thinking now of Martha toughened my resolve. I could do this. Seattle wasn't so scary.

Each morning I allowed the beautiful sunrise to renew me.

One day I got a call from Lenore in New York.

"The checks arrived today. I am couriering them to you now."

The final amount awarded almost perfectly matched the amount listed in the actuarial tables. Latent losses and economists hadn't changed a thing.

When the FedEx package arrived in Seattle, I opened it as though it were fragile, frightened to break whatever was inside. Inexplicably, there were four checks, each made out in different amounts. I sat down with a sigh, marveling at my ability to hold such a large amount of money. I ran my thumb over the amounts on the checks as though I might be able to rub them off, as though the numbers, like Arron, might suddenly disappear.

Arron would love to see these . . . Arron. I wanted to cry. These flimsy pieces of paper were meant to replace him, but they were disappointingly insubstantial. They felt tainted, and I held them like they might injure me. Or worse. I couldn't wait to get rid of them. Arron had to die for this moment to happen.

It was Friday and I couldn't deposit them until Monday. They sat inside their envelope on the kitchen counter, where I was sure they would burn through the envelope and leave a mark.

"Are we rich now?" Olivia asked as she looked at the checks.

"Yes, a little. But no. This money has to last us for the rest of our lives. It seems like a lot right now, but over a lifetime, it's not really that much. Although it might mean that I don't have to go back to work again right away."

"Goody!" Olivia clapped her hands together.

On Monday, we all traipsed downtown and walked into the city's only TD Waterhouse branch and handed over the checks. I imagined that the man who took them, photocopied them, and then wrote out the deposit slip for me to sign would remark on the quantity. Or give me a look that showed he was—what? Impressed? Sad for me? But he carried on about his business as though he deposited such amounts twenty times a day. No big deal. My hands shook as he handed me the photocopies, which I slipped into the FedEx envelope like forgeries, like one of those million-dollar bills you buy in a joke store.

"There you go. All done."

And so it was. Money in the bank.

We saw very little of Michael during our stay other than an occasional walk to the playground to push the kids on the swing, or a visit to the beach where the kids and I had camped out for the afternoon. Our conversations remained somewhat superficial but always friendly. I longed for more. I wasn't sure if it was Michael I craved or just intimacy. I was lonely. My advances were met with confusion. Either I was awkwardly rebuffed as Michael found an excuse to leave, or we attempted to re-create our passionate love-making, silently, late at night. But something was missing, and afterward, Michael would quickly dress and disappear.

One day, he called me. "I'm on my way to Madison for ten days. My father has to have surgery and I've decided that I want to be there for him."

"Oh. Ten days. That's the rest of the time that I'm here." I couldn't keep the bitter disappointment out of my voice. "Well, I guess that's it then. Your message is crystal clear."

It took a few days for my anger to really set in. "I'm only here for four weeks and he takes off for half of it?" I complained to Deirdre. "It's so clear that it was an escape for him."

"Michael can be a funny guy that way. You, the kids, it may all be too much for him."

"I'm beginning to see that."

Halfway into his trip, Michael called me from Madison.

"Can I ask you a question, Abby?"

"Sure."

"How long are you going to wear your wedding ring?" I paced outside, out of earshot of the kids, who were drawing in the kitchen. I looked down at my right hand, where my wedding ring had remained since my first date with Nick.

"I don't know, Michael. Why do you ask?" I was shocked but tried to make my voice sound neutral.

"Well, it just seems unfair that you get to keep wearing your ring." At first I thought he meant that he felt by wearing my ring, I was still too connected to Arron. I was about to sympathize with him, but then he continued. "When your spouse dies, you get all this sympathy, people support you, and you get to keep wearing your wedding ring. In divorce, especially for the guy, there's no real support and it's considered weird if you keep wearing your wedding ring. I guess I just want to keep wearing my ring, as a testament to what I had."

I didn't know what to say. I was torn between understanding Michael's point and being angry with him for feeling so sorry for himself.

"I agree that in a divorce you experience the same symptoms of loss as you do when a spouse dies. It's probably also true that you don't get as much support. I think in divorce, you're expected to get over it much sooner than with a death and that's a shame. The ring is symbolic of marriage. I guess the difference between us is that your marriage ended and mine didn't. Not really." Perhaps this was also the problem with our relationship, I thought. Michael was bitter over the ending of his marriage, whereas I felt as though mine continued, albeit one-sided.

I breathed heavily. I really cared about Michael, but these strange conversations seemed to be coming more frequently as he tried to discover what it was he wanted from life. I found them frustrating, and this one had made me mad.

Michael returned two days before we had to leave for New Jersey. He came over to the house for dinner on our last night in Seattle. After the kids were in bed, we sat awkwardly in the staged living room, sipping glasses of wine.

"I know things haven't really worked out for us, but we could have just one last night of fun. . . ." I smiled at him with a sideways glance, stroking his thigh. I was hungry for him, surprised at the strength of my desire. My anger with him had dissipated now that I had to say good-bye to him. Knowing that our romantic relationship was over, I felt desperate and clingy.

"No, I don't think that would be a good idea. I think I should go."

I took another sip of wine, as though trying to quench my own heat. But I couldn't hide my disappointment over what we had lost.

"I'll be by tomorrow to help you with your bags." His voice was businesslike. We hugged at the door and kissed for a long time, knowing it would be our last. I stared at the closed door, waiting for tears that did not come.

Despite my disappointment, I had already spent several months resigning myself to the reality that although he would always be a wonderful presence in our lives, Michael would not become the romantic partner that I had hoped for.

Another page turned.

LEAD TO GOLD

Despite holding the two memorials for Arron in New Jersey and Toronto and another two public memorials at Ground Zero, despite two anniversaries since 9/11, despite beautiful public gardens in London and Ottawa, despite TV interviews, newspaper portraits, letters of condolence from President George W. Bush, Prime Minister Jean Chrétien, and the Prince of Wales, despite copious tears and sleepless nights, I still did not feel I had honored Arron properly.

In the weeks following 9/11, "We will never forget" became a national slogan seen on bumper stickers and draped from downtown buildings. It still cuts me like a knife. As if it would ever be possible to forget Arron. The world had attempted in so many heartfelt ways to honor the 9/11 victims. There was a need, through remembrance, to understand, to make meaning where there was none. There are thousands of plaques, public statues, teddy bears, quilts, drawings, paintings, and writings memorializing the victims. They appear in the most unusual places: in the courtyard of an ancient lighthouse on Block Island in Rhode Island, or in a garden in front of a hospital in New Jersey, or, as a steel beam from the towers was, buried beneath a memorial garden in London, England.

At each monument where I sought solace, I found none. The first time I saw a bronzed eagle soaring above a big bronze open book inscribed with Arron's name at Eagle Rock Reservation, I wanted to cry. I had loved the old makeshift memorial—the poems, the flowers, the flags taped to the stone wall, now long gone. In their place I found several incongruent bronze sculptures clustered together: the eagle; a fireman's helmet on a pedestal; a young girl clutching a teddy bear; a winged angel; an African-American policeman's torso and arm, his hand clutching a lantern; the open book inscribed with names. I couldn't find any meaning in the collection. I supposed they were icons representing death, or more specifically a 9/11 death, or symbols of some sort of universal mythology, but they did not apply to the man I knew and loved.

The garden in London's Grosvenor Square had gotten me thinking. It was beautiful and simple. I discovered that the poem etched into the cement floor was by Henry Van Dyke:

> Time is too slow for those who wait,
> Too swift for those who fear,
> Too long for those who grieve,
> Too short for those who rejoice,
> But for those who love,
> Time is not.

It brought tears to my eyes. If I were ever to build a memorial, I thought, I would use that poem.

And then, there it was.

I needed to build my own memorial.

I needed to create a place where the kids and I could go to commune with Arron, a place where we felt comfortable remembering him. Typically, this would be a graveyard or a special place like a lake where a loved one's ashes have been sprinkled. With no body, there was no gravestone and no ashes to sprinkle. We had no place that was just ours and ours alone. I had to stop relying on the outside world to honor Arron for us and find a memorial that was personal and meaningful.

One morning, as I sipped my tea on the back steps, several birds sat in a nearby tree singing obnoxiously loudly. I remembered Arron joking with me—"Hey, Bird, what are those birds talking about?" My mind would always go blank trying to think of some witty repartee. At that moment, the idea for his memorial came—a birdbath.

Arron loved tiles and tiling. During our kitchen renovation, we had tiled our own backsplash in small black and white marble tiles, a project we had enjoyed together. He loved doing it so much that one of the projects on his home improvement agenda was to build a bathroom in our basement, complete with a mosaic-tiled Turkish bath. I scoffed at his plan, but I loved his whimsies. Keeping true to his whimsical nature, I decided to cover the birdbath in mosaic tiles.

Finding the right birdbath proved to be more difficult. One cold and rainy day in November, I piled the kids in the car for the ultimate New Jersey experience—a trip to "Fountains of Wayne." This landmark outlet sells every conceivable garden ornament— cement angels, elves, gnomes, donkeys, huge ornamental urns, and birdbaths—and they are incongruously displayed along a busy New Jersey highway. The place was deserted that day and I was thrilled to find that bird baths were half price. Impulsively I bought one that was covered in rosettes, with a bowl that was too flat. I realized as I learned more about tiling that it would not work well as my base. It wasn't until a spring trip to a garden center that I found the right birdbath. It was simple, smooth, with a nice deep bowl. I could finally begin my project.

Ideas for the images came slowly, over time. A butterfly in the center of the bowl representing Arron and his move into the afterlife made perfect sense when I remembered all the butterflies we saw after his death. I depicted myself as a bird hovering above the butterfly. Arron had long ago dubbed a newborn Olivia "Pickle Horse," a name derived from the lyrics of a song he made up about her, so she appears as a green horse to the left of the butterfly (she shares Arron's left-handedness). Arron named Carter "Bone Maker" due to the extraordinary quantities of milk he consumed as a baby. Given his penchant for Ovaltine, he appears as a brown cow on the butterfly's right. There is a moon for the cow to leap over, which doubles as a symbol of our love, and finally our beloved golden retriever Harley makes a cameo appearance as herself at the butterfly's "feet."

I began puzzling broken bits of glass into place to form the images. It was an exercise in trial, error, and patience. I learned to break each tile without shattering it and glued each piece individually, constantly rearranging and refitting. My hands were caked in cement adhesive and covered with many tiny cuts. One by one, over a period of nine months, each animal emerged with its own, unique character. It seemed at times that I had divine guidance as each perfectly sized piece found its way into my hand.

The underside of the bowl has a wavy, watery appearance and includes a couple of fish. I decorated the pedestal base in daisies in memory of Arron bringing his "girls" daisies on Valentine's Day, and the wonderful picture of Arron and Carter with daisies behind their ears. Finally, a bronze plaque transformed the birdbath into a true monument honoring Arron. Etched on the plaque is the poem from the London memorial by Henry Van Dyke, followed by a simple inscription from me and the kids:

Created with love for Arron, Fabbo, Daddy
1961–2001

I dedicated the birdbath to Arron in October 2004, on the third anniversary of his memorial service. On that night, forty friends and neighbors gathered in my garden as I filled the birdbath's bowl with champagne and handed everyone a silly straw to drink from. With all my friends around me, I felt not a moment of sadness. I was so happy to finally have a memorial that felt right. I sensed that Arron was happy with it, too. He would have loved its irreverence and humor and I could feel his pride in my accomplishment. I later discovered that my audience had been awed by my unique cenotaph. Many had cried during my dedication, but I had felt nothing but pleasure. I had created something that represented the universe that was my family and in doing so I had finally achieved the elusive goal of honoring Arron in a way that allowed me to let him go, but to never forget him.

11/04

One blustery November afternoon, I was driving with the kids when I broached the subject of moving with them. "So, how would you guys feel about moving to Seattle?"

"Yes! I love it there!" Olivia was quick to answer.

"Why do you like Seattle?"

"I like all the lakes and the mountains. I like that you can always be outside and there is so much to do."

"I like the mummy store!" Carter piped up. "But I don't want to live there."

"Is it because you would miss Sam?" Sam was Carter's best friend. At prekindergarten, they were inseparable. Carter spent long stretches with Sam and his dad, Temple, a kid himself, skating, playing basketball, going to movies. Temple had become a kind of surrogate dad for Carter. I knew leaving Sam and his family would be difficult for him.

"Yes." Carter's eyes began to well with tears and I choked off my own.

"That's understandable," I said.

"Mommy, if we move to Seattle, can I have a hamster?" Olivia asked suddenly. I was glad for the diversion.

"Me, too?" Carter's tears and Sam were momentarily forgotten.

"Okay . . . I guess. . . ." Suddenly the mood inside the car changed.

"I'm gonna call mine Bob!" Olivia giggled.

"Mine's gonna be Alexander!" I could hear excitement in Carter's voice.

Later, I overheard the kids begin to tell their friends of the move. "When we move to Seattle, we're gonna get hamsters. I'm gonna name mine . . ."

Since our return from Seattle, I had continued to scour the MLS listings, concentrating on the areas of Madrona and Leschi, wanting to stay close to where Deirdre lived and also hoping that Carter and Olivia might gain acceptance to the Valley School, a small, close-knit private school in the same neighborhood that Rosemary attended.

I came across a creamy yellow Italian villa–style house with a corrugated metal roof, perched on a grassy slope with serpentine gardens and views of Lake Washington. Inside, the rooms were painted in garish colors: a red dining room, chocolate-brown master bedroom, pink kitchen. The colors didn't deter me, but the price did. It was double the price of the house I would be selling in Montclair. Even selling our investment property wouldn't make up the difference. So I called Debra, my financial advisor, and told her what I was thinking. A few days later, I sat in her office as she provided me with various financial scenarios, proving that, in the long run, a house, even an expensive one, was a good investment. I walked out of Debra's office with my heart pounding at the idea of owning such a beautiful house. I wished Arron could be a part of my decision, but he would have balked at spending so much.

"Bird, do you really need to buy such an expensive house?" I imagined his look. Arms crossed. Pursed lips. A line furrowing his brow.

"No, Arron. You are not here. This is my decision. This house would be a good investment. It would be a wonderful place for the kids and me. Isn't that what matters? You know I'm right. . . ." I imagined him conceding, his silently exhaled breath ruffling his short bangs.

One day I looked online at the house again and noticed that the price had dropped. I booked a flight to Seattle for the first week of December. Selena, though despondent at this new turn of events and the prospect of us being far away, drove down to watch the kids.

I met Laura, Deirdre's niece and now my real-estate agent, on Saturday morning to begin our tour of Seattle houses. We wandered through some of the Craftsman houses I had seen online. Though delightful from the outside, once I was inside I realized that along with all their charm they would have many of the same ailments of my existing house—windows that stuck and could only be opened with the help of a rubber mallet, rotting porches, expensive paint jobs, and quirky electrical wiring and plumbing. Some of the other houses needed too much work, something I had once relished, knowing that Arron had the talent for it. Now I needed windows that I could open by myself, a house that would be easy to maintain, a simple floor plan with at least three bedrooms in the same vicinity.

Each house we saw had its charms, but none of them took my breath away. Finally, after a punishing afternoon of viewing eight different houses, we parked in the yellow house's steep sloping driveway and slowly made our way down the narrow brick steps, admiring the lush garden. Despite the cold, gray weather, fuchsias still bloomed, and there were remnants of irises, ferns, a dogwood, many rhododendrons, a camellia. As we walked through the leaded-glass front door, I knew this was our house. It had been empty for many months, but it had a clean, airy smell, untainted by past occupants. I suppressed an urge to race through the rooms, wanting to see it all as quickly as possible. I imagined painting over the ugly colors in pale shades that would reflect the stunning view of the lake. The kitchen's white cabinets and glassy cherrywood countertop gleamed. The new hardwood floors were perfect, not a nail sticking out, not a creak anywhere. The windows were big and bright with handles to crank them open and sun-blocking blinds that rolled neatly into place. There was the master bedroom that I had fantasized about, where I could wake up looking east with a view of the lake and mountains, almost the same view as the house we'd rented for a month, a few blocks away. I would have my own bathroom with a clawfoot tub situated to take advantage of the view and a long vanity with two sinks. Maybe someday that second sink will get used, I thought.

"This is it," I said impulsively to Laura as we returned to the living room. "I'm going to make an offer." By five that evening I had agreed upon a price with the seller.

The next day, I was walking around the house with the inspector I'd scheduled the night before.

"This is a really nice house. Very solid. I am not finding many issues. You may want to add some insulation in the attic and re-inforce the lug bolts on the deck, but that's about it." As the inspector poked around in the attic and the crawl spaces, I sat waiting in a folding aluminum chair in the corner of the empty, echoey living room, remembering the day that Arron and I had found our house in Montclair. As we followed the realtor up the stairs to the third floor, we gave each other a look that said it all, we agreed that this was our house. A second look from Arron told me to stay quiet so that he could do the negotiating.

As I sat there, I smelled smoke for the first time in a long while. It may have been just a neighbor lighting a fire in a nearby fireplace, but to me that smell was Arron giving me the look.

I was home.

Even Carter's early resistance to the move began to ease after another visit to Seattle in March to see the house and have an interview at the Valley School. Both kids ran around the empty house, claiming their rooms and finding a tiny door leading to a crawl space that would become their "club house." While Olivia spent a morning at the school, Carter and I went out and bought three self-inflating air mattresses.

"What are we going to use these for?" Carter asked as he helped me unpack the first one in his empty room.

"They are to sleep on when we first move here, until our furniture gets here." I plugged the motor into the socket so he could try filling the mattress up.

"I thought we couldn't bring our stuff from New Jersey," Carter said as the air mattress filled. "Cool!"

"Of course we're going to bring all of our stuff. We'll get a big truck to come to our house in New Jersey and get everything. Then the truck will drive all the way across America." I could see the lightbulb go off in Carter's mind. His eyes lit up with relief.

"You mean I can bring my own bed?" Only now could I see how worried Carter had been about the move.

Later that day, we picked Olivia up from the school. "I love that school! They taught me math in a way that I could understand!"

The next day was Carter's turn. It took some time to pry him from my leg. Connie, the first grade teacher, hovered close by, clearly experienced with such a reaction. She took Carter's hand and led him away. I made a quick retreat as Connie mouthed the words "he'll be fine" to me.

Afterward in the playground, Connie found me. "I think Carter would fit in beautifully here."

"Yes, I think he might, too. I hope they can find a place for him."

Home in New Jersey, Janet helped me to understand more of Carter's resistance to the move. "I think your trip to Seattle really helped Carter. He has been playing for several months with a Barbie camper. The camper was taped securely with duct tape and inside were 'bad guys,' who often couldn't breathe or got killed somehow. On top of the camper there was a treasure chest filled with tiny plastic babies. It was also taped shut and then taped to the top of the van. The babies often died as well."

"But ever since your trip, all the tape has come off the van. The bad guys have been freed. And now the van is a moving van, filled with all the things a house would need and two parents, a mother *and* a father, and two kids."

I began to pack up the house, making piles for the Goodwill, dropping off old computer components to charities, and creating big piles for the monthly "bulky days" that were part of our town's garbage service.

Arron's closet had held me hostage for almost four years. In the early days after his death, I would open the closet doors to see his shoes staring at me expectantly, as though longing for the warmth of his feet. I would stand inside the folding louver doors and cry into Arron's bathrobe, still smelling of his hair gel and toothpaste. I would finger his beloved but ugly striped flannel shirt. I would restack his socks that were piled impossibly high in a wire-mesh basket. His clothes waited for him, as did I. I would close the closet doors and fling myself face down onto the bed in dramatic sobs.

The closet became a test to measure my grief. Open door, cry, close door, pass test. Still grieving. Repeat in four weeks.

During a Thanksgiving visit, I saw my opportunity to bestow some of Arron's favorite items on my brother Matt, and Bruce, which seemed preferable to hauling garbage bags full to the Goodwill in preparation for the move.

My brother tried on Arron's cowboy boots that reminded me of him, tall, slender, and full of swagger. Matt shrank in my mind to a ten-year-old boy, trying on his older mentor's boots, proud, but not certain he would ever fill them. He strutted around uncertainly claiming to be honored to own them. I knew he would never wear them. Those boots were so synonymous with Arron that they would be unfathomable on anyone else. I had hoped that my brother might take on some of Arron's characteristics when he wore them, that the boots were somehow magic, but his tiptoeing inside of them, not wanting to fully plant his foot into them, revealed the truth.

Bruce pulled Arron's favorite leather jacket around his torso, trying to make the buttons meet. The coat, which had fallen to Arron's hips, reached halfway to Bruce's knees. It no longer resembled anything Arron had ever worn.

Despite the ill-fittings, I was glad for these reminders to be gone; to be the responsibility of someone else. I suspected that they would wind up at the Goodwill someday, but I didn't want to be the one who took them there.

My brother and Bruce walked off feigning pleasure at their new acquisitions, but really I think they were pleased at having helped me through a difficult process. They seemed to understand my relief at having purged a little of Arron in a loving way. Still, I hoped that they would be proud of their mementos of him.

Now as I packed, I cried, placing sweaters and shirts and the mountain of socks into garbage bags, but I also felt cleansed, free. I delicately dusted the pony shoes, made of horsehide, the ones that had always involved a little trotting dance with each wearing, and said good-bye tearfully as I placed them into the bag. The following week, we held a yard sale. I watched in agony as strange men wandered by and tried Arron's suit jackets on one by one. I made change through gritted teeth and watched as the men, pleased with their purchases, walked away with another piece of my husband.

The rack of his ties, a collection of our respective tastes—his purchases corporate and shiny, my Christmas and Father's Day gifts muted and artistic—were lovingly boxed to make the three-thousand-mile trip to our new home. I also kept the tuxedo zipped in its black plastic Brooks Brother's bag like a corpse. I would save it for Carter. I imagined the blue bathrobe hanging among my dresses in my new walk-in closet in Seattle, still dusty and mostly dry of tears. The tuxedo would remain entombed. The striped flannel shirt could have a place of honor in the shelf above. The ties would become softer with each passing month. These remnants of Arron would no longer await his return but would be kept as proof of his existence—pieces of him that we could touch and hold, talismans lovingly fondled.

Our farewell party began with loud explosions of thunder and a short torrential downpour. After the storm, I pranced around my backyard, now cleansed with a rain-fresh smell, offering drinks and replacing snacks. I greeted and hugged, I laughed. I felt no sense of remorse to be leaving all my friends behind. My life had become a series of moments in time, memories captured and held preserved, like flies in amber. I knew that I would again have moments with these friends, though they wouldn't be as frequent. Absence took on new meaning. It was no longer a permanent state. My friends and Arron would always be with me, if not in body, then in spirit. There had been some odd moments with friends who were angry with me for leaving: invitations to dinners turned down, as though preempting my absence could mask their sorrow. But most of my friends embraced me lovingly, glad for my courage to move on and glad to see excitement in my eyes. I felt like a newlywed facing a life of infinite possibilities, encouraged by the community around me. I tried to forget that I would be forging ahead alone.

And there was the tinge of sadness staining the fabric of my pure-white dress. I would need to learn to accept imperfection in my new life and not expect that a move far away could erase what was.

The movers came and emptied our house box by box, fitting them like puzzle pieces into a tiny corner of the long moving truck. My entire house took up only a third of the truck. It seemed an impossible reduction. I guided them as they packed the birdbath, wrapping it carefully in newspaper. I looked forward to setting it into my garden in Seattle, where it would enjoy the view of the lake; where I hoped Arron would enjoy the view. I walked alone through the empty house, touching everything that Arron had built. His too-high window seat, the kitchen faucet that turned the wrong way, the back porch steps, the stone wall in the back garden, the deck off the garage, the kids' treehouse.

Maureen had given me a tightly packed bouquet of dried herbs with which to "smudge" the house, cleansing it of old spirits. I lit the end of the bouquet and walked around the house feeling silly. The smell was pungent. Burning lavender and thyme filled every room. "Come on, Fab, it's time to go." I was both beckoning him to come with us to Seattle and to walk into the afterlife, leaving us to carry on without him.

The previous week, I had choked back tears as the kids hugged Janet. When it was my turn, I couldn't speak and had to turn away, tears filling our eyes. The night before, Martha had been her usual tough self. "I see you soon! I come, March maybe." I hugged her hard. "You have no idea how much you've helped me," I whispered to her. "You be fine, Abby. You strong like me." I smiled, trusting her faith in me.

On the morning that we left New Jersey, our closest friends came and bid us their farewells. Olivia had already sobbed in the car after I picked her up from horse camp the previous day. "I'm going to miss all my horses!" Now, she giggled her good-byes to her friends, while they cried. I cried seeing tears in William's eyes. He and Rachel had been my lifeline for so long. I hugged the rest of my friends before getting in the car and waving sadly as we pulled out of the drive.

The plane ride felt like a limbo between worlds. I tried to think of what lay ahead rather than what I was leaving behind. My old life seemed to vanish in the clouds.

We arrived in Seattle at almost the same time we had left New Jersey. The rental car slid neatly into the garage and we clambered excitedly down the brick steps. The house still smelled clean, the way it had when I had first seen it, six months earlier. The walls were now painted in the bright pastels I had envisioned. The kids immediately set up the air mattresses in the living room, a task they had been planning for months. Two hours later, Matt, who had left New Jersey five days earlier, driving my car and Harley across the country, arrived on the doorstep.

"Your timing is crazy! We just got here!"

"Wow. This place is beautiful, Ab," he exclaimed as we stood on the back deck looking out at the water. "That view!" The dusk was beginning to settle over the lake, and the skyline of Bellevue on the opposite shore glinted in muted colors of yellow and orange. Behind it, the Cascade Mountains shimmered in the haziness. We sipped the champagne that Laura had left in the fridge in February, when I had picked up the keys after the closing.

Two days later, the moving van arrived and I worked nonstop for most of the day reassembling the puzzle of belongings. I placed the photographs of Arron on the mantel, realizing that perhaps I had gotten my way. Arron had come with us to Seattle, but he was not etched into the framework of this house, had not built window seats and treehouses. Instead, he was in the spirit of the house. That he had played a part in getting us here was clear to me.

I looked at a picture of myself, taken a few months after September 11, looking tired and sad as I held Carter in my lap and tried hard to smile for the camera. I was glad that I no longer had that beaten-down look in my eyes and that my smile now came from genuine happiness. I felt the compassion for the woman in the photograph that others must have had for me at the time. That woman was now an ingredient of who I had become. I had endured a journey—a purification that cleansed my spirit, leaving only the essence of who I was and preparing me for who I was to become. The process had taught me that I couldn't control my fate but I could choose how I responded to it. In *After the Darkest Hour*, a book I read a couple of years after Arron's death, Ms. Brehony describes the "reddening" stage of the alchemic process: "In it, we experience a reclamation of passion, an aliveness that we have never known before. Our personality has changed. Our spirit is renewed."

The next morning, the first in my own bed, I was awoken at five by a blast of sunshine. I opened my eyes to see the first rays coming up over the bluish Cascades. The sky was a fiery salmon-gold and the color glinted off the lake like golden coins. I smiled, stretched my arms above my head and let out a sigh of appreciation.

My lead had turned to gold.

ACKNOWLEDGMENTS

Although I have dedicated this book to Arron, in many ways it is also dedicated to the army of people who helped me navigate the icy waters of my journey, helped me scale walls, slay dragons, and turn lead to gold. I doubt it will ever be possible to adequately show my gratitude toward those who participated in the incredible outpouring of sympathy, humanity, generosity, lemon gelato, and carrot soup that I received in those miserable early days. I hope that by writing this book, I am "paying it forward" by helping others who are enduring loss, and that they will find this book and be fortified by the idea that grief is ever-changing, and that with a gargantuan effort and by learning to accept the help of family, friends, and neighbors, they, too, can overcome whatever fireball life has thrown at them.

There are, of course, names that I must name. I want to thank the people who were the calm during my storm: Martha DeLeon, my rock, mother, savior. Cornelia and Bobby Carrigan, for bearing gelato and gigantic stuffed turtles, and providing wet shoulders and fatherly ministrations. William and Rachel Dunnell, for their quiet way of just being there, their Friday night dinners, and of course the cosmos. Diane, Alan, Molly, and Adam Fergurson, for the awesome baked chicken, tea at their kitchen table, Sylvia Browne books, Concetta readings, lawn mowing, and psychic babysitting. Thank you to Jeannine Cox, for somehow mustering a full-out militia to cook an entire turkey dinner and then finding someone to break into my house to serve it. Thank you to the Knoths and the entire Knoth/Chow clan for always welcoming us into your family so wholeheartedly. Thank you to all my friends and neighbors who opened their homes to my friends and family from Canada and to all those I haven't the room to name here, but who made a difference in so many ways.

I must acknowledge Tuesday's Children, and Athena Katsaros, Julia Romaine, Julie Buckley, and their Creative Insights program for nurturing the seed that became this book. They taught me that all dreams are achievable if you simply reach for them. And Maria Housden, who inspired me to write and helped me to get my very first essay published. Thank you also to Lynn and Kelly at Comfort Zone Camp for creating a place for Olivia to grieve. Also to Kim Materna, Olivia's big buddy, for being a buddy to us all. To John Muise and Tracy Clark at the Ontario Office for Victims of Crime, who buoyed Selena and me with laughter. To Maureen Girvan and Clara Hirsh at the Canadian consulate for helping arrange details from DNA tests to hotels, to passports, to getting that ziplock baggie back.

I want to recognize Sylvéne Gilchrist and Debi Goodwin at the CBC for their gentle, empathetic interviews, which ultimately led to this book being published. My agent, Denise Bukowski, who watched me on television, saw a glint of something in me that I didn't know I had, and buffed me to a polish, as one would precious metal. Susan Renouf at McClelland &

Stewart, who believed in my story enough to actually want to publish it, and Trena White, who edited her heart out, skillfully coaxing a book out of the epic that was first handed to her, bolstering my rookie-writer ego along the way.

Janet Nelson, my lifeline, confidante, surrogate mom, and receiver of my folded tissues. None of this would have been possible without her serene wisdom. Maureen Murray, whose magic touch awoke the spiritual serpent residing deep within me. John Welshons, whose book gave me hope.

Deirdre Timmons, for letting me meld myself into her life in Seattle, and for reading this book and cheering me all the way to the finish line. Theo Pauline Nestor, my memoir teacher, mentor, and reader, who helped me prove to myself once and for all that I really did have the ability to write a book. Jocelyn McNally, funeral singer extraordinaire, and ever-patient, vertically challenged girls' weekend consort. Kim Nymark, for twenty-four years of always being able to pick up where we left off. Jacquie Klan and Bruce Allan, for their pragmatic, certain friendship and turkey-inspired back bends.

"Nick," "Brian," and Michael for teaching me that I was worthy of their love and for unwittingly allowing me to expose them so publicly.

My sister, Jill, for calling me every day despite being three thousand miles away, making me sob with laughter, and pretending to find my black humor funny. Thank you for being wise beyond my wildest expectations. Dan for the fishing and baseball lessons, the brotherly protectiveness. My brother, Matt, for being brave enough to wear those boots. You have your own boots now and I am so proud of you. My mom, who despite being inadvertently forced aside in the early days, managed to persevere to help me through my loss. She taught me to be the kind of mom who battles for the well-being of her kids, and Olivia and Carter are testaments to that. She also stood by me during the writing of this book, despite her own misgivings. My dad, and his wife, Sheilagh, for remaining unwaveringly true to themselves, unflinching in the eye of a hurricane, and withstanding several of my left hooks as a result, and for their unwavering positive support in my endeavor, despite their aversion to letting it all hang out. My grandfather, who "just keeps moving" with charm and style. To Selena, my trench-mate, who cried and laughed with me through it all. Thank you for being my lifeline to Arron, for being the pragmatic voice amid the din, for setting aside your own grief to help me through mine.

Finally, to Olivia for teaching me so much about how to be graceful and strong, how to ask for what you need from the people around you, and how to laugh even when you are sad. And Carter for his dripping wet hugs, his incredible foot rubs, his ability to never miss a trick, and for keeping me on my toes as a mother and teaching me patience in spades. I love you both more than all the words in this book can say.